SOCIAL BEHAVIOR
OF THE MENTALLY RETARDED

DEVELOPMENTAL DISABILITIES
(General Editor: Manny Sternlicht)
Vol. 1

GARLAND REFERENCE LIBRARY
OF SOCIAL SCIENCE
(VOL. 175)

SOCIAL BEHAVIOR
OF THE MENTALLY RETARDED
An Annotated Bibliography

Manny Sternlicht
George Windholz

GARLAND PUBLISHING, INC. • NEW YORK & LONDON
1984

Library of Congress Cataloging in Publication Data

Sternlicht, Manny.
   Social behavior of the mentally retarded.

   (Developmental disabilities ; vol. 1.) (Garland
reference library of social science ; vol. 175)
   Includes index.
   1. Mentally handicapped—bibliography. 2. Mentally
handicapped children—Bibliography. 3. Mentally handi-
capped—Abstracts. 4. Mentally handicapped children—
Bibliography. 5. Social skills—Bibliography. 6. Social
skills—Abstracts. I. Windholz, George. II. Title.
III. Series. IV. Series: Garland reference library of
social science ; v. 175. [DNLM: 1. Social behavior—
Abstracts. 2. Mental retardation—Abstracts. W 1
DE997NH v. 1 / ZWM 307.S6 S839s]
Z6677.S74 1984 [HV3004] 016.3623   82-49140
ISBN 0-8240-9137-X (alk. paper)

Cover design by Laurence Walczak

Printed on acid-free, 250-year-life paper
Manufactured in the United States of America

CONTENTS

INTRODUCTION

In studying the social behavior of the mentally retarded, which is a highly fragmented area at present, we must first paint an overall picture of the various patterns of their social development, since within the framework of retarded behavior there are certain norms to be found.

The concept of mental retardation implies the slowdown of the development of cognitive and social adjustment functions relative to a norm (see Chapter I). In effect, the mentally retarded individual functions, by definition, on a lower developmental level than a "normal" person of comparable chronological age. Furthermore, with increasing age, the rate of development of cognitive and social adjustment functions is slower in mentally retarded people than in nonretarded individuals. This is especially the case when parents view their retarded offspring as being "sick" or "ill."

As a rule, then, the mentally retarded individual does not function intellectually and socially in daily life as effectively as the nonretarded individual. But this conclusion does not diminish the essential humanity of the mentally retarded person. A relative slowdown of a defined characteristic does not imply its absence. Mentally retarded individuals do reason and do interact with others as societal members. Though retardation applies to cognitive and social adjustment characteristics, it does not necessarily apply to certain emotional aspects, such as sexuality, fears, and aggression.

By and large, mentally retarded persons experience subjectively emotional states in a manner similar to the nonretarded, varying perhaps in intensity. It is even possible that in certain circumstances their fears and aggression are experienced more intensely than is the case with the nonretarded. The experience of fears and aggression depends, to a very large extent, on the individual's ability to deal with the environment and on the extent to which the environment is perceived as endangering the individual. Since the mentally retarded person's abilities are, developmentally, retarded, his or her helplessness—associated in part with a poor self-concept—in the face of difficult environmental conditions may increase the experience of fear and aggression. These emotions may also be accounted for by what is generally accepted as the retarded individual's relatively rigid

personality structure, which leads to a greatly reduced frustration tolerance.

The experience of emotion is subjective, or "private," and thus does not
directly affect society. Yet, since emotions have motivational properties and
thus prompt the person to behave, the behavioral expression of emotions is
subject to societal rules. These rules are usually fairly complex. The knowledge of the rules, and the formation of internal inhibitions on the behavioral expressions of emotions, demands a certain level of cognitive abilities and a certain potential for the learning of socially desirable behavior, as
well as the inhibiting of socially undesirable behavior. It is precisely in
these realms that the retardation of development manifests itself. The result
is a vicious circle. The inability to learn behaviors that correspond to the
social norm leads to a conflict with societal forces. The conflict with society,
or in general, "difficulties in living," trigger in the mentally retarded
person the subjective experiences of fear and aggression. The inability to
control the behavioral expression of fear and aggression in social situations
that prescribe such behaviors leads to a further conflict with society. The
retarded development of cognitive abilities and learning potential have,
thus, a profound impact upon the entire range of social situations in the
course of the mentally retarded person's life.

In any bibliography that attempts to be comprehensive, then, the
forces that play a key role in the retarded individual's social behavior must
be considered. Because parental and familial attitudes, values, and behavioral patterns shape the retarded child's behavior, this aspect must be
dealt with.

There is little doubt that the birth of a child has a powerful impact
upon its family members (see Chapter II). But unless the child is born with
obvious physical stigmata, as is the case with the Down's syndrome infants,
the birth of a mentally retarded child does not have an immediate impact
upon its family members. This is understandable, since mental retardation
involves, by definition, the slowdown of the development of the child's
intellectual and social abilities. The family also may not realize that their
child is mentally retarded. The family's special problems, which involve its
interaction with the mentally retarded child, occur with the recognition of
mental retardation in their child.

It is the retardation of the child's social (and sometimes physical) development that often leads to parental suspicion of abnormality. The parental apprehension may then be confirmed by professional evaluation. The
result is a profound shock that can take a variety of forms. The parents, who
may have heard of but never came directly in contact with mental retarda-

tion, may now seek information as to its causes, cures, and consequences. Regardless of what they hear about the cause, whether they understand it to be "hereditary" or "environmental," they blame themselves for their child's condition. The result is often a strong feeling of guilt. In response to the information that no magical "cure" exists, the parental reaction can take a number of forms. In some cases, the parents may use the defense mechanism of denial or some of its more intricate variants, such as the belief that the child will outgrow the handicap. Other parents, disappointed with the inability of professionals to effect an immediate improvement, may rely upon the self-styled experts' idiosyncratic advice.

Parents who confront the reality of a mentally retarded child face the option of institutionalization or home care. The first option may lead to an approach-avoidance conflict when parents wish the best for their child and feel that only a home can provide it, while at the same time believing that they will be unable to take good care of the child and that an institution staffed with specialists would be more beneficial to its welfare. As a rule, parents are more likely to institutionalize the disruptive male child or the retarded child with accompanying physically handicapping conditions. Regardless of the decision parents make, they worry about the child's future. The level of parental anxiety about their child is related to the perceived severity of retardation. Many parents worry that their child will never date, will not be able to marry, will not be able to take care of him- or herself in the future. Parents who provide their child with home care worry about what will happen to him or her when they are old or disabled.

Although parents who opt for home care worry perhaps most about their mentally retarded child's future, they also face a number of immediate problems. The mentally retarded child appears to the parents to be very helpless, requiring special protection and treatment. Mothers of mentally retarded children play, talk, and respond more often to their children than mothers of nonretarded children. Unwittingly, they may retard their children's social development by being much too protective, treating their children as if they were ill. The close relation of the parent and the mentally retarded child may also affect the emotional development of the latter.

The mentally retarded child who is taken care of by parents typically has a profound impact upon the family. The life pattern of the entire family is affected by the attention that parents pay to a member who is believed to be, sometimes realistically and sometimes not, unable to take care of himself/herself, and who has to be protected from eventual harm. The family may not be able to relax, to invite guests, or to participate in community affairs. Such a situation creates tension in a marital relationship which may have also faced unresolved conflicts in different spheres. Although parents of mentally retarded children are less likely to divorce than parents of nonretarded children, if the unresolved conflicts persist, the tensions persist, too. Many siblings of the mentally retarded also are negatively affected by their retarded brothers or sisters. The emotionally disruptive situation at home may, due to the close relationship between the mentally retarded child and his or her mother, contribute further to the emotional problems of the former.

The next logical topic to consider is the interaction between the mentally retarded and other individuals, since this too is an important determinant of social development. One of the most important consequences of the mentally retarded child's growth is increasing contact with others, especially with people outside the family (see Chapter III). Thus, the child comes into contact with other same-age children, who, within the environmental setting, are assigned a role similar to the mentally retarded child—his/or/her peers. Contact may occur in institutional settings, such as a school, or in such informal settings as the neighborhood or day-program area. The relationship of the mentally retarded persons may be either with nonretarded peers or with mentally retarded peers.

The relationship between peers encompasses attitudes toward oneself and the others, as well as behavior that is, very often, perceived by oneself and by the others. Although attitudes predispose behavior, this should not mean that attitudes dictate behavior. In considering peer relationships involving the interactions between the mentally retarded and the nonretarded, or among the retarded, the distinction between attitude and behavior must be maintained.

The attitude of nonretarded children toward the educable mentally retarded (EMR) peers in school ranges from the same attitude that is held toward their nonretarded peers to a socially undesirable stereotype. Although different studies show diverse results, no study shows a preference for the stereotype of the EMR over that held about the nonretarded peers. Though mentally retarded students may have a more positive attitude toward themselves as a group, in comparison to the attitude held by nonretarded students, nevertheless their attitude toward the nonretarded students is more socially positive than their attitude toward themselves.

Whether nonretarded children do or do not have a negative attitude toward their EMR peers, the nature of this attitude may not determine their behavior toward them. This appears to be especially true of older children who have learned that the handicapped must be treated with consideration. The nonretarded children may then find themselves in a conflictual situation: on the one hand they might not admire the EMR children—an attitude that predisposes them to reject the EMR peer—but on the other hand, they may accept the EMR peers' disagreeable behavior and offer them their friendship. The actual behavior of the nonretarded child toward his or her EMR peer differs from case to case. Apparently, this behavior is the consequence of the EMR's physical appearance and behavior, and the nonretarded peer's resolution of the conflictual situation.

The behavior of EMR children toward their peers is the consequence of conflicts as well as the existing situation. The EMR's stereotype of the nonretarded is more positive than their stereotype of themselves as a group. The EMR's behavior toward the nonretarded may be marked by the desire to be accepted. When such attempts do not bear fruit, the EMR may experience aggression. This aggression may be expressed in terms of aggressive behavior, or in behavioral forms that, though non-aggressive, are still not considered socially desirable. Undesirable behavior may in turn lead to a further rejection of the EMR person by his or her peers.

The impact of the label "mentally retarded" on peer relationships is not yet fully understood. It would seem that labelling stigmatizes the mentally retarded person as an undesirable individual in the eyes of his/her nonretarded peers. The absence of a label should therefore improve the attitude and behavior of the nonretarded toward their retarded peers. However, unattractive physical appearance, behavior that does not correspond to the norm, and the diminished scholastic performance of EMRs all tend to lead to the development in nonretarded children of a socially less desirable stereotype of their mentally retarded peers. It is, of course, quite possible that the negative label given to the mentally retarded by authorities may support the negative stereotype of the mentally retarded persons held by the nonretarded peer. But it is more likely that this stereotype is created by the mentally retarded persons' own appearance and behavior.

Mentally retarded people do associate with each other, although their contacts may be transitory. Associations with other mentally retarded peers occur more often among adults who look well, are socially skillful, and desire to associate with others. Yet, as is the case with the elderly, the establishment of social relationships in the impersonal atmosphere of large cities is by no means easy for the mentally retarded who live independently. It is possible that one of the consequences of deinstitutionalization is the separation of the mentally retarded from mutually satisfying relationships with their peers.

For the mentally retarded child, the school experience represents a watershed in life, a kind of "moment of truth." (see Chapter IV). The school experience involves a sudden, even if temporary, separation of the mentally retarded child from the protective milieu of the family, and challenges precisely those abilities in which the retarded child is so deficient. The difficulty is especially severe in families where relationships are disturbed. Not only is the mentally retarded child's school experience a problem for the child in question and his or her family, but it is also one for a society which is committed to compulsory education. No wonder that the concept of schooling for the mentally retarded sparks such heated controversies!

Although the concept of mental retardation is known in nonliterate societies, too, its problematic nature becomes more acutely felt when a child cannot keep up scholastically with other children of his or her own age. Since an important function of school is the dissemination of knowledge, the mentally retarded child's insufficient acquisition of knowledge constitutes a handicap that affects other important areas of the child's school experience. The child's social adjustment is affected as well.

The mentally retarded child's self-concept is often poor and his or her behavior may violate accepted social standards. The unacceptable behavior affects the school personnel and the other children as well. Since behavior in interpersonal situations is interactive, others react to mentally retarded childrens' behavior.

Teachers' attitudes toward the mentally retarded school child are often marked by ambivalence. Professionalism demands evenhanded treatment of all children and even sympathy toward the handicapped. However, the perception of disobedience or classroom-disturbing behavior in some mentally retarded children can bring forth teacher behavior that reflects disapproval. The perception of personal attractiveness in a child may reduce the teacher's disapproval, but not every mentally retarded child approaches his or her teacher's ideal. By and large, the mentally retarded are not preferred by teachers over normal children.

Students' attitudes toward their mentally retarded peers are often ambivalent as well. The stereotype of the mentally retarded child is not a socially desirable one. Nor do socially negative teacher reactions toward the mentally retarded child improve the stereotype of the children so labeled. Yet, both the culturally fostered demand for respect toward other persons and the occasional friendship between the normal student and his or her mentally retarded peer help to enhance the attitude toward the mentally retarded as a group. However, on the whole, it appears that the behavior of normal children toward their handicapped schoolmates is essentially that of rejection. Faced with rejection, the mentally retarded child may react defensively or aggressively, behavior patterns that do not diminish the stereotype of the mentally retarded person as an undesirable individual.

The plight of the mentally retarded child in the compulsory educational system early furthered the establishment of special classes that would provide education better suited to meet his individual needs. Subsequent failure to find evidence for the utility of self-contained education programs for the mentally retarded, combined with the egalitarian ideals of American society, led, in the post-World War II era, to the proposal for providing equal educational experience to all children of the same age. Hence the concept of mainstreaming—in its most radical form, the abolishment of special education classes for the mentally retarded and their integration in regular classes. The special needs of retarded individuals were not ignored in the proposal; nothing would prevent appropriate help for a child enrolled in the regular classroom program. The outcome of mainstreaming—in terms of its effect upon the mentally retarded individuals and other members of the educational community—has not as yet been conclusively established, and it therefore remains a controversial issue.

In considering education for the mentally retarded, two related problems must be considered. First is the problem of values; second, the efficient implementation of the accepted values. In general, the problem of values is noncontroversial as long as it is broadly stated in terms of society's desire to provide the retarded with the best possible formal education. The means of implementing these values, which in the final analysis demands concrete steps, has by no means been agreed upon. At fault is the lack of reliable and extensive knowledge in this area, and as long as this state of affairs prevails, the existing controversies on the process of education for the mentally retarded can hardly be productive.

According to the most relevant and recent studies, mentally retarded persons are more prone to have emotional problems than the nonretarded (see Chapter V). The incidence of emotional problems among mentally retarded individuals depends upon the criteria used. According to the least stringent criteria, about one third of the mentally retarded have emotional problems which range from moderate levels of anxiety and aggression to psychotic states.

This means that mentally retarded persons, as well as those significant others in their lives, do suffer. The mentally retarded suffer since their subjective emotional experiences are unpleasant, and their emotionally motivated behavior may be socially inappropriate. Such behavior often affects the significant others who not only suffer, but may also act toward the mentally retarded in an aggressive manner.

There is sufficient evidence to conclude that mental retardation and emotional problems are positively related, but this fact alone fails to indicate that there is a causal relationship. Logically, it can be argued that mental retardation and emotional problems are intrinsically related, that mental retardation causes emotional problems, or that emotional problems contribute to mental retardation.

The first possibility, that mental retardation is intrinsically related to emotional problems, assumes a general retardation factor which contains, besides the intellectual component, a social and an emotional retardation component as well. Unfortunately, the present state of studies of mental retardation sheds no light upon this possibility. In contrast, analogical research may bear upon the two alternate explanations.

It is very likely that mental retardation leads to the development of emotional problems, particularly if the mental retardation is profound or severe. Although the possibility of nonpsychogenic factors in the formation of emotional problems cannot be excluded, nevertheless the individual's interaction with the environment must be given prominent consideration in the formation of emotional problems. The mentally retarded individual faces two fundamental problems of living. First, there is the inability to solve the daily-life problems within a society formed by, and designed for, the nonretarded. Brought up in families that are often plagued by tensions or living in impersonal institutions, faced with the problem of working in organizationally sophisticated settings, mentally retarded persons must cope with social and emotional problems that would tax to the utmost the abilities of even the nonretarded. The reaction of mentally retarded people to so many obstacles is often that of fear, anxiety, aggression, or depression which may assume the forms of neuroses and psychoses. Second, the mentally retarded are often excluded from, and even discriminated by, the society at large, and under such conditions react emotionally to the perceived injustices.

It is, however, also possible that the emotional problems of the mentally retarded interfere with their social and intellectual abilities. Analogical studies, supporting the Yerkes-Dodson law, suggest that high levels of emotions interfere with the solution of more complex intellectual problems. Although the possibility that high levels of emotion cause profound intellectual and social retardation is unlikely, nevertheless strong emotional experiences lower a person's ability to deal with the environment. The individual's interactions with the environment, with its effect upon the relationship of mental retardation and emotional problems, may form a circular relationship; difficulties in dealing with the environment may lead to emotional problems, which, in turn, lower the individual's abilities to deal successfully with the environment, and thus lead to the continuation of the emotional problems. This interaction may explain the positive relationship observed between mental retardation and emotional problems.

Rationalistic arguments, with their assumption that human behavior is based uopn a conscious decision-making process, postulate a causal relationship between mental retardation and criminal or delinquent behavior (see Chapter VI). That is, if criminal and delinquent behavior is conceptualized as based upon the individual's inability to distinguish between right and wrong conduct, then the diminished intellectual abilities of the mentally retarded must result in socially inappropriate behavior.

Such rationalistic considerations have, seemingly, been confirmed by early empirical findings on the incidence of crime in relation to intellectual abilities as measured by mental tests. Thus, early in the twentieth century Goddard found that a substantial portion of the prison population was mentally deficient. But Goddard's conclusion was seriously flawed by his assumption that the prison population reflects the crimes perpetuated in the society. He neglected to take into account that the ability to escape a prison conviction may have been positively related to intellectual ability and socioeconomic status, which would have led to a greater rate of imprisonment among the mentally retarded.

More recent studies on the relationship between intelligence level and crime and delinquency indicate a slight negative relationship. That is, there is a slight tendency for the mentally retarded to be more often imprisoned than intellectually more able groups. But whether mental retardation per se leads to crime and delinquency has by no means been established. Perhaps a set of theoretical propositions may clarify this issue.

Empirical findings indicate that the mentally retarded person's criminal behavior falls into two categories. In the first are the offenses against property, involving burglary and entering. In the second are the offenses against persons, involving violence and homicide. Needless to say, the mentally retarded are seldom involved in crimes requiring considerable sophistication, such as white-collar offenses, since as the consequence of their handicap they seldom find themselves in situations which might allow such offenses.

Criminal or delinquent behavior is, from a psychological and a sociological perspective, by no means a unitary phenomenon. That is, offenses against property and offenses against people are based upon different personality characteristics of the offender and a different set of social conditions. The only common element in the mentally retarded individual's offense involves a relatively simple behavior pattern that reflects the offender's lower level of intellectual ability and a narrowly circumscribed social field of action.

Behavioral acts that involve offenses against property are most likely based upon the mentally retarded individual's quest for desirable objects which are unobtainable to him through socially acceptable means. Restraints placed upon such a behavioral tendency may be either external or internal, the first involving close supervision, the second involving adequate socialization. The mentally retarded individual's inadequate socialization, perhaps based upon his limited ability to learn, may preclude the full realization of the entire range of consequences that the behavioral act against other people's property may entail.

Behavioral acts that involve crimes against people most likely arise from the mentally retarded individual's impaired interaction with the environment. This impairment may be the result of society's attitude toward the retarded, or from the retarded individual's interaction with people who enter into a close relationship with him or her. Society's general reaction toward the mentally retarded is that of rejection or derision, to which the mentally retarded person may react with anger. However, the generality of the situation by and large does not provide the mentally retarded individual with a defined target against whom retaliation is possible. Furthermore, even inadequate socialization aimed at restraining aggression may be sufficient to prevent the aggressive act. The situation is different when the mentally retarded individual's interaction with special people—such as family members or peers—involves conflicts that lead to the intense experience of anger. A specific provocation by a known person, in contrast to a general provocation by society, may not only involve an intense level of anger, but also provide a well-defined target for aggression. The inability to resolve the conflict because of inadequate verbal or social skills, coupled with the mentally retarded individual's difficulty in envisioning the long-range consequences of a violent act, may lead to the relatively primitive act of physical aggression and to a subsequent criminal conviction.

Having discussed already the social behavior of mentally retarded persons in the classroom, their behavior in the institution and in the community must now be considered. In both the institution and the classroom, the retarded individual, despite the shortcomings of institutionalization, is in an essentially protective environment. However, once in the community he has more freedom and better opportunities for growth, though he also faces more stress-producing situations. Thus, social behavior in the community needs to be dealt with in terms of those adjustments that must be made in living in a complex and sophisticated environment and in coping with this environment.

Historically, the policy of institutionalizing the mentally retarded arose out of society's ambivalent attitude toward this handicapped group (see Chapter VII). It was, on the one hand, society's humanitarian concern for the well-being of the mentally retarded and, on the other hand, society's fear of their behavior that led to the establishment of large, out-of-the-way custodial facilities for the retarded.

The humanitarian concern should not be belittled. The mentally retarded seldom represented the society's more desirable members. They were often subjected to parental neglect or rejection and exposed to derision or cruelty by more fortunate members of society. Urban society, especially in the throes of the Industrial Revolution, was not characterized by kindness to individuals whose behavior deviated from the accepted standard of a "successful" person, and very few mentally retarded approached that ideal. Hence the belief of well-meaning individuals that supervised, custodial care for the mentally retarded—offering them a roof over the head, a bland diet, and protection from severe abuse—was preferable to their life outside the institution.

But, at the same time, societal members, convinced that the lack of intellectual abilities was tantamount to asocial behavior, believed that the mentally retarded would be better off if they were held in custodial care in buildings located far away from urban population centers. The inability of some parents to control their children and the belief in the relationship between mental retardation and criminal behavior further strengthened the trend toward institutionalization.

Society's ambivalent attitudes toward the retarded extend to present patterns of institutionalization in large facilities. At the same time that there is a trend toward deinstitutionalization, there is a desire to improve the services provided by the institutions. Basically, deinstitutionalization involves preventing the establishment of, and the abolishment of, large institutions for the mentally retarded, and either the return of the mentally retarded individual into society, or, if it should become necessary, the placement of the individual in community-based houses, in foster care, or under the supervision of local social agencies. Opposed to deinstitutionalization is the view that institutionalized mentally retarded individuals are better off than noninstitutionalized ones, but only provided that the institution serve as a rehabilitation agency aimed at allowing the client to become, sooner or later, an integral society member.

While the debate continues, the practice of institutionalization persists. Hence, the question arises as to how the institutionalized fare. To begin with, it must be realized that a lack of normal intellectual abilities does not, per se, constitute a sufficient condition for institutionalization. The decision to institutionalize a mentally retarded person is either in the hands of parents or societal authorities. It is best understood as the reaction of others to the mentally retarded person's behavior. The parents' belief that they cannot take care of their mentally retarded child, the disturbance in familial relationships attributed to the mentally retarded member, the inability of the mentally retarded person to take care of himself or herself in a manner considered to be appropriate in the society, are some of the reasons for institutionalization.

In 1966, MacAndrew and Edgerton provided a vivid description of the daily existence of profoundly retarded adults in an institutional ward. The sounds, smells, and behavior of the residents graphically communicated the dreary reality of institutionalized life. More objective research findings confirm this description.

The wards are noisy, which makes communication difficult, especially for residents who have a language handicap. Although residential care is not related directly to the size of the institution, the care that is received plays an important role in the mentally retarded person's life. No man is the master of his fate, and this is especially true for the institutionalized mentally retarded individual, who has to depend upon the good will of the staff. By and large, staff members fail to respond to behavior initiated by mentally retarded individuals, but when they do respond, it is often in terms of encouraging socially appropriate behavior and discouraging socially inappropriate behavior. The attitude of the staff toward mentally retarded people's sexual behavior is especially telling: it follows the pattern of middle class standards, ranging from the condemnation of all forms of sexual behavior to the toleration of masturbation in a non-public setting. On the whole, the quality of care differs from institution to institution and from case to case.

In the ward, the mentally retarded can establish a relatively permanent territory. Their relationships with peers are marked by a dominance hierarchy, and friendships are transitory. The nature of adjustment ranges from cooperation to aggressive behavior, the latter negatively related to available space. The activities of the mentally retarded vary; they are, to a large extent, determined by intellectual abilities and personality characteristics. Some of the mentally retarded show little complex behavior; others help to care for their peers. Some are cooperative, while others are rebellious.

The mentally retarded leave an institution in a variety of ways, often by moving into the community. This course of action is not uncommon among the mentally retarded who were admitted during their adolescence. De-institutionalization tendencies further this, although with different outcomes for different individuals, dependent at least in part on the types of community programs and services that are available.

Over the last one hundred years our society's treatment of the mentally retarded has undergone a number of changes. Rejected and feared by society's nonretarded members, the mentally retarded had been left, by and large, to live either in distant institutions or in the community according to their own devices. Society's recognition that they need protection and care, coupled with society's fears, led to the establishment of large-scale institutions at a "safe" distance from communities. More recently, society's attitude toward the mentally retarded has changed; it is now recognized that they are as human as are the nonretarded and therefore should become integral members of the community. In practice, this has led to deinstitutionalization, that is, to the attempt to abolish (large-scale) institutions (see Chapter VIII). The abolishment of such institutions confronted society with the issue of what should happen to its mentally retarded residents. One solution was that of independence—the mentally retarded individual's life pattern was to be similar to that of other normal members of society. However, the recognition that not all mentally retarded residents are capable of such a radical transition in their lifestyle suggested the establishment of small-scale care facilities located within the geographical limits of a community.

The advocates of the latter approach argued that this arrangement would benefit both mentally retarded people and the community as a whole. The integration of the mentally retarded individual within the community would restore his or her essential humanity, so badly damaged by depersonalizing experiences in a large-scale institution. By living in a community, the mentally retarded person would be provided with the opportunity to become an integral member of society. The consciousness of the normal community members would be enriched by their acceptance of the less fortunate others. Finally, the community resources would be less strained by a small-scale facility located within a community.

The success of community programs for the mentally retarded is by no means clear-cut. Although the initial opposition by a neighborhood to a small facility housing the mentally retarded may give way to tolerance, the actual acceptance of its inhabitants into the informal social setting is by no means assured. The placement of the mentally retarded in high-crime neighborhoods of a large city may have unpleasant consequences for the less resourceful mentally retarded people. Little evidence is presented that the many services provided by the community to the mentally retarded living in the community are more cost-efficient than similar services provided by the large-scale institutions. Nor can it be asserted that the placement of the mentally retarded in small-scale care facilities located in the community involves qualitatively better care than that provided in large-scale institutions.

At best, the establishment of care facilities within communities represents a change of attitude, and sometimes of behavior, of the society at large toward mentally retarded people. Institutionalization implied the near-ultimate rejection of the mentally retarded. The establishment of community-based care facilities involves society's admission of the existence of mentally retarded people, and with it the possibility of their acceptance as integral members of the community.

The problems of vocational and occupational adjustments and leisure-time pursuits also need to be considered and taken into account. And finally, penultimate and ultimate variables associated with independent living must be understood and acknowledged.

Not only does the mentally retarded person's gainful employment free society from supporting him, but it also gives him the status of an integral member of the society. Gainful employment improves the mentally retarded person's self-concept and his sense of value, and wins him respect in the eyes of others (see Chapter IX). Yet, the mentally retarded person faces considerable obstacles before the goal of gainful employment can be realized. There is little doubt that the same goal taxes the resources of normal people, and this is especially true for the handicapped.

The obstacles which a mentally retarded person faces are fourfold. First, he or she must be able to get a job. Second, he or she must be able to perform the job regularly. Third, the mentally retarded person must be able to perform the job in a competitive situation. Fourth, he or she must behave on the job in a socially appropriate manner.

In regard to the mentally retarded person's ability to obtain gainful employment, it must be realized that not many employers, especially in times of unemployment, are willing to hire a handicapped person. Hence, the mentally retarded person initially has first to convince an employer of his or her ability to do the job satisfactorily. Once the mentally retarded person has obtained the position, he/she has to come to work regularly and on time, a task by no means easy, since many often unexpected obstacles lie between the individual's home and the place of employment. Once on the job, even when the mentally retarded person knows how to perform relatively simple and routine tasks, unexpected and novel problems may arise at any moment, and the employee must be able to deal with these in a satisfactory manner. Then too, any work situation is a social situation; the mentally retarded person has to deal not only with the demands of the supervisor but also with the idiosyncrasies of fellow employees.

In view of these circumstances, social agencies are obliged to provide the mentally retarded person with the training necessary for the individual's successful employment. That process involves three steps: first, vocational guidance; second, job and social training; and third, aid in finding a job.

Vocational guidance involves a thorough physical examination and psychological assessment. The aim is to determine the physical and mental potentialities and limitations of the client as these pertain to a future position in the world of work. Severe physical handicaps and profound mental retardation greatly limit the possibility of employment, whereas good health and mild retardation provide a good basis for future employment. In the latter cases, the task of vocational guidance is to determine specifically the mentally retarded individual's range of abilities. The guidance counsellor must note that the major factor in vocational success is not so much the intelligence level of the mentally retarded person as such things as physical appearance, absence of physical disabilities, and social skills.

Perhaps an on-the-job program would be the most efficient way to teach the mentally retarded individual the appropriate job-related behavior, but not many employers are willing to undertake this task. Hence, the sheltered workshop approach is widely used. It involves a situation, under the control of a social agency, in which a mentally retarded person, under supervision, can learn the specific skills required on the job. In other words, the sheltered workshop provides the mentally retarded person with an environmental situation designed to develop the skills required in the future work situation. The sheltered workshop is thus a stepping stone to the world of work.

The sheltered workshop, of course, has to enable the mentally retarded person to acquire job-related skills, but it must also provide training in social skills. These include, to begin with, training for punctuality, the proper way of reacting to the supervisor's commands, considerate behavior toward fellow workers—social training is a part of the job-learning process.

Yet, the sheltered workshop may contain hidden dangers. It may be too specific, too protective, and too rigid. It may be too specific in that its program allows the learning of skills that do not transfer to the actual work situation in which the mentally retarded person finds himself. It may be too protective in terms of defending the mentally retarded individual from the many taxing situations found in the competitive work situation. It may be too rigid in its demands upon the mentally retarded person's social behavior in work situations that demand flexibility. Only to the extent that the training given within a sheltered workshop approximates the real situation encountered by the mentally retarded employee does the workshop accomplish its task.

The social agency's responsibility toward the mentally retarded person does not end with a successful completion of the training program. It is not easy to find a job in the complex industrial societies. Hence it is the task of social agencies to assume the role of employment agencies and, in addition, to supervise the mentally retarded person during the initial phase of employment.

Although the activities subsumed under the term "leisure" cannot be strictly differentiated from other complex activities such as work or familiar relationships, it is nevertheless possible to define leisure as activities that are pleasant in themselves, rather than elicited and maintained by external rewards (see Chapter X). Structurally, leisure involves complex activities rather than simple ones (such as reflexes) that are delineated by the individual's ability and the societal norms.

Child's play may be the simplest form of leisure. Since the concept of mental retardation involves, functionally, the retardation of normal cognitive development, the mentally retarded child's play assumes less complex forms in comparison to that of other children of the same chronological age. And the severely retarded adult's leisure behavior in institutional settings is usually organized in terms of relatively simple play activities as well.

The leisure activities of mildly retarded persons approximate the leisure activities of intellectually normal people. Yet, the leisure activities of the mentally retarded are restricted by personal characteristics and social aspects. To a very large extent, the leisure activities of the mentally retarded tend to be passive rather than active. They involve the role of a spectator, rather than that of an active participant. Attending a sports event, watching TV programs, and going to a movie are some of the examples of mentally retarded people's leisure pursuits. Active participation in leisure activities is more limited by a variety of factors. First, the physical handicaps often associated with mental retardation frequently limit participation in many socially approved leisure pursuits. Thus, some mentally retarded persons may find it difficult to engage in the more taxing sports activities unless they compete among themselves (special olympics). Second, leisure activities that demand a higher level of intellectual attainment may preclude the participation of mentally retarded persons. Where personal characteristics allow the mentally retarded person's participation in leisure activities, social conditions may restrict it. Thus, many leisure activities are connected with financial expenses which the mentally retarded person can ill afford. Then, too, active leisure pursuits often involve interrelationships with others. If the significant others are nonretarded, then they may reject the mentally retarded person as an unequal participant. If the significant others are mentally retarded as well, their behavior within society may violate societal norms. Hence, the active leisure patterns of the mentally retarded create problems which demand special arrangements—often provided by social agencies—which are designed to meet the special needs of the retarded. Since the distinction between leisure and other complex activities, such as work or social relationships, is tenuous at best, the organization of leisure activities by social agencies may approximate the complex activities found in the society at large, and thus aid in the integration of the mentally retarded with the mainstream.

The ultimate goal of deinstitutionalization is normalization—when the mentally retarded individual's independent living pattern is essentially identical to that of the normal members of a society (see Chapter XI). Yet, while the normal society member's life pattern defines the societal norms, the independently living mentally retarded individuals, who may have spent years in an institution, face the problems of living up to the norm. Hence, the question of definition of independent living is germane.

The definition "to be able to take care of oneself" is certainly too broad. The minute description of the mentally retarded person's socially defined ideal behavior is impractical. Hence the description of independent living must take into consideration what mentally retarded persons can do and what society expects them to do. The mentally retarded person's intellectual abilities are, of course, restricted and his or her social behavior may be unpleasant. On the whole, society expects that mentally retarded people will adhere to the rules for respecting the rights and feelings of others, and that they will support themselves so as not to be a burden to society. Within these limits, the independent living pattern of the mentally retarded may take on as many expressions as that of other society members. Yet society also realizes that it would be too unrealistic to expect that people who have spent years in the protected environment of an institution will suddenly, without any further aid, live up to these demands. Hence the society, usually through special institutions, is willing to help the mentally retarded live in its midst.

By and large, mentally retarded adults do meet most of society's demands. In fact, many do pretty well. Some mentally retarded individuals merge into the population of the nonretarded, while others live in small supervised groups. To a very large extent, the mentally retarded adult's quality of life outside the institution depends upon his/her IQ, social skills, and training in how to deal with the encountered problems.

Most mentally retarded adults' independent living patterns approximate those of people within the lower socioeconomic stratum. If the mentally retarded person works, either within a commercial enterprise or in a sheltered workshop, the remuneration is by no means high and neither is the standard of living. Their jobs belong usually in the unskilled category, for example, dishwashing. Some mentally retarded may be unemployed or on welfare. Many of them have difficulties in establishing satisfactory social relationships, while others are able to enter into successful marriages or family relationships. Their leisure activities are by no means sophisticated, yet neither do these differ greatly from that of the lower socioeconomic classes. The mentally retarded may be politically active and may take college-level courses suited to their abilities and interests.

For most mentally retarded persons, independent living is not easy. They may have difficulties in handling the many problems that they encounter in daily life. Their lives may be marked by loneliness. While they are more often asocial rather than antisocial, they may nevertheless, unless closely supervised, violate some societal norms. Living in a highly complex society, they may often feel helpless. But by and large, mentally retarded people living independently and dealing with the many problems that baffle even the nonretarded prefer their life in the community to one in an institutional setting, particularly if there is a trusted adult "helper" available to them.

Social Behavior
of the Mentally Retarded

CHAPTER I:
PATTERNS OF SOCIAL DEVELOPMENT

1. Adams, M. *Mental Retardation and Its Social Dimensions*.
    New York: Columbia University Press, 1971.

    Presents mental retardation from the social perspective
and in relation to social work intervention.

2. Ando, H., & Yoshimura, I. "Effects of Age on Communica-
    tion Skill Levels and Prevalence of Maladaptive Behaviors
    in Autistic and Mentally Retarded Children." *Journal
    of Autism and Developmental Disorders,* 1979, 9, 83-93.

    Investigated the effect of age on communication and mal-
adaptive behavior in autistic and MR children. The cross-
sectional method was used to compare junior and senior groups,
and ratings on communication skills and maladaptive behaviors
were obtained from teachers. It was found that the skills of
comprehension and conversation in autistic children improved
significantly with age, and speech improved somewhat. In
spite of this improvement in communication skills, maladaptive
behaviors in the autistic children, other than hyperactivity,
did not change significantly with age. Withdrawal improved
significantly with age in the MR children but not in the
autistic children.

3. Ando, H., Yoshimura, I., & Wakabayashi, S. "Effects of
    Age on Adaptive Behavior Levels and Academic Skill
    Levels in Autistic and Mentally Retarded Children."
    Journal of Autism and Developmental Disorders, 1980,
    10, 173-184.

    For 47 autistic (A) and 128 MR children, cross-sectional
comparisons were made between junior (ages 6-9 years) and
senior (ages 11-14 years) groups using ratings obtained from
teachers on adaptive behaviors and academic skills. Results

show that the levels of toilet training, eating skills, participation in group activities, and self-control in the As improved significantly with age. Number concepts skills also improved significantly with age in this group. However, these adaptive and academic levels were in general significantly lower than those of the MRs. The levels did not improve significantly, but were lower in the As.

4. Barclay, A. "Longitudinal Changes in Intellectual and Social Development of Noninstitutionalized Retardates." *American Journal of Mental Deficiency,* 1969, 73, 831-837.

This study investigated longitudinal changes in intellectual and social development among young noninstitutionalized retardates. Chronological age largely accounted for changes in intellectual and social maturity but, at earlier ages, age increase did not entirely account for changes in social maturity. At later ages, observed asymptomatic levels of intellectual and social functioning suggested that while absolute increments in mental age and social age do occur, the rate is slow. The occurence of absolute increments in mental and social age is, however, offset by faster rates of chronological age increments, resulting in asymptomatic levels of intellectual function reflected in derived measures, such as the IQ and SQ.

5. Bartak, L., Rutter, M., & Cox, A. "A Comparative Study of Infantile Autism and Specific Developmental Receptive Language Disorder: I. The Children." *British Journal of Psychiatry,* 1975, 126: 127-145.

Forty seven boys (5 to 10 years old) with a severe developmental disorder of receptive language were examined to determine whether language disorder is necessary for the development of infantile autism. Ss, who had no apparent neurological dysfunction, hearing loss, or MR, were evaluated through standard tests of cognitive, linguistic, and social behavior; and standardized interviews administered to parents. Nineteen children were classified as autistic, 23 were diagnosed as having uncomplicated developmental language disorder (dysphasia), and 5 Ss with some atypical autistic features were considered "mixed." Children diagnosed as autistic were shown to have more severe comprehension defect, more extensive language disability, and a defect in the social usage of language. Very few differences among groups were noted in the pattern of nonlinguistic skills. The development of autism seems to be associated with a distinctive type of language disability

6. Bass, M.S., ed. *Sexual Rights and Responsibilities of the Mentally Retarded*. Santa Barbara: Channel Lithograph, 1973.

     Selection of different chapters dealing with the sexuality of MR persons, and of their sexual rights.

7. Bender, L. "The Life Course of Children with Autism and Mental Retardation." In F.J. Menolascino, ed. *Psychiatric Approaches to Mental Retardation,* 149-190, New York: Basic Books, 1970.

     Follow-up study of 50 autistic childrens' life courses shows that the surviving persons may show a wide range of schizophrenic disorders and organically defective disorders in adulthood. Twenty-four percent of the patients made social adjustments in the community as adults in a variety of settings.

8. Bergsma, D., & Pulver, A.E., eds. *Developmental Disabilities: Psychologic and Social Implications*. New York: Liss, 1976.

     Includes chapters dealing with the social aspects of MR, emphasizing the psychosocial adaptation and specific special needs of retarded children and adolescents.

9. Blacher-Dixon, J.B. "Social Cognition in Early Childhood: A Study of Fundamental Communication Skills in Young Retarded and Nonretarded Children." Doctoral dissertation, University of North Carolina at Chapel Hill, 1979, summarized in *Dissertation Abstracts International,* 1980, 40, 4996A-4997A. (University Microfilms No. 80-05016).

     Determined fundamental social-congnitive skills in retarded children, and the developmental factors of such skills.

10. Brody, G.H., & Stoneman, Z. "Social Competencies in the Developmentally Disabled: Some Suggestions for Research and Training." *Mental Retardation,* 1977, 15(4), 41-43.

     Offers suggestions for the development and instruction of social competencies in developmentally disabled children. The conceptualization of social competencies is based upon the beliefs that: (a) effective social functioning involves

a complex network of psychological processes, elucidated by
cognitive social learning theory; (b) social behaviors occur
within a context of frequently changing environmental settings;
and (c) effective social functioning requires social behavior
patterns to change qualitatively as the child matures.

11.   Burns, E.G. "The Social Preferences and Interpersonal
      Relations of Retarded and Normal Children." Doctoral
      dissertation, University of Michigan, 1971, summarized
      in *Dissertation Abstracts International,* 1972, 32,
      6245A. (University Microfilm No. 72-14820).

      This study investigated whether the ability of the MR
children to maintain preferences to group members of varying
levels of mental ability is related to the child's mental
ability. Found that the reliability and transitivity of social
preferences is related to mental ability.

12.   Capobianco, R.J., & Cole, D.A. "Social Behavior of
      Mentally Retarded Children." *American Journal of Mental
      Deficiency,* 1960, 64, 638-651.

      Studied the social behavior of EMR and TMR boys and
girls in institutional and noninstitutional settings. Found
that mental age, unlike IQ, does not seem to influence the
pattern of social behavior in the MR.

13.   Chatagnon, P.A. "Retardation of the Organization and
      Development of Mental Functions in the Human: I. Mental
      Retardation and Social Capacity." *Annales Medico-Psycho-
      logiques,* 1970, 2, 497-544.

      The degree to which mental capacity affects social ca-
pacity is subject to great variation. The extreme mental
defects are easily recognized, but more benign forms are difficult to differentiate from the normal and are far more numerous. Social incapacity cannot be easily expressed in terms
of MA, yet the regular linkages found between low intelligence
and the social problems of poverty, crime, illness, and delinquency underline its causal nature. Much attention has
been directed to early detection and special education, as
it is now recognized that most of the problem is biological
or social, rather than pathological in nature. This study
presents a modest sample of 20 children or adolescents, chosen
at random, in considerable detail with the intent to provide
guidelines for the handling of the many, from reflections
arising from an intensive study of a few.

14. Clancy, H., & McBride, G. "The Isolation Syndrome in
     Childhood." *Developmental Medicine and Child Neurology*,
     1975, 17, 198-219.

     Suggests a diagnostic category, the isolation syndrome,
which occurs in institutional settings due to traumatic separation from the mother, disturbance in family, and the family's
reaction to the child's disability.

15. Collins, H.A., Burger, G.K., & Doherty, D. "Self-Concept
     of EMR and Nonretarded Adolescents." *American Journal
     of Mental Deficiency*, 1970, 75, 285-289.

     This study compared the self-concept of EMR adolescents
with a control group of nonretarded adolescents attending a
public high school. The Tennessee Self-Concept Scale was used
as the measurement instrument. It was hypothesized that EMR
adolescents would have significantly more negative self-concepts than the nonretarded subjects. Significant differences
were found for the variables of self-criticism, identity, social
self, family self, and moral-ethical self scales. All differences in the hypothesized direction.

16. Cornwell, A.C., & Birch, H.G. "Psychological and Social
     Development in Home-Reared Children with Down's Syndrome
     (Mongolism)." *American Journal of Mental Deficiency*,
     1969, 74, 341-350.

     Data of 44 home-reared children with Down's syndrome
(mongolism) on the Stanford-Binet and on the Vineland Social
Maturity Scale revealed a broad range of both intellectual
and social competence. IQ scores decreased with age whereas
SQ scores did not decline as systematically. The age-specific
patterns indicated a slow accretion of certain social functions and concomitant impoverishment in advanced social skills.
Severe limitations in language and conceptualization were
noted throughout. The data supported the hypothesis that in
Down's syndrome there is both a developmental lag and an
arrest of certain psychological and social capacities.

17. Di Nola, A.J. "Moral Judgment in the Mentally Retarded."
     Doctoral dissertation, Yeshiva University, 1972, sum-
     marized in *Dissertation Abstracts International,* 1973,
     33, 3433A. (University Microfilms No. 73-1089).

     Attempted to determine the relationship between the
Piagetian concept of moral judgment and a number of characteristics of MR children. Found that moral judgment was positively related to the child's mental age and role-taking
activities.

18. Edmonson, B., McCombs, K., & Wish, J. "What Retarded
     Adults Believe About Sex." *American Journal of Mental
     Deficiency,* 1979, 84, 11-18.

     Information was presented from results of administration
of the Socio-Knowledge and Attitudes Test to retarded persons
aged 18 to 41 (equal sex distribution), most of whom were
moderately or severely retarded. One-half of the sample were
residents in a state institution, and the other half lived
in their own or in group homes in an urban community. Little
relationship was found between subjects' ages and response
scores, but, on certain subtests, there were significant relationships between sex-knowledge score and subject's IQ,
adaptive behavior level, sex, and/or place of residence.

19. Edmonson, B., & Wish, J. "Sex Knowledge and Attitudes
     of Moderately Retarded Males." *American Journal of
     Mental Deficiency,* 1975, 80, 172-179.

     In semi-structured interview sessions, 18 moderately
retarded men undergoing deinstitutional training were questioned to determine their understanding of pictures of homosexual embrace, masturbation, dating, marriage, intercourse,
pregnancy, childbirth, drunkenness, and their knowledge of
anatomical terminology. The frequencies of various response
categories revealed a range of comprehension, the lowest
answering only 10 percent correctly, the median consisting
of 28 percent correct, and only 1 subject correctly answering
as many as one-half of the items. Correct conceptual responses significantly correlated with WAIS Full Scale and
Verbal IQs and were also significantly related to the Adaptive Behavior Scale domains of Language, Socialization, and
Responsibility. Serious errors of fact and conceptual confusion, though most prevalent in responses by the low compre-
henders, were found in at least some responses by all of the
men.

20. Eyman, R.K., & Arndt, S. "Life-Span Development of
     Institutionalized and Community-Based Mentally Retarded
     Residents." *American Journal of Mental Deficiency,* 1982,
     86, 342-350.

     Life-span development of MR residents in institutional
and community settings was examined. Results showed that significant growth in adaptive behavior occurred for all groups
of residents regardless of their level of retardation. Furthermore, the shapes of these growth curves were parallel
across the different levels of retardation over the age-range
studies (5 to 50 years). Measures of the quality of the environment were available for institutionalized residents and
were found to be unrelated to adaptive behavior growth; however,
environmental quality was associated with initial levels of adaptive behavior, suggesting that for institutionalized residents,
adaptive behavior competence may determine the type of environment provided.

21. Francis, S.H. "Behavior of Low-Grade Institutionalized
     Mongoloids: Changes with Age." *American Journal of
     Mental Deficiency,* 1970, 75, 92-101.

     With increasing age, low-grade institutionalized mon-
goloids exhibit an increase in self-oriented behavior, in
postures, in rocking, and in diffuse movements, and a decreasing interest in the external world (as measured by the focus
of their visual attention, manipulation of objects, and the
amount of social contact in which they are engaged). More
changes in behavior occur between the ages of 4 and 13 years
and after 30 years than at other ages. It is suggested that
the behavioral changes are due to institutionalization rather
than to aging.

22. Gottlieb, J. *Introduction to Mental Retardation: Social
     and Behavioral Aspects.* Baltimore: University Park, 1978.

     Considers the issues of mild and moderate mental retarda-
tion to be primarily social problems, which affect these mentally retarded individuals' psychological development.

23.   Gunzburg, H.C. *Social Competence and Mental Handicap.*
      London: Bailliere, Tindall & Cassell, 1968.

      Deals with some aspects of remedial action designed to
ease the burden imposed on society by the MR, and also discusses the assessment of social knowledge in this group, as
well as the development of social competence.

24.   Hall, J.E., & Morris, H.L. "Sexual Knowledge and Attitudes
      of Institutionalized and Noninstitutionalized Retarded
      Adolescents." *American Journal of Mental Deficiency,*
      1976, 80, 382-387.

      Sixty-one noninstitutionalized and 61 institutionalized
MR adolescents were psychometrically assessed on three measures:
sexual knowledge, sexual attitudes, and self-concept. The two
groups differed on total score on sex knowledge only, with the
noninstitutionalized groups being more knowledgeable. With
regard to sexual attitudes and self-concept, the two groups
did not differ in terms of total correct statements. Intercorrelations of relevant variables for each group (10 for the
noninstitutionalized, 13 for the institutionalized) produced
several significant correlations. Results were discussed with
reference to the development of a standardized instrument for
assessing sex-education programs for mentally retarded persons.

25.   Hall, J.E., Morris, H.L., & Baker, H.R. "Sexual Knowledge
      and Attitudes of Mentally Retarded Adolescents." *American
      Journal of Mental Deficiency,* 1973, 77, 706-709.

      Sixty-one noninstitutionalized mildly and moderately
retarded adolescents were psychometrically assessed in reference to self-concept, sexual ethics, and knowledge of sex.
In addition, parents tried to predict their retarded adolescents' responses in these areas. Parents and teachers provided
additional information through, respectively, a social history
form and a behavior rating scale. Analysis included (a) normalization of scores, evaluation for internal consistency, and
tests for significant differences between means; and (b) inter-
correlation of 32 variables on each subject (e.g., sex, IQ,
self-concept score). The retarded respondents were significantly more liberal in sexual ethics than their parents predicted, but parents accurately predicted the scores of the
adolescents on knowledge and self-concept.

26. Heshusius, L. "Sexuality, Intimacy, and Persons We
     Label Mentally Retarded: What They Think--What We Think."
     Mental Retardation, 1982, 20, 164-168.

     Naturalistic research, in which persons labeled mentally
retarded express their perceptions of intimacy and sexuality,
is reviewed. Statements which interpret these aspects of life
primarily as positive and essential are categorized according
to their ascribed meanings, and are contrasted with professional
practices which typically do not allow for privacy and the expression of sexuality. Data on normal sexual development and
beneficial effects of sexual contact are discussed, along with
cultural comparisons and psychological and anthropological
data on the importance of touch and sexual expression in human
development. We are urged to re-examine our ideas about "sex
and the mentally retarded," as well as our professional practices and attitudes.

27. Kahn, J.V. "Moral and Cognitive Development of Moderately
     Retarded, Mildly Retarded, and Nonretarded Individuals."
     American Journal of Mental Deficiency, 1976, 81, 209-
     214.

     The relationships of moral maturity, cognitive reasoning,
MA and CA were investigated with three IQ groups. The subjects
were 20 moderately retarded, 20 mildly retarded, and 20 nonretarded individuals matched for MA. The findings indicated
that moderately retarded individuals are at lower levels of
cognitive reasoning and moral maturity than MA-matched mildly
retarded and nonretarded individuals. The findings also indicated a stronger relationship between moral maturity and
cognitive reasoning than between MA and moral maturity of MA
and cognitive reasoning.

28. Kriger, S.F. "On Aging and Mental Retardation." In
     J.C. Hamilton & R.M. Segal, eds. *Proceedings of the
     Consultation Conference on the Gerontological Aspects
     of Mental Retardation.* Ann Arbor: University of Michigan,
     1975.

     Presents data dealing with the life styles of MR senior
citizens.

29. Mayhew, G.L., Enyart, P., & Anderson, J. "Social Reinforcement and the Naturally Occurring Social Responses of Severely and Profoundly Retarded Adolescents." *American Journal of Mental Deficiency,* 1978, 83, 164-170.

Findings suggest that deficits in the social behavior of severely retarded persons may be due to failure of their environment to maintain such behavior.

30. Meyerowitz, J.H. "Sex and the Mentally Retarded." *Medical Aspects of Human Sexuality,* 1971, 5(11), 94-118.

A review of literature on the sex-related problems of the MR from the developmental perspective.

31. Morgan, S.B. "Development and Distribution of Intellectual and Adaptive Skills in Down's Syndrome Children: Implications for Early Intervention." *Mental Retardation,* 1979, 17, 247-249.

This study presents data on the systematic decline in IQs and Social Quotients in Down's syndrome children from infancy to adolescence. An analysis of the distribution of IQs within different age ranges is also presented. The implications of the findings are discussed in terms of factors that might contribute to this decline and variability in functioning.

32. Morgenstern, M. "The Psychosexual Development of the Retarded." In F.F. de la Cruz & G.D. LaVeck, eds. *Human Sexuality and the Mentally Retarded.* New York: Brunner/Mazel, 1973.

Describes the psychosexual stages of normal and MR children, and reports results of a study comparing the sex-role perceptions and family relationships of 7- to 20-year-old normals and retardates.

33. Rosenheim, H.D., & Ables, B.S. "Social Deprivation and 'Mental Retardation'." *Child Psychiatry and Human Development,* 1974, 4, 216-226.

It is proposed that the relative effects of social deprivation may be useful in understanding psychological and etiological factors in MR. Social deprivation is viewed as resulting from the difference between predeprived and deprived levels of adults' social stimulation, and as being greatly affected by the rate of change. A case history approach illustrated the way in which the relative social deprivation thesis can contribute to a better understanding of the child's emotional and intellectual development as well as treatment techniques.

34. Schroeder, S.R., & Henes, C. "Assessment of Progress of Institutionalized and Deinstitutionalized Retarded Adults: A Matched-Control Comparison." *Mental Retardation,* 1978, 16, 147-148.

The Progress Assessment Chart (PAC) was given to group home residents recently placed from a regional mental retardation facility and their matched control counterparts who had remained at the institution. When the PAC was readministered after a year, group home placements showed more gains in their post-test scores, especially in communication. These gains were negatively related to the length of deinstitutionalization but unrelated to chronological age, mental age, or length of institutionalization.

35. Shastri, A.S.I., & Misra, A.K. "Assessment of Social Functioning of 56 Mentally Retarded Children." *Indian Journal of Mental Retardation,* 1974, 7(1), 31-35.

Assessed the social functioning of 56 MR schoolchildren on the basis of 4 criteria: (a) social interaction; (b) levels of communication; (c) self-responsibility; and (d) social behavior and its level of functioning in relation to the level of impairment. Results reveal that mildly retarded children function more in the lower level of social interaction; as the amount of intellectual impairment decreases, an average or satisfactory level of social functioning can be observed. It is concluded that since intellectual impairment affects the basic channels of communication, parents and teachers should be more involved in developing the social behavior of retarded children.

36.   Sternlicht, M. "Adolescent Retardates' Values, As
      Gleaned from Sentence-Completion Responses." Paper
      presented at the annual meeting of the Eastern Psycho-
      logical Association, Boston, April 1967.

      Using the Sentence Completion Test, the values, percep-
tions of the world, and attitudes of MR institutionalized
adolescents were obtained.

37.   Sternlicht, M. "Fears of Institutionalized Mentally
      Retarded Adults." *Journal of Psychology,* 1979, 101,
      67-71.

      The patterns of fears of institutionalized MR adults
were studies in a sample of 22 moderately retarded men and
women between the ages of 21 and 49. The direct questioning
method was employed. Two interviews were held, two weeks
apart; the first interview elicited the Ss' fears, while the
second concerned the fears of their friends. A total of 146
responses were obtained, and these were categorized according
to the types of fears: supernatural-natural events, animals,
physical injury, psychological stress, egocentric responses,
and no fears. The Ss displayed a higher percentage of fears
in the preoperational stage than in the concrete operational
stage. In a comparison of male to female fears, only one
category, that of fears of animals, reached significance.
The study suggested that the same developmental trend of
fears that appears in normal children appears in the retarded
as well, and these fears follow Piaget's level of cognitive
development, proceeding from egocentric perceptions of causal-
ity to realistic cause-and-effect thinking.

38.   Sternlicht, M. "Perceptions of Ugliness in the Mentally
      Retarded." *Journal of Psychology,* 1978, 99, 139-142.

      Thirty male and female retarded adults were asked to
draw a picture of a person and then to draw a picture of an
ugly person, in order to determine whether broader facial
features are a measure to ugliness (as found by McCullers
and Staat). Additionally, measures of broadness of facial
outline and body outline of the drawings were taken. Although there were no significant differences, there was a
trend to exaggerate the drawing of the ugly person, and the
rationale of this was discussed.

39. Sternlicht, M., & Deutsch, M.R. *Personality Development and Social Behavior in the Mentally Retarded.* Lexington, Mass.: Lexington Books, 1972.

Volume dealing with general issues in social behavior and development, including chapters on Social Behavior and Social Problems, Behavioral Adjustments in the Classroom, and the Adult Retardate.

40. Switzky, H., Rotatori, A.F., Miller T., & Freagon, S. "The Developmental Model and Its Implications for Assessment and Instruction for the Severely/Profoundly Handicapped." *Mental Retardation,* 1979, 17, 167-170.

The normative developmental model was discussed in terms of its implications for assessment and instruction for severely/profoundly handicapped children. Normative development sequences cannot provide educational program contents in a direct fashion as educational objectives. Educators are now deemphasizing "normal development" and are taking a remedial approach to strengthen specific skills regardless of hypothesized "developmental sequences and readiness."

41. Throne, J.M. "Normalization through the Normalization Principle: Right Ends, Wrong Means." *Mental Retardation,* 1975, 13(5), 23-25.

To speak of normalizing the retarded by treating them normally is a contradiction in terms; treating them normally will leave them functioning as retarded. Retarded by definition means retarded under ordinary conditions. Only extraordinary conditions—non-normal ones—can result in diminishing retarded states, i.e., making the retarded more normal.

42. Woodward, M. "Early Experiences and Later Social Responses of Severely Subnormal Children." *British Journal of Medical Psychology,* 1960, 33, 123-132.

One-third of MR children 3 to 10 years old living in a hospital responded with avoidance behavior to an unfamiliar person in an unfamiliar room. This response was associated with previous adverse environment.

CHAPTER II:
FAMILIAL INTERACTIONS

43. Affleck, G., Allen, D., McGrade, B.J., & McQueeny, M.
     "Home Environments of Developmentally Disabled Infants
     as a Function of Parent and Infant Characteristics."
     American Journal of Mental Deficiency, 1982, 86, 445-
     452.

     Variables from three categories were inspected as cor-
relates of HOME Inventory ratings for 43 severe perinatal
risk or developmentally disabled infants at 8 to 9 months
post-expected date of delivery. These variables were maternal
perceptions of the infant's temperament, maternal self-reported
mood, and interactional characteristics of the infant as rated
by a home observer. Stepwise regression analysis of HOME
total scores showed that infants who were viewed by their
mothers as more active and by the observer as less irritable
were particularly likely to experience more optimal developmental practices in the home. Significant predictors in regression equations for various of the HOME subscales were:
maternal ratings of the infant's mood, approach, adaptability,
and rhythmicity; maternal self-reported depression, tension,
and confusion; and infant pleasure in physical contact.

44. Alcorn, D.A. "Parental Views on Sexual Development and
     Education of the Trainable Mentally Retarded." *Journal
     of Special Education,* 1974, 8, 119-130.

     A questionnaire aimed at determining the sexual history
of the MR in terms of their parents' knowledge about them
and at assessing parental attitudes toward sex education and
the possibility of married family life for their TMR children
is evaluated in 206 cases. Parents reported much concern regarding the TMR's future sexual behavior. About two-thirds
of the subjects did not appear to their parents to be percep-
tive enough of sex differences to reveal any interest. Marriage for the TMR was supported by only a few of the parents,
but the wish for a happy relationship was expressed by a number

of parents. Most of the parents had little faith in the
ability of the TMR to use contraceptives. The results of
the study suggested that parents may be less inclined to
support voluntary sterilization in their own child than in
the MR in general.

45.   Barsch, R.H. *The Parent of the Handicapped Child*.
      Springfield, Ill.: C.C. Thomas, 1968.

      Presents a study of the child-rearing behavior pattern
of parents of MR children.

46.   Berger, M., & Foster, M. "Family-Level Interventions
      for Retarded Children: A Multivariate Approach to
      Issues and Strategies." *Multivariate Experimental
      Clinical Research*, 1976, 2(1), 1–21.

      Considers issues and strategies of household-level
interventions for families of retarded children. A perspective regarding retardation and a statement of the relevant
levels of analysis is set forth. Section 1 considers the
specific issues facing families with retarded children.
Section 2 (a) reviews the literature concerning interventions
aimed at families with retarded children, and (b) offers suggestions for future research and intervention efforts.

47.   Berger, M.I. "Stress, Family Competence, and Family
      Response to Stress." Doctoral dissertation, George
      Peabody College for Teachers, 1974 summarized in,
      Dissertation Abstracts International, 1975, 35, 6086B–
      6087B. (University Microfilms No. 75-12,434).

      This study provides evidence that families with a re-
tarded child are more likely to avoid conflictual or high
affect situations than families with a non-retarded child.
Also, families with a retarded child find child-rearing to
be more upsetting than families of a nonretarded child.

48. Buck, C., Valentine, G.H., & Hamilton, K. "A Study of Microsymptoms in the Parents and Sibs of Patients with Down's Syndrome." *American Journal of Mental Deficiency,* 1969, 73, 683-692.

A comparison of 110 families in which there occurs a subject with Down's syndrome with 100 control families gave no evidence that fathers, mothers, brothers, or sisters of affected subjects show consistently mongoloid deviations of 22 physical characteristics implicated in the microsymptoma-tology of that condition. The relation between this result and that of the previous comparison of the reproductive histories of mothers in the mongol and control families has been discussed.

49. Cleveland, D.W., & Miller, N. "Attitudes and Life Commitments of Older Siblings of Mentally Retarded Adults: An Exploratory Study." *Mental Retardation,* 1977, 15(3), 38-41.

Data from a survey of 90 men and women who were siblings of 72 MR adults suggested that a majority of the respondents did not suffer adverse affects upon their life commitments by having an MR brother of sister. A positive adaptation was made to the MR sibling; and in the majority of cases, the respondents indicated their parents had approached the problem of raising an MR child in an adaptive manner. However, in a minority of cases, the sex roles of the normal siblings influenced their reaction to the situation. In contrast to the normal male sibling, whose responses revealed a lack of information about the MR child, the female sibling's responses showed a close relationship to the MR, perhaps because of being assigned more parent-surrogate responsibilities. This, in turn, might have led to a greater effect on adult commitments.

50. Cummings, S.T. "The Impact of the Child's Deficiency on the Father: A Study of Fathers of Mentally Retarded and of Chronically Ill Children." *American Journal of Orthopsychiatry,* 1976, 46, 246-255.

Two hundred and forty fathers, 60 fathers each of MR children, chronically physically ill children, neurotic children, and healthy children, were assessed for the psychological impact of their children's handicaps. Test measures were selected to permit assessment of the fathers' prevailing

mood, their self-esteem, their interpersonal satisfaction in
relating to family members and others, and their child-rearing
attitudes. The fathers of the MR and chronically ill children
revealed significant negative effects from the experience of
fathering a health-deficient child, with fathers in the first
group showing the greater negative impact.

51. Dashiff, C.J. "Mother-Child Relationships in Retarded
     and Normal Children." Doctoral dissertation, Florida
     State University, 1977, summarized in *Dissertation
     Abstracts International,* 1978, 38, 4149B-4150B. (Univ-
     ersity Microfilms No. 7801470).

     Mothers of 2 and 3-year-old mildly MR children, in
comparison to mothers of normal children, tend to overassess
the child's development, and were less submissive, cooperative,
and conversant.

52. Davis, H., & Oliver, B. "A Comparison of Aspects of the
     Maternal Speech Environment of Retarded and Nonretarded
     Children." *Child Care, Health & Development,* 1980, 6,
     135-145.

     Eight mothers were observed in interaction with their
retarded children and compared with 8 mothers of nonretarded
infants. Ss had been matched in terms of various socioeconomic
indices (e.g., nationality, marital status, and type of housing)
and language behavior. The mothers of retarded children were
found significantly more stimulating vocally, more responsive,
and less directive than controls. Findings are discussed in
terms of possible reasons for such differences and the implications for the child.

53. Dimperio, T.L. "Psychological Adjustment of Fathers of
     Young Retarded Children." Doctoral dissertation, The
     University of Texas Health Science Center at Dallas,
     1975, summarized in *Dissertation Abstracts International,*
     1976, 36, 5757B. (University Microfilms No. 76-11,834).

     The study is concerned with the impact of a MR child on
the psychological adjustment of fathers. Although the fathers'
overall personality functioning may not be reduced by the
birth of a MR child, the fathers' psychosocial adjustment is
likely to be negatively affected.

54. D'Onofrio, A., Robinson, B., Isett, R.D., Roszkowski, M.J., & Spreat, S. "Factors Related to Contact between Mentally Retarded Persons and Their Parents during Residential Treatment." *Mental Retardation,* 1980, 18, 293-294.

Factors concerning the degree of parental involvement with institutionalized MR offspring are identified. Significant bivariate correlations are found between the duration of family visits and 11 parent or offspring variables. A linear combination of years of prior institutionalization, parents living together, presence of convulsive disorders, and the ABS Psychological Disturbances domain results in a multiples correlation of .42 with the duration of parental visits. A weak correlation between client adaptive behavior and parental contact is revealed.

55. Dunlap, W.R., & Hollinsworth, J.S. "How Does a Handicapped Child Affect the Family? Implications for Practitioners." *Family Coordinator,* 1977, 26, 286-293.

Notes the growing concern for families of the handicapped, with emphasis on the problems of the parents and recognition of the stress created in the family by such a child. The present study was based on data gathered in interviews with 404 families with a developmentally disabled family member. The vast majority of the families interviewed did not perceive the disabled member as having substantial effects on them. Results indicate that the adjustment of family members had been good and indicate no serious consequences to their family.

56. Dupras, A., & Tremblay, R. "Path Analysis of Parents' Conservatism toward Sex Education of Their Mentally Retarded Children." *American Journal of Mental Deficiency,* 1976, 81, 162-166.

Investigated three probable reasons why parents of MR children would be opposed to sex education being offered as a school subject: general sexual attitudes, specific sexual attitudes, and prejudices against the retarded child's own sexuality. A questionnaire was given to 60 parents of retarded children and 62 parents of nonretarded children. A correlation analysis revealed evidence of all three kinds of reasons and led to a causal model of conservatism on sex education. A path analysis revealed that (a) sexual prejudices are a major obstacle to sex education, and (b) each group of parents represents a specific dynamic of conservatism on sex education.

57. Eheart, B.K. "A Comparative Observational Study of
     Mother-Child Interactions with Nonretarded and Mentally
     Retarded Children." Doctoral dissertation, University
     of Wisconsin-Madison, 1976, summarized in *Dissertation
     Abstracts International,* 1977, 37, 5033A. (University
     Microfilms No. 76-25,556).

The play interaction between mothers and nonretarded
children was compared with the play interaction between
mothers and their MR children. It was found that many of
the mothers of the MR children dominated the free play
sessions more than did mothers of the non-MR children. It
is suggested that mothers of MR children are apt not to foster social competency skills in their children.

58. Eheart, B.K. "Mother-Child Interactions with Nonretarded
     and Mentally Retarded Preschoolers." *American Journal
     of Mental Deficiency,* 1982, 87, 20-25.

Comparisons of mother-child interaction patterns exhibited during free-play sessions were made between 8 mother-
child dyads and 8 mother-nonretarded child dyads. Mothers'
perceptions of randomly selected interactions were also examined. The children were matched for cognitive level on the
basis of play behavior. The mean age of the retarded children was 46.5 months; of the nonretarded children, 27.2 months.
Results indicated that mothers of children dominated the play
sessions more than did the comparison mothers. In addition,
they perceived themselves as trying to change their children's
behavior more often than did the comparison mothers. The MR
children responded less frequently to their mothers' invita-
tions than did the nonretarded children, and they initiated
less than half as many interactions.

59. Eheart, B.K., & Ciccone, J. "Special Needs of Low-Income
     Mothers of Developmentally Delayed Children." *American
     Journal of Mental Deficiency,* 1982, 87, 26-33.

The needs that were created or intensified for 36 low-
income mothers in the first years after learning that they
were the parents of a developmentally delayed child were investigated, and intervention strategies to help these mothers
meet their special needs were identified. Results suggest
that the overwhelming need of these mothers was to learn how
to cope with the many unknowns about their child's future, and
that an effective intervention strategy might be the establishment of groups run by and for parents in conjunction with early
intervention programs for the children.

60. Ellis, N.R., Bostick, G.E., Moore, S.A., & Taylor, J.J. "A Follow-up of Severely and Profoundly Mentally Retarded Children after Short-Term Institutionalization." *Mental Retardation,* 1981, 19, 31-35.

A follow-up study of profoundly and severely MR children after a period of institutionalization was conducted. The study consists of evaluation of institutional records and an assessment of functioning on the ABS. The average length of institutionalization is 10.5 months. The institutional/training experience seems to lead some parents to keep their child at home and others to place their child in an institution on a long-term basis, contrary to early plans and intent.

61. Evans, E.C. "The Grief Reaction of Parents of the Retarded and the Counsellor's Role." *Australian Journal of Mental Retardation,* 1976, 4(4), 8-12.

Although grief may be experienced by some parents of minimally MR children, this reaction is probably more universal among parents of moderately MR children. The process of grief may be divided into the 5 primary stages of shock, protest, despair, detachment, and acceptance. Most parents of the MR child suffer chronic grief throughout their lives regardless of whether the child is kept at home or institutionalized. The intensity and expression of grief vary with the person and the situation, but in all cases the parent's suffering may be alleviated by counseling.

62. Farber, B. "Effects of a Severely Mentally Retarded Child on Family Integration." *Monograph of the Society for Research in Child Development,* 1959, No. 71

Mothers were asked to rate their oldest sibling on a scale designed to measure the role tension of a normal sibling as it related to various aspects of a younger, MR child. The results indicated that, as perceived by the mother, a high degree of role tension in the normal sibling was related to the mother's tension, regarding the MR child as highly dependent.

63.   Farber, B. "Family Adaptations to Severely Mentally
      Retarded Children." In M.J. Begab & S.A. Richardson,
      eds. *The Mentally Retarded and Society: A Social Science
      Perspective*, 247-266. Baltimore: University Park Press,
      1975.

      Discusses the form of the family adaptation process to
severely MR children, and the appropriateness of adaptations.
Also discusses the part played by family values in determining
the suitability of the particular adaptation, and methods for
determining the "rationality" of any given adaptation.

64.   Farber, B., & Ryckman, D.B. "Effects of Severely Men-
      tally Retarded Children on Family Relationships."
      Mental Retardation Abstracts, 1965, 2, 1-17.

      Describes the diverse reactions of parents to their MR
child.

65.   Featherstone, H. *A Difference in the Family*. New York:
      Basic Books, 1980.

      Describes the experiences of parents of disabled children.

66.   Ferrara, D.M. "Attitudes of Parents of Mentally Retarded
      Children toward Normalization Activities." *American
      Journal of Mental Deficiency,* 1979, 84, 145-151.

      Parents of MR children were surveyed via a 5-point
Likert scale to determine their attitudes toward normalization
activities in general and in relation to their child. Results
indicated significant differences in response, with the more
positive attitudes being those associated with a general (the
mentally retarded population) rather than specific (my child)
referent. Within the general referent group, parents of TMR
children displayed the most positive attitudes. Age, sex, and
level of retardation had an effect on child-specific responses.

67. Fowle, C.M. "The Effect of the Severely Mentally Retarded
     Child on His Family." *American Journal of Mental Defi-
     ciency,* 1968, 73, 468-473.

     Compared the marital integration and sibling role tension
in families that retained their MR children at home to those
that placed the MR children in institutions. Differences
were found in the siblings' role tensions.

68. Freeman, R.D. "Psychological Management of the Retarded
     Child and Its Family." *Psychiatric Annals,* 1973, 3(7),
     11-22.

     Proposes that the later functioning of most retarded
persons depends more on socialization than IQ. Early relationships between physician and such families are instrumental in
providing the necessary home support.

69. Gath, A. "The Impact of an Abnormal Child upon the
     Parents." *British Journal of Psychiatry,* 1977, 130,
     405-410.

     Thirty families with a newborn mongol baby were matched
with thirty families with a normal baby. Both groups were
followed for eighteen months to two years and interviewed
six times. Few differences could be found in the mental or
physical health of the two groups of parents, but marital
breakdown or severe marital disharmony was found in nine of
the mongol families and in none of the controls.

70. Goldenberg, I. "Acquiescence to a Social Label." *American
     Journal of Orthopsychiatry,* 1974, 44, 190.

     The acquiescence of low-status individuals to a social
label is discussed, focusing on problems of MR mothers, infant stimulation and social intervention. MR mothers acquiesce
to their social label by appearing incompetent to provide their
children with adequate social and cognitive stimulation. The
presence of experiments influences lower-class MR mothers to
function far below their capacity as mothers. An infant stimulation program, based on the repertoire of behaviors observed
by the experimenter, might overlook skills that the mother
possesses. Social intervention programs should reflect a
realistic evaluation of individual capacities with no experimenter bias.

71. Goodman, D.M. "Parenting an Adult Mentally Retarded
     Offspring." *Smith College Studies in Social Work,* 1978,
     48, 209-234.

     Studied the feelings, attitudes, views problems, and
practices of 23 parents of 16 MR adults. Respondents were
46 to 78 years old. They were administered a 62-item questionnaire during interviews. Almost all said they felt uncomfort-
able leaving their offspring alone, whether supervised or not.
More than half felt that the retardate's presence at home had
little effect on their social life. All expressed a wish for
more job-related programs for the retarded. Almost all said
that they got along well with the retarded individual, but
certain problems in the relationships were noted. What should
happen to the retarded person when the parent(s) died was a
major source of anxiety and two-thirds of the respondents said
they needed help or guidance in planning their child's future.

72. Goodman, L., Budner, S., & Lesh, B. "The Parents' Role
     in Sex Education for the Retarded." *Mental Retardation,*
     1971, 9(1), 43-45.

     Presents results of the social work section of an inter-
disciplinary survey concerned with selected aspects of the
sexual development and education of the mildly retarded. Fifteen parents of retarded adolescents were interviewed in depth.
An attempt was also made to synthesize extensive clinical experience in dealing with the problem. The necessity for
parent participation in programs concerned with sex education
is highlighted.

73. Graliker, B.V., Fishler, K., & Koch, R. "Teenage Reaction
     to a Mentally Retarded Sibling." *American Journal of
     Mental Deficiency,* 1962, 66, 838-843.

     Presents the results of a study performed with 21 teen-
age siblings of 16 retarded children, which suggest that these
teenagers, on the whole, lead a normal life with adequate
social outlets and positive relationships with their peers.
Their relationships within the home were good, and they accepted their retarded sibling.

74. Granat, J.P. "Marital Disintegration among Parents of
     Mentally Retarded Adults and Adolescents: Implications
     for Psychological Counseling." Doctoral dissertation,
     University of Michigan, 1978, summarized in *Dissertation
     Abstracts International,* 1978, 39, 3469A. (University
     Microfilms No. 7822900).

     Studied marital behavior of parents of MR persons.
Found that the divorce rate of parents of MR persons is lower
than it is among parents of nonretarded persons. Parental
disorder rates are greater in families with more children.
Parents in intact marriages have a greater frequency of parental disorders than parents who experienced divorce or separation.

75. Greene, E.G. "A Comparative Study of Perceptions of
     Parents toward Their Mentally Retarded Children."
     Doctoral dissertation, University of Alabama, 1970,
     summarized in *Dissertation Abstracts International,*
     1971, 31, 3372A. (University Microfilms No. 71-1242).

     Studies parents' perceptions of their EMR children and
trainable MR children. Found that the perception of parents
of their MR children depended on the severity of the child's
retardation. Furthermore, found that parents of EMR retarded
children were more anxious than parents of trainable MR children.

76. Gumz, E.J., & Gubrium, J.F. "Comparative Parental Per-
     ceptions of a Mentally Retarded Child." *American
     Journal of Mental Deficiency,* 1972, 77, 175-180.

     Several studies have explored mothers' perceptions of
and behavior toward their MR child. This research compares
the retarded child's perceptions of mothers and fathers util-
izing the instrumental-expressive role framework of Parsons
and Bales. Although not consistently statistically significant, evidence from a sample of 50 families with a retarded
child showed that there is a tendency for fathers to perceive
their child more instrumentally than mothers, the latters'
perceptions being more expressive.

77. Hastings, D. "Some Psychiatric Problems of Mental Defi-
     ciency." *American Journal of Mental Deficiency,* 1948,
     52, 260-262.

     Holds that parents of MR children should receive the help
of professional personnel in taking care of their children.

78. Holroyd, J., & McArthur, D. "Mental Retardation and
     Stress on the Parents: A Contrast between Down's
     Syndrome and Childhood Autism." *American Journal of
     Mental Deficiency,* 1976, 80, 431-436.

     Mothers of autistic, Down's syndrome, and outpatient
psychiatric clinic children completed a questionnaire about
their attitudes toward the identified child and the effect
of the child on themselves and their families. Results revealed a general retardation/social dependency factor separating
the mothers of the two retarded groups from the clinic group.
The autism group was differentiated from the Down's syndrome
group by scales measuring the severity of the child's handicap
and family integration problems more than by scales measuring
stress on the mother. Mothers of autistic children reported
more problems than the mothers in both of the other groups.

79. Jamison, C.B., Attwell, A.A., & Fils, D.H. "Parent vs.
     Teacher Behavior Ratings of TMR Pupils." *American
     Journal of Mental Deficiency,* 1971, 75, 746-751.

     The Test Behavior Observation Guide (TBOG) was completed
by 65 mothers and 28 teachers of 65 TMR pupils to permit a
comparison of the parent and teacher behavior ratings of the
boys and girls. Significant differences between parent and
teacher ratings were found in Motor Activity and Amount of
Speech (for the girls) and in Effort and Cooperation (for
the boys).

80. Katz, E. *The Retarded Adult at Home: A Guide for Parents.*
     Seattle, Wash.: Special Child Publications, 1970.

     General baedeker for parents of MR adults, including
available community services.

81. Kennett, K.F. "The Family Behavior Profile: An Initial
     Report." *Mental Retardation,* 1977, 15(4), 36-40.

        Aware that much of what each individual learns is the
product of observing the behavior of others, especially those
of the immediate family, the AAMD Adaptive Behavior Scale
was extended by the development of the Family Behavior Profile.
The Family Behavior Profile provides behavior patterns of
related individuals and a family constellation as an aid in
identifying deficiencies in the home environment, in developing appropriate training programs to increase awareness of
the importance of the home environment, to provide behavioral
information relevant to cultural and familial aspects of
etiology, to aid in developing realistic goals, and to aid in
devising modelling techniques in a real situation.

82. Kershner, J.R. "Intellectual and Social Development in
     Relation to Family Functioning: A Longitudinal Compari-
     son of Home vs. Institutional Effects." *American Journal
     of Mental Deficiency,* 1970, 75, 276-284.

        Forty-two MR children were tested before entering an
institution and 1 year later on measures of SQ (Vineland) and
IQ (Stanford-Binet) and their families pre- and post interviewed to assess the adequacy of family functioning. Comparisons were made with 27 community-based families and their
children who were of similar CA and IQ. Family functioning,
SQ, and IQ/SQ discrepancy were found to be related to family
decisions to seek long-term residential placement. Community
families and children showed decreases over the year on all
measures taken, whereas institutional families tended to improve in functioning. In the community group, a significant
positive correlation was found between IQ, decrement and
family pre-posted losses. In the institution group, a significant negative correlation was found between low initial SQ
and family increments in functioning. Results point up the
important reciprocal relations existing between the retarded
child and his family.

83. Koch, R., & Dobson, J.C., eds. *The Mentally Retarded
     Child and His Family: A Multidisciplinary Handbook.*
     2nd ed. New York: Brunner/Mazel, 1976.

        A broad treatment of the problem, causative factors,
and the multidisciplinary approach to mental retardation.

84. Kogan, K.L., & Tyler, N. "Mother-Child Interaction in
     Young Physically Handicapped Children." *American Journal
     of Mental Deficiency,* 1973, 77, 492-497.

     Observational techniques combining verbal and nonverbal
behaviors were employed to analyze interactions between 10
physically handicapped children and their mothers. The patterns were compared to those of 15 nonhandicapped and 6 MR
mother-child pairs. Behaviors were analyzed according to
their relative status, affection, and involvement components.
Mothers of the physically handicapped children displayed a
greater incidence of assertive control and warm behaviors
than did the comparison mothers and showed no differences
from the mothers of mentally retarded children. The physically
handicapped children interacted at low involvement levels more
frequently than the nonhandicapped, but they displayed a greater
number of assertive controlling behaviors than the retarded
children.

85. Kohler, C., & Didier, P. "Reflections on the Problems
     Posed by Children of Mentally Handicapped Parents."
     *Revue de Neuropsychiatrie Infantile et d'Hygiene Mentale
     de l'Enfance,* 1974, 22(1-2), 53-64.

     Presents a longitudinal study of 5 children of MR parents.
It is noted that the sparse literature available on normal children of retarded couples focuses on their affective and character problems, and their slowness in language development. Case
histories of the 5 Ss revealed a high incidence of instability
in the parental relations and of general disinterest in the
child. It is suggested that disturbances in the parent-child
relations in families with retarded parents make the children
highly vulnerable to ego disorders. It is concluded that
social service agencies need to be more aware of the problems
of MR couples and their normal children.

86. Marshall, N.R., Hegrenes, J.R., & Goldstein, S. "Verbal
     Interactions: Mothers and Their Retarded Children vs.
     Mothers and their Nonretarded Children." *American
     Journal of Mental Deficiency,* 1973, 77, 415-419.

     Compared 20 MR and 20 nonretarded 3 to 5-year-olds and
their mothers on frequency of 4 verbal operants, which were
obtained from a tape-recorded 15-minute play session involving
each mother and her child. Nonretarded and MR children differed quantitatively with regard to verbal operants: tacts,

mands, and intraverbals occurred with greater frequency with nonretarded children. The only difference between mothers was a higher mand rate for mothers of retarded children. With the exception of echoics by the retarded children, the order of usage of verbal operants was the same between mothers and between children.

87. McKinney, J.P, & Keele, T. "Effects of Increased Mothering on the Behavior of Severely Retarded Boys." *American Journal of Mental Deficiency,* 1963, 67, 556-562.

Twenty-four severely retarded boys received increased physical attention from older, mildly retarded women. The boys' behavior, primarily purposive behavior and language communication, improved.

88. Miller, S.G. "An Exploratory Study of Sibling Relationships in Families with Retarded Children." Doctoral dissertation, Columbia University, 1974, summarized in *Dissertation Abstracts International,* 1974, 35, 2994B-2995B. (University Microfilms No. 74-26,606).

Probed the relationship between siblings in families with one retarded child and one or more normal siblings. Found that there are differences between the way the normal children related to normal siblings and the way they related to retarded siblings. The effect of the retardate on his normal siblings can be either positive or negative.

89. Moric-Petrovic, S. "The Mentally Retarded Child in the Family." *Psihijatrija Danas,* 1974, 6, 179-184.

Mental retardation is defined as lack of ability to learn and mature socially at the usual rate because of factors that have existed before and at the time of conception, during pregnancy and birth, and during the developmental period. The importance of allowing the MR child to establish a meaningful relationship with his/her mother is emphasized.

90. Nihira, K., Meyers, C.E., & Mink, I.T. "Home Environment
     Family Adjustment, and the Development of Mentally Re-
     tarded Children." *Applied Research in Mental Retardation,*
     1980, 1(1-2), 5-24.

     Examined the longitudinal effect of educational and resi-
dential environments on personal, social, and cognitive development of 114 trainable (TMR) and 152 EMR children (mean IQs 42.2
and 66.4, respectively) and their families. All Ss resided in
their natural homes with married parents. Some environmental
variables included parental behavior and attitude, psychosocial
climate, and demographic and structural characteristics. Measures of family adjustment included the S's effect on the family
and the family's capacity to cope with mental retardation.
Child characteristics were described in terms of adaptive and
maladaptive behavior, psychological and social adjustment, and
self-concept, using the Adaptive Behavior Scales. Canonical
correlation analyses indicated conceptual and statistical linkages between home environment, family adjustment, and competency
of MR children.

91. Pancheri, P. "A Study of the Reaction of a Group of
     Mothers of Retarded Children Using the Parental Attitude
     Research Instrument (PARI)." *Revista di Psichiatria,*
     1971, 6, 394-407.

     Administered the PARI to 2 groups of 30 Ss each. One
was composed of mothers of children with no serious physical
deficiency but with mild mental deficiency, and the other of
mothers with normal children. On some items significant differences were found between the 2 groups. Results are interpreted as signs of maternal maladjustments to extra-familial
social environment or as the acceptance of maternal duties.

92. Pecci, E.F. "Parents and Siblings of the Retarded."
     In E. Katz, ed. *Mental Health Services for the Mentally
     Retarded.* 155-171. Springfield, Ill.: C.C. Thomas, 1972.

     Discusses the effects of the retarded child upon family
autonomy, particularly those stresses placed upon the mother
as the primary caretaker. Also, deals with the emotional
reactions of parents and siblings toward the retarded child,
and concludes with some words on therapy with the parents
and siblings.

93. Price-Bonham, S., & Addison, S. "Families and Mentally Retarded Children: Emphasis on the Father." *Family Coordinator,* 1978, 27, 221-230.

In this review, literature is summarized that is relevant to persons who work with MR children and their families. However, the major emphasis is on the relationship between fathers and their MR children. It is suggested that fathers should be more involved with their MR child, and this can be achieved through education, counseling, and various programs.

94. Ramey, C.T., Mills, P., Campbell, F.A., & O'Brien, C. "Infants' Home Environments: A Comparison of High-risk Families and Families from the General Population." *American Journal of Mental Deficiency,* 1975, 80, 40-42.

Home environments of 30 infants at high-risk for developmental retardation were compared with those of 30 infants from the general population (matched for age, sex, and parity) by means of the Home Observation Measurement of the Environment. Fifteen high-risk infants attended a day-care intervention program; 15 did not. The Home Observation for Measurement of the Environment showed significant differences between the high-risk groups and the general population, favoring the general population on all factors (maternal warmth, absence of restriction and punishment, organization of the environment, appropriate toys, maternal involvement, and opportunities for variety); but showed none between the two high-risk groups.

95. Reeder, D.A. "A Model of Family Characteristics for Problem-Solving Behavior in Families with a Mentally Retarded Child." Doctoral dissertation, Boston University Graduate School, 1973, summarized in *Dissertation Abstracts International,* 1973, 34, 1758B. (University Microfilms No. 73-23,510).

Attempted to develop a model of family characteristics hypothesized as being operationally helpful for problem-solving behavior in families with a MR child. The model was tested on one family that managed the problems efficiently, and one family that did not. Several conclusions emerged in regard to the father's role and the family's flexible approach to problem solving.

96.   Ricci, C.S. "Analysis of Child-Rearing Attitudes of
      Mothers of Retarded, Emotionally Disturbed, and Normal
      Children." *American Journal of Mental Deficiency,* 1970,
      74, 756-761.

      Found that mothers of retarded, emotionally disturbed,
and normal children differ on the Authoritarian-Control and
the Warmth dimensions.

97.   Smith, H.M., & Sykes, S.C. "Parents' Views on the Develop-
      ment of Social Competencies in Their Mildly Intellectually
      Handicapped Adolescents." *Australian Journal of Develop-
      mental Disabilities,* 1981, 7(1), 17-26.

      Developed and administered an interview schedule to par-
ents of 43 16- to 21-year-old mildly MR adolescents attending
a work preparation center. The schedule provided insights
into home background influences and underlying parents' perceptions and expectations. This determined the extent of the
need for parental involvement, support, and subsequent directions for programming. The responses revealed that many Ss
were still home-based and family-dependent. Some parents were
prolonging the dependence of their children rather than reinforcing the independent living-skills training at the center.
Parents were aware of important deficiences in Ss' lack of
friends and leisure time interests but needed guidance in
helping in these areas.

98.   Tavormina, J.B., Henggeler, S.W., & Gayton, W.F. "Age
      Trends in Parental Assessments of the Behavior Problems
      of Their Retarded Children." *Mental Retardation,* 1976,
      14(1), 38-39.

      Fifty-two mothers with an MR child living at home each
voluntarily provided a list and description of the 3 most
pressing problems she currently faced in the management of
her child. Responses were categorized into 12 problem areas
and analyzed by age groups (2 to 4 years, 4 to 6 years, 8 to
12 years, and 12 to 17 years). The category of disobedience,
stubbornness, and noncompliance was the most pressing issue
and occurred with greatest frequency in all age groups except
adolescence. There was a trend for most issues to decrease
with age. These included (a) eating problems; (b) talking and
communication problems; (c) mobility-walking problems; (d)
impulsiveness, sensitivity, and "temperamental" behavior; (e)
aggressiveness toward others; and (f) personal hygiene and

dressing problems. In contrast, problems with social interaction peaked in the oldest age group. Concern with toileting
and toilet training existed across all age groups and was listed
by 45 percent of mothers.

99. Tizard, J., & Grad, J.C. *The Mentally Handicapped and
    their Families, a Social Survey.* London: Oxford Univ-
    ersity Press, 1967.

Discusses the relationship of the MR with their families,
and specific interactional patterns.

100. Tomkiewicx, S. "Tolerance and Stability of Parents of
     The Backward Child." *Bulletin de Psychologie,* 1971-1972,
     25, 1040-1047.

Discusses 2 ideas of critical importance in working with
parents of backward children, especially in cases where the
parents are rejecting or hyperprotective: tolerance or the
attitude which maximizes the integration of the backward child
into the family, and family stability or the quality which
protects the needs and desires of all members of the family.
The concept of levels of tolerance and stability are elaborated
and the difficulty of estimating these levels are discussed.

101. Turchin, G. "Sexual Attitudes of Mothers of Retarded
     Children." *Journal of School Health,* 1974, 44, 490-492.

Attitudes of 44 mothers of TMR children toward the sexual
behavior, sex education, birth control, marriage, and dating
of these children were assessed. Religion proved to be an
influence in the mothers' attitudes toward masturbation and
marriage. Although many mothers expected that their children
would develop the ability to date, most of them felt that
their children would never be able to marry. The mothers
wanted sex education taught in the schools, and parent groups
to be formed to aid them in understanding the sexuality of
their children.

102. Villecheneoux-Bonnafe, M.Y. "The Young Backward Child
      and His Family: The Persistence of Ties Between Parents
      and the Child Even When the Child Has Been Removed from
      the Home." *Revue de Neuropsychiatrie Infantile et
      d'Hygiene Mentale de l'Enfance,* 1974, 22(1-2), 41-51.

      Discusses patterns of interpersonal relations in the
families of retarded children. The presence of a severely
MR child is a traumatic situation for the family, and can
lead to conflicts between parents, conflicts in the retarded
child's siblings, and loss of social status for the family.
It is suggested that the ties between a retarded child and
his family continue to be strong even if he is removed from
the family and institutionalized. It is concluded that the
institutionalized retarded child can make real progress only
when his teachers are convinced that the parents desire his
progress.

103. Wadsworth, H.G., & Wadsworth, J.B. "A Problem of Involve-
      ment with Parents of Mildly Retarded Children." *Family
      Coordinator,* 1971, 20, 141-147.

      Parents of these mildly or borderline retarded children
have not organized in an effort to receive better services.
Several reasons are suggested for this lack of involvement
by the parents: (a) unwillingness to admit to a significant
intellectual problem with their child, (b) indifference, and
(c) dependence on special education programs of the school.
Questionnaires were sent to parents of mildly retarded children in special education classes to try to involve these
parents in their child's education. Two conclusions are
discussed: (a) Significant differences were found between
respondents and nonrespondents on socioeconomic status and
children's IQ level. (b) Those who did respond evidenced
intense feelings toward the problem of the classificatory
labeling of the children.

104. Weller, L., Costeff, C., Cohen, B., & Rahman, D. "Social
      Variables in the Perception and Acceptance of Retarda-
      tion." *American Journal of Mental Deficiency,* 1974, 79,
      274-278.

      In Israel, the effects of country of origin (Jews of
European or Eastern descent), social class of parents, and
level of retardation of the child on parental guilt feelings,
perception of the retardation, and acceptance of the child

were studied. Seventy-six mothers of retarded children were interviewed. Results show no effect for country of origin. Middle-class parents and parents of severely retarded children more accurately perceived the retardation than lower-class parents or parents whose children were less severely retarded. There were no differences by social class or level of retardation for parental guilt feelings or acceptance of the child.

105. Wikler, L., & Stoycheff, J. "Parental Compliance with Postdischarge Recommendations for Retarded Children." *Hospital & Community Psychiatry,* 1974, 25, 595-598.

Used parental compliance with postdischarge recommendations as the criterion for successful intervention in a study conducted on a short-term in-patient ward for retarded children. Parents' attitudes and the extent to which they had followed the recommendations were assessed in telephone interviews at least 3 months after the child was discharged. Results indicate that 3 variables were significantly correlated with compliance: agreement with the diagnosis, postdischarge contact with the ward, and preadmission stresses of caring for the child.

106. Willer, B.S., Intagliata, J.C., & Atkinson, A.C. "Crisis for Families of Mentally Retarded Persons Including the Crisis of Deinstitutionalization." *British Journal of Mental Subnormality,* 1979, 25(1), 38-49.

Examines the literature on reactions of families of MR persons to a number of crisis events: initial diagnosis, burden of care, institutionalization, and deinstitutionalization. Research on each crisis indicates that reactions to diagnosis, such as severe grief, do not necessarily have long-term effects. Studies of burden of care indicate that deleterious effects on family functioning and the mental health of the mother are more related to how the family perceives the need for care than to the actual level of developmental handicap. Institutionalization, often chosen as a solution to earlier crises such as diagnosis and burden of care, was found to be a poor solution and, in fact, represented a crisis event for families as well.

107.   Willer, B.S., Intagliata, J.C., & Atkinson, A.C. "De-
       institutionalization as a Crisis Event for Families
       of Mentally Retarded Persons." *Mental Retardation,*
       1981, 19, 28-29.

       Structured interviews were conducted to determine the
extent to which families of the MR experience a crisis upon
deinstitutionalization of a family member. The results indicate that approximately 50 percent of the families experience a crisis, even if their family member is not returned
to their home. Highly structured families, as measured by
the Family Environment Scale, are the least likely to experience crisis.

108.   Wolf, L.C., & Whitehead, P.C. "The Decision to Institu-
       tionalize Retarded Children: Comparison of Individually
       Matched Groups." *Mental Retardation,* 1975, 13(5), 3-7.

       A group of 24 institutionalized MR children was individu-
ally matched on the basis of sex, socio-economic status, I.Q.,
and A.A.M.D. diagnostic category, with a group of 24 retarded
children who remained at home. Results indicated that the
sex of the child and the amount of disruption perceived by
the family, as caused by the child, are significant factors
in determining the course of institutionalization.

109.   Wolfensberger, W., & Kurtz, R.A. "Use of Retardation-
       Related Diagnostic and Descriptive Labels by Parents
       of Retarded Children." *Journal of Special Education,*
       1974, 8, 131-141.

       Parents of handicapped and primarily MR children were
administered a list of 57 diagnostic or descriptive labels
historically associated with handicap or MR, and the meaning
of the terminology was explained. The data suggest that
parental reactions to a list of MR and MR-related terms are
emotionally based and that parents had considerable difficulty
accepting any label for their MR children. Parents rejected
terms which are clearly negative in social desirability; in
a context where parents do not have to label their children
with any terms, or where the labeling process is not emphasized, judgments of their children are handled without difficulty.

110. Zuk, G.H. "Autistic Distortions in Parents of Retarded
      Children." In T.E. Jordan, ed. *Perspectives in Mental
      Retardation,* 35-43. Carbondale: Southern Illinois Univ-
      ersity, 1966.

      A study of parental perception of handicapped and non-
handicapped MR children.

CHAPTER III:
PEER AND OTHER INTERACTIONS

111.   Bedrosian, J.L., & Prutting, C.A. "Communicative Perform-
       ance of Mentally Retarded Adults in Four Conversational
       Settings." *Journal of Speech & Hearing Research,* 1978,
       21, 79-95.

       Conducted a sociolinguistic analysis of the communica-
tive performances and social interactions of 4 MR 24 to 28-
year-olds. Role relationships were examined in various con-
versational settings. Recordings were made of Ss' conversation
while discoursing with their speech-language pathologists,
peers, parents, and a normal young child. Results show that
Ss, though not always able to hold a dominant position in a
conversation, were capable of expressing the same types of
control as normal adults. Findings suggest that a socio-
linguistic approach provides important information regarding
the MR adult's communicative performance.

112.   Berger, W. R. "The Effect of Competition on the Self-
       Concept, Peer Social Acceptance and Work Productivity
       of Mental Retardates in Vocational Training." Doctoral
       dissertation, University of Connecticut, 1976, summar-
       ized in *Dissertation Abstracts International,* 1977,
       38, 153A. (University Microfilms No. 77-14,449).

       Participation in sport competition by MR in vocational
training failed to change the self-concept, yet improved
social acceptance and work productivity. Winners were more
accepted by peers than losers.

113. Berkson, G., & Romer, D. "Social Ecology of Supervised
      Communal Facilities for Mentally Disabled Adults:
      I. Introduction." *American Journal of Mental Deficiency*,
      1980, 85, 219-228.

      The social relationships among mentally disabled adults
who worked in four sheltered workshops were described. In
this paper, procedures for observing and interviewing clients
and staff members were described, and data on reliability and
general levels of behavior were reported. Reliability of
social behavior was significant across time and situations.
Social choice estimates were not very consistent across staff,
clients, and observations. Clients spent about 40 percent
of their time in informal socializing, primarily in conversation.

114. Borys, S.V., & Spitz, H.H. "Effect of Peer Interaction
      on the Problem-Solving Behavior of Mentally Retarded
      Youths." *American Journal of Mental Deficiency*, 1979,
      84, 273-279.

      EMR young adults were given one-bit problems (Experiment
1) or a test of conversation (Experiment 2). Subjects were
classified as either high or low performers. In a second
session the low performers were paired with the high performers, and the dyads were required to agree on the solution to
the problems presented. A control group of low performers
was simply tested individually in a second session. One
month later all the low performers were retested on the same
logic problems or on an alternate form of the conservation
test. No differences were observed in Experiment 1. In
Experiment 2, the conservation scores of subjects who participated in the peer interaction were higher than those of controls on the posttest; however, based on responses to the lie
item, authors concluded that the experimental subjects had
simply learned to respond "same" and to parrot a verbal statement. No such mimiking was possible in the logic problem.
Results suggest that peer interaction is not a particularly
effective method for enhancing the problem-solving ability
of MR individuals.

115. Bowman, R.A., & Dunn, J.M. "Effect of Peer Pressure on Psychomotor Measures with EMR Children." *Exceptional Children,* 1982, 48, 449-451.

The psychomotor performance of EMR children increases in the presence of their passive peers and an adult observer.

116. Bruininks, R.H., Rynders, J.E., & Gross, J.C. "Social Acceptance of Mildly Retarded Pupils in Resource Rooms and Regular Classes." *American Journal of Mental Deficiency,* 1974, 78, 377-383.

Sociometric questionnaires were administered to 1,234 nonretarded peers to determine the social acceptance of mildly retarded children enrolled in regular classes and resource centers within urban and suburban school settings. When rated by children of the same sex, mildly retarded urban children achieved significantly higher peer ratings than nonretarded children, whereas suburban mildly retarded children received lower ratings than nonretarded children. However, no appreciable differences were obtained between retarded and nonretarded samples in level of peer acceptance in either setting when ratings of boys and girls were combined. Variations in personal characteristics and in value orientations of suburban and urban school children, as well as differences in methods of analyzing peer choices, were cited as possible explanations for differences between these results and those of previous reports.

117. Budoff, M., & Siperstein, G.N. "Judgments of EMR Students toward Their Peers: Effects of Label and Academic Competence." *American Journal of Mental Deficiency,* 1982, 86, 367-371.

To test the relative potency of a clinical label and behavioral competence on the judgments of EMR students, the authors asked special-class students to evaluate a target child (labeled "mentally retarded" or "regular" student) who performed competently or incompetently on an academic task, controlling the sex of the target. The EMR students rated the target child in a manner similar to that of nonretarded raters. They responded most negatively to the incompetent retarded target child, while expressing positive affect toward the other three target children, in ascending order: the incompetent nonlabeled, competent retarded, and competent nonlabeled child. For these subjects competence was valued highly, and more potently determined their expressed attitude than did the assigned label.

118.   Budoff, M., & Siperstein, G.N. "Low-Income Children's
       Attitudes toward Mentally Retarded Children: Effects
       of Labeling and Academic Behavior." *American Journal
       of Mental Deficiency,* 1978, 82, 474-479.

       Effects of the label "mentally retarded" and academic
competence on low-income sixth-grade children's attitudes
toward peers were examined. Attitude was defined in terms
of children's affective feelings and behavioral inclinations.
The results showed that low-income children expressed more
favorable attitudes toward a competent than an incompetent
child and, paradoxically, toward a labeled than a nonlabeled
child. The data also revealed that an academically incompetent
child who was not labeled as retarded evoked negative attitudes,
especially from boys, whereas an incompetent child who was
labeled as retarded evoked positive attitudes. The findings
were discussed in terms of the pros and cons of the current
trend toward delabeling.

119.   Cimler, L.L. "A Descriptive Analysis of Self-referent
       Responses of Developmentally Disabled Individuals."
       Doctoral dissertation, Montana State University, 1974,
       summarized in *Dissertation Abstracts International,*
       1974, 35, 815A. (University Microfilms No. 74-18,299).

       This study shows that a group setting can be created
in which certain MR adults will openly discuss personal
aspects of their private lives, and that such psychometrically
valid statements can be used to infer the individual's world
as he experiences it.

120.   Clark, D.F. "Visual Feedback in the Social Learning of
       the Subnormal." *Journal of Mental Subnormality,* 1960,
       6, 30-39.

       Describes a technique that assesses the effects of know-
ledge of results shown visually, in regard to social discrimination among MR adolescent boys.

121.   Clark, E.T. "Children's Perception of a Special Class
       for Educable Mentally Retarded Children." *Exceptional
       Children,* 1964, 30, 289, 295.

       Children's perception of a special class in their school
was studied. Interviews were held with 163 children in 3
fourth and 3 fifth grade classes in which 134 gave descriptions
of the special class of the pupils in the class. Six percent
of the total content of Ss' reports were derogations, whereas
27 percent were designations of the class either by its teacher's name or as special. Found that the majority of children
in the regular grades do not derogate the special class, nor
do the children in the special class consider themselves as
victimized.

122.   Edmonson, B. "Measurement of Social Participation of
       Retarded Adults." *American Journal of Mental Deficiency,*
       1974, 78, 494-501.

       Compared 2 methods of obtaining social participation
information from 25 adult retarded males. A questionnaire
yielded retrospective information, and an illustrated diary
format yielded a record of current everyday activities. Three
dimensions of participation were scored: the range of participation within and outside the home, the average level of responsibility in outside settings, and the frequency of participation within and outside the home. Found that competence ratings
were correlated with level of responsibility scores from the
questionnaire and with range and frequency of participation
scores from the diaries.

123.   Farina, A., Thaw, J., Felner, R.D., & Hust, B.E. "Some
       Interpersonal Consequences of Being Mentally Ill or
       Mentally Retarded." *American Journal of Mental Deficiency,*
       1976, 80, 414-422.

       This study was carried out at an institution for MR
persons where the subjects (college students) were transported.
Under the guise of being "normal," mentally ill, or MR, each
of four confederates met three independent groups of subjects.
The verbal reports of the subjects did not vary a great deal as
a function of condition, but amount of pain inflicted in an
experimental task was strikingly different. In the mentally
retarded confederate condition, shocks delivered were shorter
and less intense than those given in the "normal" or mentally
ill confederate conditions. Since subjects had to teach the

confederate, they might have been kinder in the mentally retarded confederate condition because less was expected of the
learner. Evidence was also found suggesting that the social
impact of stigmas depends on the personal characteristics of
the stigmatized person.

124.   Geske, F.D. "The Effects on Follower Behavior of Inequity
       in Reinforcement for Cooperative Responding in Mentally
       Retarded Adult Males." Doctoral dissertation, University
       of Wisconsin, 1973, summarized in *Dissertation Abstracts
       International,* 1973, 34, 1316A. (University Microfilms
       No. 73-20,995).

       Assessed the effects on follower behavior of inequity
in reinforcement for cooperative responding in MR adults.
Found that after the inequity in reinforcement, social fol-
lowers emitted a high frequency of emotional and avoidance
behavior.

125.   Gibbons, F.X., & Gibbons, B.N. "Effects of the Institu-
       tional Label on Peer Assessments of Institutionalized
       EMR Persons." *American Journal of Mental Deficiency,*
       1980, 84, 602-609.

       The "group concept" of educable EMR persons was examined
in a study in which 51 institutionalized males and females
evaluated a target person either labeled as institutionalized
or not labeled. Contrary to expectations, the institutionalized person was rated as favorably as the noninstitutionalized
person on all of the adjective traits (e.g., "friendly"); however, all Ss showed a preference for the noninstitutionalized
person on 2 social-distance items ("live near" and "work with").
In addition, when asked in a series of questions to compare
an institutionalized and noninstitutionalized target person,
male Ss preferred the noninstitutionalized person. Results
are discussed in terms of Ss' reactions to the institutional
label.

126.   Gottlieb, J. "Attitudes toward Retarded Children: Effects
       of Labeling and Behavioral Aggressiveness." *Journal of
       Educational Psychology,* 1975, 67, 581-585.

       Examined effects of label "mentally retarded" on atti-
tudes of peers among 48 third graders. Half of the Ss were
shown a videotape of an actor displaying acting-out behavior,

while the remaining half were shown a videotape with the same
actor engaging in passive behavior. Half of the Ss in each
of these 2 groups were told that the actor was a fifth grader,
and the other half were told that he was a mentally retarded
boy in a special class. Analysis of variance results revealed
a significant interaction between label and behavior, which
indicated that Ss responded more negatively to the "mentally
retarded" actor who displayed acting-out behavior than to
the same actor who exhibited identical behavior but was not
labeled. It is concluded that labels should be considered
only as they interact with specific behavior.

127. Gottlieb, J., Cohen, L., & Goldstein, L. "Social Contact
     and Personal Adjustment as Variables Relating to Atti-
     tudes toward EMR Children." *Training School Bulletin,*
     1974, 71, 9-16.

     Attitudes of intellectually average children toward EMR
pupils were studied. The study was replicated 4 months later
in schools serving and not serving EMR pupils to determine
how social contact and personal adjustment related to attitudes
toward EMR children. Both sets of findings indicate that attitudes were more favorable when the raters had little school
contact with EMR children. A prediction that well adjusted
non-EMR pupils would express more favorable attitudes than
poorly adjusted children was not supported by the findings.
Difficulties of using the contact hypothesis to predict attitudes toward MR persons are discussed.

128. Gottlieb, J., & Davis, J.E. "Social Acceptance of EMR
     Children during Overt Behavioral Interactions." *American
     Journal of Mental Deficiency,* 1973, 78, 141-143.

     The purpose of this study was twofold: (a) to determine
whether EMR children are rejected during overt interactions
with non-EMR children, and (b) to determine whether EMR children who were integrated full-time in a nongraded school are
perceived by their non-EMR peers to be similar to segregated
EMR children. Forty-two fourth, fifth, and sixth graders
were asked to select one of two children as a partner to help
them win a prize at a bean-bag toss game. Depending upon
the treatment, the other two children were either: (a) a segregated EMR child and a non-EMR child, (b) an integrated EMR
child and a non-EMR child, or (c) a segregated EMR child and
an integrated EMR child. The results indicated that both
integrated and segregated EMR children were chosen less often
than non-EMR children, and that integrated and segregated EMR
children were selected equally often.

129. Guralnick, M.J. "Social Interactions among Preschool Children." *Exceptional Children,* 1980, 46, 248-253.

Investigated the nature and extent of social interactions among 37 preschool children at different developmental levels. Communicative and parallel play interactions
of mildly, moderately, severely, and nonhandicapped Ss were
observed during free play across 2 time periods. Nonhandicapped and mildly handicapped Ss interacted with each other
more frequently than expected on the basis of availability,
and they interacted with moderately and severely handicapped
Ss less frequently than expected. Moderately and severely
handicapped Ss interacted with all 4 groups as expected by
availability.

130. Jaffe, J. "Attitudes of Adolescents Toward the Mentally Retarded." *American Journal of Mental Deficiency,* 1966, 70, 907-912.

Ss' views of a person described as an EMR were compared
on four measures with those of a person identical in personal,
social, and vocational characteristics but not retarded. No
differences were found for the semantic differential Evaluative
factor, and adjective checklist Favorability rating, or a
social distance Acceptability score. The retarded sketch
person, however, received a lower score on the semantic differential Strength-Activity factor. Findings also show that (a)
the label "mentally retarded" was evaluated less favorably
and with greater variability than the retarded sketch person,
(b) Ss having a previous contact with the EMR attributed a
greater number of favorable traits to the retarded sketch
person but similarly evaluated such person on the other measures
(c) indices of Ss' intelligence and socioeconomic status were
not related to any attitude measures, and (d) girls attributed
a greater number of favorable traits to the retarded sketch
person than did boys.

131. MacMillan, D.L., Jones R.L., & Aloia, G.F. "The Mentally Retarded Label: A Theoretical Analysis and Review of Research." *American Journal of Mental Deficiency,* 1974, 79, 241-261.

Literature pertaining to the effect of the mentally retarded label was reviewed critically. Few studies were found
in which labeling was isolated, thus enabling differences
between labeled and unlabeled groups to be attributed to the

label, per se. The evidence uncovered failed to provide
support for the notion that labeling has long-lasting and
devastating effects on those labeled. In fact, it was concluded that while there may be detrimental effects of labeling,
the research to date does not reflect sufficent appreciation
for the complexity of the dynamics of how the label operates.
In the second half of the article, consideration was given
to factors hypothesized to alter the effect of the label.

132. Madsen, M.C., & Connor, C. "Cooperative and Competitive
     Behavior of Retarded and Nonretarded Children at Two
     Ages." *Child Development*, 1973, 44, 175-178.

     Assessed cooperative-competitive interaction between
18 pairs of retarded and 16 pairs of nonretarded children.
In a situation in which competitive interaction was non-
adaptive in terms of reward attainment, the retarded group
was significantly more cooperative than the nonretarded
group, and the 6- to 7-year old retarded group was more
cooperative than the 11- to 12-year old retarded group.
Results are discussed in relation to previous developmental
studies of cooperation-competition and placed in the context of cognitive and reinforcement theories of social development.

133. Miller, R.V. "Social Status and Socioemphatic Differ-
     ences among Mentally Superior, Mentally Typical, and
     Mentally Retarded Children." *Exceptional Children*,
     1956, 23, 114-119.

     Using 120 Ss enrolled in fourth and sixth grades, it
was found that the mentally superior were considered to be
the most popular by their peers, followed by the typical,
and then the retarded students.

134. Peterson, G.F. "Factors Related to the Attitudes of
     Nonretarded Children toward Their EMR Peers." *American
     Journal of Mental Deficiency*, 1974, 79, 412-416.

     Four hundred and twenty nonretarded children of both
sexes attending grades five through eight in a suburban public school system were administered two attitude scales to
determine the possible effects of contact, IQ, CA, and the
educational level of the respondents' parents on attitudes
toward their EMR peers. On one of the instruments, subjects
who had contact with EMR peers reported more favorable attitudes, while on the other instrument no differences were found.

Of the subjects having contact, no differences were observed
among high- and low-IQ groups. In general, the older the
subjects, the more favorable were their attitudes. No differences were reported between male and female subjects. In
all groups studied, the higher the level of educational attainment of the subjects' parents, the more negative were
the subjects' attitudes toward their retarded peers.

135. Renz, P., & Simensen, R.J. "The Social Preception of
     Normals toward Their EMR Grade-Mates." *American Journal
     of Mental Deficiency,* 1969, 74, 405-408.

     This study compared the social perception and attitude
of normal adolescents toward two types of grade-mates: normals
and special class EMRs; 14 special class EMRs and 14 randomly
selected normals were rated and described by 57 randomly
selected normal grade-mates. Contrary to many previous findings, (a) special class EMRs were not rejected with greater
frequency than their normal grade-mates, (b) normal subjects
used the same variables to describe EMRs that they used to
describe normals, and (c) normal subjects used the same con-
tinua to perceive and describe EMRs that they used for other
normals.

136. Romer, D. & Berkson, G. "Social Ecology of Supervised
     Communal Facilities for Mentally Disabled Adults: II.
     Predictors of Affiliation," *American Journal of Mental
     Deficiency,* 1980, 85, 229-242.

     The behavior of 304 mentally disabled adults were ob-
served in five settings (one residence, four sheltered workshops) during periods when they were free to affiliate with
peers. Regression analyses using settings, personal traits
(age, sex, IQ, and diagnosis), and mediating variables (e.g.,
physical attractiveness, desire for affiliation, and length
of institutionalization) were conducted to predict various
aspects of affiliative behavior. Settings accounted for 16
to 63 percent of the predictable variation independent of personal and mediating variables. Although older and mentally
ill clients affiliated less extensively, neither degree of
retardation, length of previous institutionalization, use of
medication, or other physical disabilities appeared to affect
affiliation independent of other variables. In general,
clients who were physically attractive, desired affiliation,
and had intelligent peers in their programs affiliated more
extensively and intensively with peers.

137. Romer, D., & Berkson, G. "Social Ecology of Supervised
      Communal Facilities for Mentally Disabled Adults: III.
      Predictors of Social Choice." *American Journal of Mental
      Deficiency*, 1980, 85, 243-252.

      Studies social preference behavior of mentally disabled
adults in community settings. Found that clients prefer peers
to whom they had more exposure, same-sex peers, and peers of
similar attractiveness.

138. Schlottmann, R.S., & Anderson, V.H. "Social and Play
      Behaviors of Institutionalized Mongoloid and Nonmongo-
      loid Retarded Children." *Journal of Psychology*, 1975,
      91, 201-206.

      Observed 24 retardates, 12 mongoloid (Down's syndrome)
and 12 nonmongoloid in dyadic interaction with peers in a
free-play situation. A number of specific peer-social and
nonsocial behaviors were recorded as they occurred. Differences between mongoloid and nonmongoloid Ss were most apparent
in several social behavior categories which support the stereotypic conception of mongoloids as more sociable and gregarious.
Differences were most apparent for the mongoloid males. The
possible influence of tranquilizer drugs and cottage placements
on the observed differences is discussed.

139. Shellhaas, M.D. "Sociometric Status of Institutionalized
      Retarded Children and Nonretarded Community Children."
      American Journal of Mental Deficiency, 1969, 73, 804-808.

      This report utilized the well-established relationship
between mental ability and sociometric status to predict the
choice patterns of institutionalized MR children and nonretarded community children in a summer day camp. Cross-choices
developed between the two groups, and the relationship between
mental ability and sociometric status emerged after five days
of participation at the camp.

140. Shellhaas, M.D. "The Effects of Small Group Interaction
      on Sociometric Choices of Day Campers." *American Journal
      of Mental Deficiency*, 1969, 74, 259-263.

      This report demonstrates that small group interaction in
a day camp setting increased sociometric choices within the
small groups. Cross-choices between institutional retarded

campers and nonretarded community campers were also facilitated
by the small group interaction. The findings are in support
of Homans' theory of a quantitative relationship between interaction and sentiment under generally favorable situational conditions.

141. Stamm, J.M., & Gardner, W.I. "Effectiveness of Normal
      and Retarded Peers in Influencing Judgments of Mildly
      Retarded Adolescents." *American Journal of Mental Defi-
      ciency*, 1969, 73, 597-603.

      Conformity behavior of groups of male and female mildly
retarded adolescents was evaluated in a simulated group atmosphere. During a simple cognitive task, social models depicted
as retarded and normal peers provided discrepant judgments.
Female retardates were more influenced by female models depicte
as retarded. In contrast, male retardates were more influenced
by normal male peers.

142. Sternlicht, M., & Siegel, L. "Time Orientation and Friend
      ship Patterns of Institutionalized Retardates." *Journal
      of Clinical Psychology*, 1968, 24, 26-27.

      In an attempt to assess the time orientation and friend-
ship patterns of the MR, 30 institutionalized MR children
were administered a story-completion technique and a friendship
pattern measure over a four-week interval. The results demonstrate that retardates are present-orientated, and have unstabl
friendship patterns.

143. Strichart, S.S. "Effects of Competence and Nurturance on
      Imitation of Nonretarded Peers by Retarded Adolescents."
      American Journal of Mental Deficiency, 1974, 78, 665-673.

      Investigated the effects of competence and nurturance on
imitation of 128 nonretarded peers by 128 retarded adolescents,
and whether nonretarded peers would imitate retarded Ss. All
Ss were 12 to 20 years old and enrolled in junior and senior
high school classes. Retarded Ss were paired with nonretarded
peers, whom they had previously named as liked (nurturant) or
disliked (nonnurturant), on a task manipulated by E so that
levels of competence for all participants could be controlled.
For both retarded and nonretarded Ss, competent models were
imitated more than noncompetent models, and noncompetent observers were more imitative than were competent observers.

No significant effects were found for nurturance. Implications concerning various peer tutoring pairings of retarded and non-retarded children are discussed.

144. Voeltz, L.M. "Children's Attitudes toward Handicapped Peers." *American Journal of Mental Deficiency*, 1980, 84, 455-464.

As services for severely handicapped children become increasingly available within neighborhood public schools, children's attitudes toward handicapped peers in integrated settings warrant attention. Factor analysis of attitude survey responses of 2,392 children revealed four factors underlying attitudes toward handicapped peers: social-contact willingness, deviance consequation, and two actual contact dimensions. Upper elementary-age children, girls, and children in schools with most contact with severely handicapped peers expressed the most accepting attitudes. Results of this study suggest the modifiability of children's attitudes and the need to develop interventions to facilitate social acceptance of individual differences in integrated school settings.

145. Voeltz, L.M. "Effects of Structured Interactions with Severely Handicapped Peers on Children's Attitudes." *American Journal of Mental Deficiency*, 1982, 86, 380-390.

Regular-education children participated in structured social interactions with severely handicapped children, and an attitude survey was administered to measure the effects of this intensive contact upon them and their classroom peer group. Results over two semesters of the program revealed significantly higher acceptance of individual differences on three attitudinal dimensions by children at an experimental school in comparison to children from schools where no severely handicapped children were enrolled and schools with severely handicapped children enrolled but without the interaction program. Results support the development of personalized, peer-interaction interventions to facilitate social acceptance of child variance in integrated school settings.

146. Willey, N.R., & McCandles, B.R. "Social Stereotypes for
      Normal, Educable Mentally Retarded, and Orthopedically
      Handicapped Children." *Journal of Special Education*,
      1973, 7, 283-288.

      While fifth grade students described their EMR peers
less positively, the latter, in contrast, described the nonretarded peers positively. Yet, each group attributed to
itself more positive characteristics than the other group.

147. Wisely, D.W., & Morgan, S.B. "Children's Ratings of
      Peers Presented as Mentally Retarded and Physically
      Handicapped." *American Journal of Mental Deficiency*,
      1981, 86, 281-286.

      Third- and sixth-grade children were shown slides and
tapes presenting target children as either (a) physically
nonhandicapped and nonretarded, (b) physically handicapped
only, (c) mentally retarded only, or (d) physically handicapped and mentally retarded. All children were rated more
favorably by third graders than sixth graders and more favorably by boys than girls. Physically handicapped target
children were rated more favorably than were nonhandicapped
children on behavioral intentions measures but were not rated
differently on an attitude scale; retarded children were also
rated more favorably than were nonretarded children on the
former measures but less favorably on the attitude scale.
Significant interactions were noted and implications of the
results discussed.

148.   Aloia, G.F., Effects of Physical Stigmata and Labels
        on Judgments of Subnormality by Preservice Teachers."
        Mental Retardation, 1975, 13(6), 17-21.

        Randomly selected full-time students in a teacher train-
ing program participated in a study to determine the impact
that the label "mentally retarded" and physical attractiveness
has on individual judgments of subnormality. The students
examined a series of photographs of children that had been
selected along a continuum of physical attractiveness with
the two extremes, the physically attractive and the physically
unattractive photographs, being used in the design. Discussion
examined the impact of the physical appearance and teacher
judgments on the educational outcome of the child.

149.   Aloia, G.F., Beaver, R.J., & Pettus, W.F. "Increasing
        Initial Interactions among Integrated EMR Students
        and Their Nonretarded Peers in a Game-Playing Situation."
        American Journal of Mental Deficiency, 1978, 82, 573-579.

        Two ways of increasing the initial interaction among EMR
students and their nonretarded classmates in a game-playing
situation were examined. Three hundred and four randomly
assigned intermediate school students observed classmates about
to play a simple game and were asked to select partners and
opponents from two pairs of students matched on sex and grade.
The experimental pair had 1 EMR student and 1 nonretarded
student; the control pair had 2 nonretarded students. The
subjects' past knowledge of the pair members served as a covariate in the design to determine whether past knowledge influenced
their selection of pair members. Each subject was also provided
information regarding the competency level of each pair member
in relation to the particular game. Results indicated that the
covariate was not a significant factor in the selection process;

however, the appended competency statement and the game-playing option were found to be highly significant in influencing selection of the pair members and increasing the selection of the EMR child by his nonretarded classmate.

150. Aloia, G.F., Maxwell, J.A., & Aloia, S.D. "Influence of a Child's Race and the EMR Label on Initial Impressions of Regular-Classroom Teachers." *American Journal of Mental Deficiency*, 1981, 85, 619-623.

Regular-classroom elementary school teachers were shown a photograph of an 11-year-old black, Mexican-American, or white child and were told that the child was either EMR or attended a fifth-grade class. Three dependent measures were used to assess the teachers' initial impressions of the child's attractiveness and his academic and behavioral potential. Data indicated that the race of the child significantly influenced the teachers' initial expectations. The EMR label yielded significant results when the teachers assessed the child's intellectual potential. A significant interaction was found on the behavioral measure between race and label, indicating that the race and label of a child can differentially influence a teacher's initial impressions of his or her behavior.

151. Bacher, J.H. "The Effects of Special Class Placement on the Self-Concept, Social Adjustment, and Reading Growth of Slow Learners." Doctoral Dissertation, New York University, 1964, summarized in *Dissertation Abstracts International,* 1965, 25, 7071 (University Microfilms No. 65-6570).

Found that in and of itself special class placement of MR children does not produce differences between the self-concepts of the children placed in special and regular classes. Yet, the social adjustment in school of the MR children can be more positive when they are placed in a special class.

152. Ballard, M., Corman, L., Gottlieb, J., & Kaufman, M.J. "Improving the Social Status of Mainstreamed Retarded Children." *Journal of Educational Psychology*, 1977, 69, 605-611.

Thirty-seven mainstreamed EMR children in Grades 3, 4, and 5 were randomly assigned to a control group or to an experimental treatment given during regular class activities for the purpose of improving their social status among nonretarded classmates. Each experimental EMR pupil worked in a small cooperative group with 4 to 6 nonretarded classmates on highly structured, manipulative tasks using multimedia materials. The treatment was provided in two cycles which lasted a total of 8 weeks. Sociometric tests were given before and after treatment to pupils in classes with experimental and control EMR subjects. Within 2 to 4 weeks of the completion of the treatment, the nonretarded children's social acceptance of their experimental peers improved significantly more than that of the control children.

153. Berry, R., & Marshall, B. "Social Interactions and Com-
     munication Patterns in Mentally Retarded Children."
     American Journal of Mental Deficiency, 1978, 83, 44-51.

     An observational approach and video recordings were used to investigate a group of four MR kindergarten children with minimal language development. Results showed that when a facilitator (teacher) was present, there were more social interactions and vocalizations, but there was no significant increase in meaningful verbal content. Nonverbal communication rose sharply in the presence of the facilitator. The findings indicate that an observational analysis of patterns of inter-action is useful in planning intervention programs in the area of social and communication development.

154. Blacher-Dixon, J., Leonard, J., & Turnbull., A.P. "Main-
     streaming at the Early Childhood Level: Current and
     Future Perspectives." *Mental Retardation*, 1981, 19, 235-
     241.

     An updated empirical and conceptual review of pre-school mainstreaming is presented. Specific topics addressed include rationale, program outcomes, child outcomes, teacher variables, and effects on parents. Potential areas for future research are also identified.

155. Bruininks, R.H., Rynders, J.E., & Gross, J.C. "Social
     Acceptance of Mildly Retarded Pupils in Resource Rooms
     and Regular Classes." *American Journal of Mental Defi-
     ciency*, 1974, 78, 377-383.

     Sociometric questionnaires were administered to 1,234 nonretarded peers to determine the social acceptance of mildly retarded children enrolled in regular classes and resource

centers within urban and suburban school settings. When rated
by children of the same sex, mildly retarded urban children
achieved significantly higher peer ratings than nonretarded
children, whereas suburban mildly retarded children received
significantly lower ratings than nonretarded children. However, no appreciable differences were obtained between retarded and nonretarded samples in level of peer acceptance
in either setting when ratings of boys and girls were combined.
Variations in personal characteristics and in value orientations
of suburban and urban school children, as well as differences
in methods of analyzing peer choices, were cited as possible
explanations for differences between these results and those
of previous reports.

156.   Bryan, T.H., & Wheeler, R.A. "Teachers' Behaviors in
       Classes for Severely Retarded–Multiply Trainable Mentally
       Retarded, Learning Disabled and Normal Children." *Mental
       Retardation*, 1976, 14(4), 41-45.

Teachers' behaviors in classes for severely retarded–
mulitply handicapped, trainable mentally retarded, learning
disabled and normal children were recorded using an Interaction
Process Analysis. This time sampling technique allowed recording of such behaviors as teachers' verbalizations to individual children and to the group, teachers' emission of positive
and negative reinforcements, and the responses of children to
the teachers. Significant differences were found among the
four groups of teachers in a number of interaction categories.
The differences in interaction patterns are discussed in terms
of their effects upon children and current notions about educational placements for handicapped children.

157.   Budoff, M. "The Mentally Retarded Child in the Mainstream
       of the Public School." In P. Mittler, ed. *Research to
       practice in mental retardation*, Vol. 2, 307-313. Baltimore
       University Park, 1977.

Discusses the effects of the mainstreamed MR child in
terms of his relationships to the school administration, his
teachers, and his age-mates. Concludes that retarded children
do appear to act differently than do their normal controls.

158. Budoff, M., & Gottlieb, J. "Special-Class EMR Children Mainstreamed: A Study of an Aptitude (Learning Potential) Treatment Interaction." *American Journal of Mental Deficiency*, 1976, 81, 1-11.

Academic, personal, and social growth were compared for special-class EMR children who were assigned randomly to regular grades or retained in special classes at three time intervals: prior to the assignment, and at the conclusion of the school year. There were no significant differences between the two groups prior to or 2 months after reintegration. After one school year, the reintegrated children were more internally controlled, had more positive attitudes toward school, and were more reflective in their behavior. The hypothesis that the more able students by the learning potential criterion would benefit more from regular than special-class placement was supported. These students expressed more positive feelings toward themselves as students, felt others preceived them as more competent, and behaved more reflectively when they were integrated than when assigned to special class. The high-able (learning potential) students performed more competently academically than the low-able (learning potential) students, regardless of placement.

159. Burns, E. "Consistency of Cyclic Social Preferences of Retarded and Nonretarded Subjects." *Psychological Reports*, 1974, 34, 478.

Examines the consistency of cyclic sociometric pair-comparison triples .of 72 retarded and nonretarded 8.5- to 16.9-year-old students. The proportion of consistent triples suggests that cyclic social preferences of retarded and nonretarded Ss were most likely the results of judgmental errors and do not represent a systematic method for ordering other group members.

160. Carsrud, A.L., Carsrud, K.B., Henderson, D.P., Alisch, C.J., & Fowler, A.V. "Effects of Social and Environmental Change on Institutionalized Mentally Retarded Persons: The Relocation Syndrome Reconsidered." *American Journal of Mental Deficiency*, 1979, 84, 266-272.

The "relocation syndrome" in multiply-handicapped, institutionalized MR residents was examined in an observational study. Weight change and the initiation and duration of constructive and nonconstructive behavior were observed, as well as resident-staff interactions before and after relocation to a new living unit. The hypothesis that there would be an increase in behavior deleterious to the health of clients after relocation, when compared to two premove baseline periods of crowding, was not totally supported. Although relocation did cause significant changes in a variety of behaviors, not all were deleterious (i.e., no mortalities, weight gains).

161.   Carvajal, A.L. "An Analysis of Predictors of Four Criteria of Self-Concept in Educable Mentally Retarded Adolescents. Doctoral dissertation, University of Northern Colorado, 1971, summarized in *Dissertation Abstracts International*, 1971, 32, 810A. (University Microfilms No. 71-20,717).

The study investigated the effect of segregated or integrated special education settings on the self-concept of white, EMR male and female adolescents. The results indicate that physical setting, whether integrated or segregated by itself, is not a significant variable in the development of the self-concept of EMR adolescents.

162.   Carvajal, A.L. "Predictions of Four Criteria of Self-Concept in Educable Mentally Retarded Adolescents." *Exceptional Children*, 1972, 39, 239.

This study shows that physical setting, whether integrated or segregated, is not a significant variable in the development of the self concept of white EMR adolescents.

163.   Cavallaro, S.A., & Porter, R.H. "Peer Preferences of At-Risk and Normally Developing Children in a Preschool Mainstream Classroom." *American Journal of Mental Deficiency*, 1979, 84, 357-366.

Social interactions and peer preferences in a preschool mainstream classroom containing normally developing and at-risk children were studied using the ethological method of direct observation. Data on social play and on gaze orientation indicated that normally developing children and at-risk children interacted primarily with children from the same group (other normally developing and at-risk children, respectively). Data on selection of game partner and on preference of seat neighbor, however, revealed peer preference by normally developing children only.

164. Feuerstein, R., Rand, Y., Hoffman, Ma., Hoffman, Me., & Miller, R. "Cognitive Modifiability in Retarded Adolescents: Effects of Instrumental Enrichment." *American Journal of Mental Deficiency*, 1979, 83, 539-550.

Compared the 2-year progress of 57 matched pairs of 12- to 15-year-old MRs, socioculturally deprived Ss who were exposed to 2 different programs. One group in a residential center and 1 group in a day center received Instrumental Enrichment (IE), a program designed by the first author to modify the cognitive functions of retarded adolescents in Israel; another group from each of the 2 settings received General Enrichment (GE). Results show significantly better performance by the IE groups than by the GE groups on tests of specific cognitive functions, on scholastic achievement, and on some classroom interaction scales.

165. Foley, J.M. "Effect of Labeling and Teacher Behavior on Children's Attitudes." *American Journal of Mental Deficiency*, 1979, 83, 380-384.

Seventy-eight fourth-grade subjects from a rural school containing an integrated special-education program viewed one of two videotapes that depicted a child demonstrating various kinds of academic and social behavior. On one tape, the teacher reacted positively to the child's behavior; on the other negatively. The subjects were told that the child on the tape was either a "normal," MR, or learning-disabled fourth grader. The subjects were randomly assigned to one of two teacher conditions (positive or negative) and one of three labeling conditions. After viewing the videotape, the subjects filled out a peer-acceptance questionnaire concerning the child on the videotape. Results indicated that across all labeling conditions the subjects rated the child higher on the questionnaire when the child was reacted to positively by the teacher and, further, that the "mentally retarded" label led to significantly higher peer-acceptance ratings than did the "normal" or "learning-disabled" label.

166. Frankel, F., & Graham, V. "Systematic Observation of Classroom Behavior of Retarded and Autistic Preschool Children." *American Journal of Mental Deficiency*, 1976, 81, 73-84.

Observed 6 autistic Ss and 6 retarded Ss for 7 20-minute sessions. The following environmental parameters were manipulated: teacher-to-child ratio, presence of food reinforcement,

and skill area being presented. Behavior under observation
fell into 30 classes: adaptive performance (percentage response
and percentage correct), attention, and maladaptive behavior.
Results suggest that food reinforcement and the 1:1 teacher-
to-child ratio may not generally enhance adaptive performance
but may have an effect upon attention and tantrum behavior;
attention to task is more predictive of adaptive behavior than
attention to teacher; and interactions were generally lacking
between the above parameters and diagnostic group, while level
of functioning did show such interactions. Results support
the practice of individual behavioral assessment of autistic
and retarded children. The present procedure, coupled with
statistical analysis for individual Ss, may provide educational
prescriptions for individual children.

167. Gampel, D.H., Gottlieb, J., & Harrison, R.H. "Comparison
     of Classroom Behavior of Special-Class EMR, Integrated
     EMR, Low IQ, and Nonretarded Children." *American Journal
     of Mental Deficiency*, 1974, 79, 16-21.

The classroom behavior of 12 segregated and 14 integrated
EMR children, who were all formerly segregated and then randomly
assigned to their present class placements, were compared to
those of a low-IQ group who had never been identified for
special-class placements and to an intellectually average
group of children. The method was a time-sampling observational one, using 12 behavior categories. The data indicated
that 4 months after the school year began, the integrated EMR
children behaved more similarly to nonlabeled EMR children
than to their segregated peers. The results were discussed
in terms of appropriate peer models influencing classroom
behavior of EMR children.

168. Goodman, H., Gottlieb, J., & Harrison, R.H. "Social
     Acceptance of EMRs Integrated into a Nongraded Elementary
     School." *American Journal of Mental Deficiency*, 1972,
     76, 412-417.

Twenty intermediate unit and 16 primary unit non-EMR
children, equally divided between the sexes, were administered
sociometric questionnaires to determine their social acceptance
of 3 groups of children: non-EMR children, EMR children who
were integrated into the academic routine of a nongraded school,
and EMR children who remained segregated in the nongraded
school's only self-contained class. The results indicated that
both integrated and segregated EMR subjects are rejected significantly more often than non-EMR subjects, that young subjects are

more accepting of others than older subjects, that male subjects express more overt rejection than females, and that
integrated EMR children are rejected significantly more often
than segregated ones by male subjects but not by females.

169. Gottlieb, J. "Attitudes toward Retarded Children: Effects
     of Labeling and Behaviorial Aggressiveness." *Journal of
     Educational Psychology*, 1975, 67, 581-585.

     Effects of the label "mentally retarded" on attitudes of
peers were examined among 48 third-grade pupils. Half of the
subjects were shown a videotape of an actor displaying acting-
out behavior, while the remaining half were shown a videotape
with the same actor engaging in passive behavior. Half of
the subjects in each of these two groups were told that the
actor was a fifth-grade pupil, and the other half were told
that he was a mentally retarded boy in a special class. Analysis of variance results revealed a significant interaction
between label and behavior, which indicated that subjects responded more negatively to the "mentally retarded" actor who
displayed acting-out behavior than to the same actor who exhibited identical behavior but was not labeled. It was concluded that labels should be considered only as they interact
with specific behavior.

170. Gottlieb, J. "Mainstreaming: Fulfilling the Promise?"
     American Journal of Mental Deficiency, 1981, 86, 115-
     126.

     Four assumptions that propelled the movement away from
self-contained classes for EMR children and towards mainstreaming were presented. Available data were provided for each
assumption that indicated the extent to which the initial
assumption has been realized. Overall, the data did not indicate major improvement in the caliber of education provided
to EMR children as a consequence of the mainstreaming movement. The limitations of present conceptions of mainstreaming
were cited, as was the possibility of a need to redefine the
concept of least restrictive environment.

171. Gottlieb, J., & Budoff, M. "Social Acceptability of
      Retarded Children in Nongraded Schools Differing in
      Architecture." *American Journal of Mental Deficiency*,
      1973, 78, 15-19.

      The social position of integrated and segregated EMR
children in a traditional school building was compared to
that of EMR children in a no-interior-wall school. Found
that while EMR children in the unwalled school were known
more often by their non-EMR peers, they were not chosen as
friends more often. Retarded children in the unwalled school
were rejected more often than children in the walled school.
Also, integrated EMR children were rejected more than segregated EMR children.

172. Gottlieb, J., & Gottlieb, B.W. "Sterotypic Attitudes
      and Behavioral Intentions toward Handicapped Children."
      American Journal of Mental Deficiency, 1977, 82, 65-71.

      Fifty-six junior high school pupils were asked about
their attitudes toward MR and crippled children. Same- and
opposite-sex ratings of stereotypes and behavioral intentions
were obtained. Results indicated a significant main effect
for handicap condition, with stereotypic attitudes toward the
crippled child being more favorable than attitudes toward the MR
child. No differences in attitudes toward the two handicapping
conditions emerged on the measure of behavioral intentions. Sex
of the subject and sex of the handicapped child being rated did
not affect attitude scores in this study.

173. Gottlieb, J., Semmel, M.I., & Veldman, D.J. "Correlates
      of Social Status among Mainstreamed Mentally Retarded
      Children." *Journal of Educational Psychology*, 1978,
      70, 396-405.

      The relative contribution of misbehavior, academic in-
competence, and exposure to nonretarded children to the ex-
planation of retarded children's sociometric status were explored. Teachers and peers rated MR children on the dimensions
of behavior and academic performance. The results indicated
that perceiving academic incompetence was associated with EMR
children's level of social acceptance, whereas perceived misbehavior was associated with retarded children's social rejection by peers. Amount of exposure to nonretarded children
did not relate to retarded children's social status.

174. Gottlieb, J., & Switzky, H.N. "Development of School-Age Children's Stereotypic Attitudes toward Mentally Retarded Children." *American Journal of Mental Deficiency*, 1982, 86, 596-600.

The developmental changes in the structure of attitudes toward MR children in elementary-school-aged students was investigated. Four orthogonal factors characterized their responses: general negative evaluation, general positive evaluation, likeability, and unhappiness. For the most part, increased age was associated with a decrease in negative stereotypes and an increase in specific stereotype.

175. Gresham, F.M. "Misguided Mainstreaming: The Case for Social Skills Training with Handicapped Children." *Exceptional Children*, 1982, 48, 422-433.

Holds that mainstreaming is based in part upon three faulty assumptions: (a) placement of handicapped children in regular classrooms will result in increased social interaction between the handicapped and nonhandicapped children; (b) placement of handicapped children in regular classrooms will result in increased social acceptance of handicapped children by their nonhandicapped peers; (c) mainstreamed handicapped children will behave like their nonhandicapped peers because of increased exposure to them. The reviewed research fails to support these assumptions. It is suggested that handicapped children should learn the requisite social skills for effective social interaction and peer acceptance, and that social skill curricula for use by both special and regular education teachers be established.

176. Gunzburg, H.G. "Further Education for the Mentally Handicapped." In A.M. Clarke & A.D.B. Clarke, eds. *Mental deficiency, the changing outlook*, 3rd ed. 669-707. New York: Free Press, 1974.
    Advocates education for MR adults in a variety of social and vocational areas.

177. Harbin, G.L.J. "A Comparison of the Effects of the
      Use of Single versus Dual Criteria on the Number of
      Black Children Judged Eligible for Classification as
      Educable Mentally Retarded." Doctoral dissertation,
      University of North Carolina at Chapel Hill, 1980,
      summarized in *Dissertation Abstracts International*,
      1980, 41, 1456A-1457A. (University Microfilms No.
      8022462).

      Found that the use of adaptive behavior measurement
drastically reduced the number of black children who would
be eligible for the EMR program.

178. Hart, V. "The Blind Child Who Functions on a Retarded
      Level: The Challenge for Teacher Preparation." *New
      Outlook for the Blind*, 1969, 63, 318-321.

      Incorporated theoretical concepts for preparation of
teachers of multihandicapped children into a 5-week pilot
training program involving 11 3- to 9-year-old children
considered uneducable, and 3 teachers, each handling a different area of functioning. A variety of educational strategies were used. Teacher recognition of the children's potentialities is important in obtaining of positive results.

179. Hayes, C.S., & Prinz, R.J. "Affective Reactions of
      Retarded and Nonretarded Children to Success and Failure."
      American Journal of Mental Deficiency, 1976, 81, 100-102.

      After performing a simple motor task, 208 mildly retarded
children pointed to photographs of modeled affective facial
expressions to indicate how they felt, wished to feel, and
thought their teachers would feel about their performance.
Children in both IQ groups frequently attributed positive affect to themselves and their teachers after success, although
younger retarded children were less positive than were nonretarded children in teacher affect attributions. Following
failure, retarded subjects were less frequently negative than
were nonretarded subjects in affect attributions to themselves
and particularly to their teachers.

180. Iano, R.F., Ayers, D., Heller, H.B., McGettigan, J.F.,
     & Walker, V.S. "Sociometric Status of Retarded Children
     in an Integrative Program." *Exceptional Children*, 1974,
     40, 267-271.

     Established the sociometric status in elementary school
regular classes of former special-class EMR children in an
integrative resource room program. Found that the EMR children were not better accepted in regular classes than were
EMR children in earlier studies for whom such supportive resources room services were not provided. Overlap in sociometric acceptances and rejections was found between EMR children and other children in regular classes.

181. Joyner, D.E. "An Investigation of the Social Relation-
     ships of Educable Mentally Retarded Children in Negro
     Schools in Five School Districts of Northeast Louisiana."
     Doctoral dissertation, University of Cincinnati, 1970,
     summarized in *Dissertation Abstracts International*, 1971,
     31, 4586A. (University Microfilms No. 71-6413).

     Attempted to determine the social position of the EMR
black children in regular northeast Louisiana classrooms. The
retarded children are rejected by other children and considered
by teachers as having less desirable personality traits than
the typical children.

182. Kern, W.H., & Pfaeffle, H. "A Comparison of Social Ad-
     justment of Mentally Retarded Children in Various Edu-
     cational Settings." *American Journal of Mental Deficiency*,
     1962, 67, 407-413.

     Compared the social adjustment of MR children in special
classes, special school, and regular classes. Found that the
special school children showed the best overall social adjustment, followed by special classes, and regular class children.

183. Klein, N.K. "Least Restrictive Alternative: An Educational
     Analysis." *Education and Training of the Mentally Retarded*,
     1978, 13(1), 102-114.

     Discusses the history of public school education and how
various reforms and strategies have affected the status of
children with special needs. Compliance with PL 94-142 and
the availability of "least restrictive alternatives" for these

children are examined. Children cannot continue to be arbi-
trarily divided between special and regular education, because
such practices are restrictive and allow few if any alternative
choices.

184.   Kurtz, P.D., Harrison, M., Neisworth, J.T., & Jones,
       R.T. "Influence of 'Mentally Retarded' Label on Teachers'
       Nonverbal Behavior toward Preschool Children." *American
       Journal of Mental Deficiency*, 1977, 82, 204-206.

       Twelve teachers were assigned to social interaction with
either a labeled or a nonlabeled preschool child. All children were, in fact, nonhandicapped and had no diagnosis or
record of MR. After reading a labeled or nonlabeled description of the child's developmental status, each teacher read
the child a story. Results indicate a positive bias toward
children labeled "mentally retarded." Teachers leaned for-
ward toward labeled children significantly more than toward
nonlabeled children. It is possible that the teachers' motivation and interest were aroused and expressed nonverbally
through greater immediacy in an effort to compensate for the
child's presumed handicap.

185.   Kuveke, S.H. "School Behaviors of Educable Mentally
       Retarded Children." Doctoral dissertation, Yeshiva
       University, 1978, summarized in *Dissertation Abstracts
       International*, 1978, 39, 1476A. (University Microfilms
       No. 7816115).

       Attempted to find the causes for the rejection of EMR
children in regular classes. Teachers' ratings show that
the behavior of EMR children is more socially unacceptable;
namely, their behavior is more anxious and hostile isolating,
than that of the normal children.

186.   Lambert, N.M., & Nicoll, R.C. "Dimensions of Adaptive
       Behavior of Retarded and Nonretarded Public-School
       Children." *American Journal of Mental Deficiency*, 1976,
       81, 135-146.

       The AAMD Adaptive Behavior Scale Public School Revision
was administered to 2,618 elementary-school children from 7
to 13 years of age. The sample of children included white,
black, and Spanish-surname groups from regular and special-
education classes. Factor analyses of domain scores indicated

four dimensions of adaptive behavior: Functional Automony, Interpersonal Adjustment, Social Responsibility, and Intrapersonal Adjustment. Comparison of factor structure across school classification and age groups revealed the same four dimensions for all groups.

187.   Lax, B., & Carter, J.L. "Social Acceptance of the EMR in Different Educational Placements." *Mental Retardation*, 1976, 14(2), 10-13.

A review of the social consequences of various educational placements of MR children was undertaken. The results indicated that much more research needs to be done before any definite conclusions can be obtained. However, a general conclusion by a majority of the researchers concerned with the problem gave support to the special classroom as being the most efficacious placement for the social and personal development of the EMR child.

188.   MacMillan, D.L. *Mental Retardation in School and Society*. Boston: Little Brown, 1977.

Discusses the advances made by the school and society in dealing with mental retardation. Deals with the effects of labeling, and the social learning and affective characteristics of mentally retarded persons. Also discusses alternative placements.

189.   MacMillan, D.L., Jones, R.L., & Meyers, C.E. "Mainstreaming the Mildly Retarded: Some Questions, Cautions and Guidelines." *Mental Retardation*, 1976, 14(1), 3-10.

Current interest in mainstreaming of mildly handicapped learners has resulted in activity directed toward the integration of exceptional children into regular programs. In this paper, the authors raise questions that need answering in order that children not be harmed in this wave of well-intended, but sometimes naive, acceptance of mainstreaming. A distinction is made between the principle of mainstreaming and its implementation, and an attempt is made to examine roadblocks that exist in general education to its implementation. It is noted that children other than the mainstreamed children are affected by such action, and perspectives on evaluation of programs are explored. Finally, several guidelines are proposed based on the points raised in the first part of the paper.

190.   MacMillan, D.L., & Morrison, G.M. "Correlates of Social
       Status among Mildly Handicapped Learners in Self-Con-
       tained Special Classes." *Journal of Educational Psychol-
       ogy*, 1980, 72, 437-444.

The contributions of perceived congitive competence and
misbehavior to the variance in the sociometric status of educable mentally retarded and educationally handicapped children
in self-contained special classes were studied.   Teachers and
peers rated the target children on each of two dimensions:
academic competence, and misbehavior.   The results indicated
that the combined teacher ratings of these two dimensions
accounted for the most variance in both acceptance and rejection
of EMR children, whereas ratings of academic competence were
associated with both acceptance and rejection of educationally
handicapped children.   The results are discussed in terms of
differential factors associated with social status of mildly
handicapped learners in special classes versus regular classes.
In addition, the data suggest the importance of differences
in the characteristics of children doing the rating of both
independent and dependent variables.

191.   Malone, D.R., & Christian, W.P., Jr. "Adaptive Behavior
       Scale as a Screening Measure for Special-Education
       Placement." *American Journal of Mental Deficiency*, 1974,
       79, 367-371.

The utility of the Adaptive Behavior Scale in the special-
education placement of 126 institutionalized MR children and
adolescents was examined.   An investigation of relationships
among Adaptive Behavior Scale (Part I) scores, Wide Range
Achievement Test scores, and IQ scores revealed a significant
relationship between Adaptive Behavior Scale scores as well
as between IQ scores and achievement test scores.   Adaptive
Behavior Scale and IQ were the most effective scores in providing significant discrimination between the special-education
training levels.   Adaptive Behavior Scale subdomain percentage
scores were discussed as criteria for a computer-assisted placement of MR students in a special-education program.

192. Marburg, C.C., Houston, B.K., & Holmes, D.S. "Influence of Multiple Models on the Behavior of Institutionalized Retarded Children: Increased Generalization to Other Models and Other Behaviors." *Journal of Consulting and Clinical Psychology*, 1976, 44, 514-519.

After being pretested to determine base levels of imitation, institutionalized retarded children were reinforced for imitating a model in nine training sessions. Children in a single model condition were reinforced by the same model across all sessions, whereas children in a multiple model condition were reinforced by three different models (three sessions per model). A posttest to assess levels of imitation was then conducted by a model with whom the children had not had contact and who demonstrated a new set of behaviors. Results obtained during training sessions indicated that (a) children learned to imitate, and this learning was not inhibited by mulitiple models; and (b) children generalized and imitated nonreinforced behaviors, and this response generalization was facilitated by multiple models. Most important, pretest-posttest comparisons indicated that generalized use of the new response class (imitation) with new models was eight times greater for children trained with multiple, as opposed to single, models.

193. Meyerowitz, J.H. "Self-Derogations in Young Retardates and Special Class Placement." In T.E. Jordan, ed. *Perspectives in Mental Retardation*, 260-269. Carbondale: Southern Illinois University, 1966.

Described the self-concept of EMR children. Found that EMRs make a greater number of derogatory statements about themselves than normal children.

194. Morlock, D., & Tovar, C. "Sex Education for the Multiple Handicapped As It Applies to the Classroom Teachers." *Training School Bulletin*, 1971, 68, 87-96.

Considers that areas of sexuality and sex education in a comprehensive way, including all the degrees of variations that can be seen between the 2 poles of the continuum, i.e., the normal, the profoundly retarded, and the multiple handicapped. The authors accept the Freudian contention that sexuality is at the core of all emotional disturbances or behavioral deviations. The difference is that more emphasis is placed on confusion and bewilderment about sexuality than in the Freudian entities of castration anxiety, Oedipal conflict, and similar

concepts accepted by psychoanalytical theory. It is further
emphasized that the participation of classroom teachers, as
one of the poles, has an important influence in the psychological elements of sexuality in the pupil.

195. Newman, H.G. "The Social Adaptability of the Trainable
      Mentally Retarded Child." Doctoral dissertation, Emory
      University, 1971, summarized in *Dissertation Abstracts
      International*, 1971, 32, 1948A. (University Microfilms
      No. 71-27,791).

      The study suggests that increased social interaction
in an environment of high teacher-expectation helps to increase the performance level of the TMR.

196. Newman, H.G., & Doby, J.T. "Correlates of Social Compe-
      tence among Trainable Mentally Retarded Children."
      American Journal of Mental Deficiency, 1973, 77, 722-
      732.

      The performance of 110 school age TMR children was meas-
ured using a Likert scale for social competence. Measures of
biological genetic potential, motivational factors, and situational factors were used as independent variables. Using a
multiple step wise regression, chronological age, interaction,
IQ, and teacher expectation explained 65 percent of the variance in social competence. It is indicated from these results
that biological-genetic factors (IQ and age) and experience
with the environment (social interaction) are the primary
independent variables. This suggests that increased social
interaction in an environment of high teacher-expectation
would increase the performances and adaptability of the TMR
child.

197. Nihira, K., Mink, I.T., & Meyers, C.E. "Relationship
      Between Home Environment and School Adjustment of TMR
      Children." *American Journal of Mental Deficiency*, 1981,
      86, 8-15.

      The relationship between the home environment and school
adjustment of 104 TMR children was examined. Results revealed
that specific factors of home were related to the adjustment
of TMR children in school, including (a) harmony and quality
of parenting, (b) educational and cognitive stimulation available at home, (c) emotional support for learning, and (d) co-
hesiveness of family members.

198. Parashar, O.D. "Disturbed Classroom Behavior: A Comparison between Mentally Retarded, Learning-Disabled and Emotionally Disturbed Children." *Journal of Mental Deficiency Research*, 1976, 20, 109-120.

Attempted to identify and measure the nature and prevalence of disturbed classroom behavior in 56 MR children, and to compare them with 51 learning disabled and 65 emotionally disturbed children. Eleven types of disturbed classroom behavior (defined as behavior which interfered with learning) were studied. Ss were rated by their teachers on the Devereux Elementary School Behavior Rating Scale. Results show that the 3 groups exhibited significant differences on their profiles of the cumulative 11 disturbed classroom behavior factors. They also differed on the individual factors of classroom disturbance, disrespect-defiance, external blame, achievement anxiety, comprehension disorders, irrelevant responsiveness, and lack of creative initiative. The MR Ss exhibited more comprehension disorders than did Ss of the other 2 groups. The emotionally disturbed Ss showed higher classroom disturbance, disrespect-defiance, external blame, achievement anxiety, inattentive-withdrawal, and irrelevant-responsiveness but lower comprehension disorders and lack of creative initiative than did the MR.

199. Parashar, O.D. "Investigation of the Academically Relevant Disturbed Classroom Behaviors of the Clinically Diagnosed Mentally Retarded, Learning Disabled and Emotionally Disturbed Children as Measured by the Devereux Elementary School Behavior Rating Scale." Doctoral dissertation, University of Cincinnati, 1973, summarized in *Dissertation Abstracts International*, 1974, 34, 5758A-5759A. (University Microfilms No. 73-29,458).

This study was designed to identify and measure the nature and prevalence of academically relevant disturbed classroom behavior factors of the clinically diagnosed MR, learning disabled, and emotionally disturbed children. Classroom disturbance was found to be related to impatience, disrespect-defiance, and a number of other characteristics.

200.   Patrick, J.L., & Reschly, D.J. "Relationship of State
        Educational Criteria and Demographic Variables to School-
        System Prevalence of Mental Retardation." *American Jour-
        nal of Mental Deficiency*, 1982, 86, 351-360.

        A survey of state departments of education revealed wide
variations in mental retardation terminology, definition, and
classification variables. The relationship of survey variables
and demographic characteristics of states with school-system
prevalence of mental retardation definition was analyzed. Surve
variables such as MR definition, adaptive behavior measurement,
and IQ cutoff score were largely unrelated to school-system prev
alence. Demographic characteristics based on summary data for
states on variables such as per capita income, educational leve.
and rate of illiteracy were highly related to school-system prev
alence. Caution was recommended in interpretation of results
based on ecological correlations, i.e., correlations based on
group summaries rather than individual data. The results were
seen as further indication of the relative social-system nature
of mild mental retardation.

201.   Paul, J.L., Turnbull, A.P., & Cruickshank, W.M. *Main-
        streaming: A Practical Guide*. New York: Schocken, 1979.

        Discusses the rationale of mainstreaming, which is to
provide the most appropriate education for all students in the
least restrictive setting, and its effective planning and
implementation, offering practical guidance in this latter
area.

202.   Petersen, G.A., Austin, G.J., & Lang, R.P. "Use of Teache
        Prompts to Increase Social Behavior: Generalization Effec
        with Severely and Profoundly Retarded Adolescents." *Ameri
        can Journal of Mental Deficiency*, 1979, 84, 82-86.

        In a single-subject design with replication across sub-
jects, teacher prompts were used in an attempt to increase the
rate of social behavior of three severely and profoundly retarded adolescents who were legally blind. Training took place
in the classroom on successive school days with the teacher
prompting each subject to engage in positive social interaction
with each peer. Observations for generalization effects im-
mediately followed each training session. The remaining class
members were brought into the room, and social interactions
were observed in a free-play setting while the teacher was
absent. During both phases, observers recorded the behavior
of the three subjects for 5 minutes and recorded all units of

social exchange that each subject initiated or responded to.
Increased rates of social behavior were obtained for all three
subjects during both training and generalization. Major factors
that contributed to the generalization effects were discussed.

203. Raber, S.M., & Weisz, J.R. "Teacher Feedback to Mentally
      Retarded and Nonretarded Children." *American Journal of
      Mental Deficiency*, 1981, 86, 148-156.

      To understand earlier findings on helplessness of re-
tarded children, the feedback was given during reading training to retarded and nonretarded children of third- to fourth-
grade reading ability. The helplessness-inducing pattern of
feedback identified in previous research on learned helplessness was more pronounced among retarded than nonretarded children. Retarded children were more likely to receive negative
feedback than were nonretarded children. The findings suggest
that retarded children's susceptibility to helplessness may
result partly from the feedback they receive in school.

204. Richmond, B.O., & Dalton, J.L. "Teacher Ratings and
      Self-Concept Reports of Retarded Pupils." *Exceptional
      Children*, 1973, 40, 178-183.

      This study examines the relationship between self ratings
and teacher ratings of 100 children in classes for the EMR.
The results indicate that the self images of these pupils are
positively related to the teachers' image of their academic ability. The teachers' ratings of each pupil's social and emotional
behavior were not correlated significantly with the child's perception of his social or emotional relationship. In addition,
the EMR subjects in this study did not perceive their standing
among peers to be positively correlated to academic success.
Implications of these findings for the pupils' educational program are suggested.

205. Ross, M.B., & Salvia, J. "Attractiveness as a Biasing
      Factor in Teacher Judgments." *American Journal of Mental
      Deficiency*, 1975, 80, 96-98.

      A doubled-blind experiment to evaluate the effect of
facial attractiveness on teacher judgments was performed.
Given identical information, teachers systematically rated
attractive children more favorably than unattractive children. In the case of unattractive children, teachers were
more willing to recommend special-class placement and held
lower expectations for future academic and social development.

206. Sajwaj, T., Twardosz, S., & Burke, M. "Side Effects of
      Extinction Procedures in a Remedial Preschool," *Journal
      of Applied Behavior Analysis*, 1972, 5, 163-175.

      Undertook behavior-modification procedures with a 7-year-
old retarded boy who engaged in excessive conversation with his
preschool teacher. When the teacher ignored his initiated conversation during free-play periods, it decreased. In addition,
social behavior relative to children increased, and use of girls
toys decreased during free play. In a second study, the teacher
alternated conditions of praise and ignoring for talking with
children. Talking with children varied accordingly. In addition, use of girls' toys and group disruptions rose during
the ignoring condition. Appropriate behaviors dropped. Lastly,
a time-out procedure was used to eliminate the undesirable side
effects of disruptions and use of girls' toys. Apparently, a
response class may have member behaviors that covary directly
and/or inversely. Some covariations may be socially desirable,
others undesirable. The appearance of undesirable side effects
can be controlled using behavior modification techniques.

207. Salova, Zh.S. "Increase in Cognitive Activity and Indepen-
      dence in Pupils of the Auxiliary School in Programmed
      Teaching." *Defektologiya*, 1971, 3(1), 60-64.

      Argues for the incorporation of elements of programmed
instruction in teaching Russian to mentally retarded children in order to increase both cognitive activity and self-
reliance. Presents a detailed illustration of a programmed
lesson.

208. Shapiro, E.S. "Self-Management in Educating Emotionally
      Disturbed, Mentally Retarded Children." Doctoral disser-
      tation, University of Pittsburgh, 1978, summarized in
      Dissertation Abstracts International, 1978, 39, 1145A.
      (University Microfilms No. 7816814).

      Provided token reinforcement for preacademic task be-
havior of 6 to 9-year-old MR/emotionally disturbed children
in classroom situation, aimed at establishing self-management
behavior. Study shows that the established self-management
behavior, involving high rates of task-related behavior and
low frequencies of disruptive behavior, persisted in an 8-week
follow-up period after the completion of the initial training
period.

209. Sheare, J.B. "Social Acceptance of EMR Adolescents in
      Integrated Programs." *American Journal of Mental Defi-
      ciency*, 1974, 78, 678-682.

      Four hundred nonretarded ninth-grade students from three
suburban junior high schools were randomly assigned to experimental and control groups of equal size. In the experimental
condition, nonretarded children and EMR adolescents from the
special classes in each school were integrated in nonacademic
classes, and social and athletic activities. Control groups
were not integrated. An Acceptance Scale was devised and administered to all subjects at midyear. A three-way analysis
of variance revealed that the experimental groups consistently
gave more positive ratings to EMR adolescents than did the
control groups, and that female subjects rated more positively
than males in all groups.

210. Siperstein, G.N., Budoff, M., & Bak, J.J. "Effects of
      the Labels 'Mentally Retarded' and 'Retarded' on the
      Social Acceptability of Mentally Retarded Children."
      American Journal of Mental Deficiency, 1980, 84, 596-
      601.

      Effects of the labels "mentally retarded" and "retarded"
on fifth- and sixth-grade children's attitudes toward peers
were studied. Results indicated that children's feelings and
behavioral intentions were more positive toward the child
labeled "mentally retarded" than toward those labeled "retarded."
The children's reactions to the two labels were, in part, a
function of the physical appearance and academic achievement
of the rated peer. Children had the most negative attitudes
toward a child labeled "retarded" who appeared to be normal.
In contrast, children reacted favorably to the child labeled
"mentally retarded," even when he or she was academically
incompetent. Boys were more negative than were girls toward
the labeled child, especially when the child was labeled "retarded."

211. Siperstein, G.N., & Gottlieb, J. "Physical Stigma and
      Academic Performance as Factors Affecting Children's
      First Impressions of Handicapped Peers." *American Journal
      of Mental Deficiency*, 1977, 81, 455-462.

      The effects of four variables on attitudes toward chil-
dren were studied: the sex and social status of the rater and
the physical appearance and academic competence of the rated

child. Results indicated that competent and physically non-
stigmatized children were rated more favorably than incompetent
and physically stigmatized children. Girls had a more positive
stereotype than did boys of a competent male target child, but
boys were more willing to be in physical proximity to the male
target child. Popular children rated the attractive and competent target child less favorably than children who were not so
popular. However, the popular children rated the attractive
and incompetent target child more favorably than the less popular children did.

212.   Soule, D. "Teacher Bias Effects with Severely Retarded
       Children." *American Journal of Mental Deficiency*, 1972,
       77, 208–211.

       Examined the effect of experimentally induced teacher
bias, or expectancy, on the subsequent behavior of institutionalized severely retarded children when the bias effects were
a result of optimistic psychological reports to cottage parents.
No effect of teacher bias was found.

213.   Stager, S.F., & Young, R.D. "Intergroup Contact and
       Social Outcomes for Mainstreamed EMR Adolescents."
       American Journal of Mental Deficiency, 1981, 85, 497–
       503.

       The prediction of the contact hypothesis, that contact
between nonretarded and EMR adolescents would result in the
EMR adolescents being viewed as more competent, likeable, and
socially acceptable, was examined. Subjects were 26 mainstreamed EMR adolescents. Likeability, competency, and acceptability scores were computed for each subject on the basis of
responses by nonretarded and EMR classmates to a survey questionnaire. Intergroup contact did not significantly modify the
attitudes of nonretarded classmates toward the EMR subjects,
who were viewed as significantly more competent, likeable,
and socially acceptable by EMR classmates in the special class
than by nonretarded classmates in the mainstream class.

214.   Strain, P.S., & Cooke, T.P. "An Observational Investigation of Two Elementary-age Autistic Children During Free-Play." *Psychology in the Schools*, 1976, 13(1), 82-91.

Two observational systems were employed to measure the behavior patterns of two elementary-age autistic children and their classroom peers during a free-play period. Results obtained from the total behavior repertoire system indicate that the subjects spent the majority of the free-play period manipulating various toys and objects. Data obtained from the social interaction system reveal that the subjects' encounters with peers typically were negative. Additionally, the subjects were observed to respond more frequently to verbal social behavior by peers than they were to motor gestural responses.

215.   Voeltz, L.M. "Children's Attitudes toward Handicapped Peers." *American Journal of Mental Deficiency*, 1980, 84, 455-464.

As services for severely handicapped children become increasingly available within neighborhood public schools, children's attitudes toward handicapped peers in integrated settings warrant attention. Factor analysis of attitude survey responses of 2,392 children revealed four factors underlying attitudes toward handicapped peers: social-contact willingness, deviance consequation, and two actual contacts with severely handicapped peers expressed the most accepting attitides. Results of this study suggest the modifiability of children's attitudes and the need to develop interventions to facilitate social acceptance of individual differences in integrated school settings.

216.   Warner, F., Thrapp, R., & Walsh, S. "Attitudes of Children toward Their Special Class Placement." *Exceptional Children*, 1973, 40(1), 37-38.

The attitudes of 369 EMR children toward their special class placement were explored. The majority of children, especially the younger ones, expressed their satisfaction at being in a special class.

217. Werbel, C.S. "A Library Program for the Severely Retarded
      Education and Training of the Mentally Retarded, 1980, 15
      315-318.

      Designed and administered a behaviorally-based library
program to teach adaptive skills to residents at a large public institution for the mentally retarded. The 15 participants
ranged in CA from 22 to 62 years and had a mean IQ of 41. Results show Ss learned to behave properly in a library, causing
very little, if any, disruption and to utilize story hours and
films.

218. Wingert, M.L. "Effects of a Music Enrichment Program in
      the Education of the Mentally Retarded." *Journal of
      Music Therapy*, 1972, 9, 13-22.

      Studied the effects of a music-enrichment program on the
measured intelligences, basic knowledges, communicative abilities, and social behaviors of 10 control Ss at the same school.
A program of musical activities was conducted for a 40-minute
period, twice weekly, for 18 weeks-36 sessions and approximatel}
24 hours. Controls, although having some musical participation
in their regular classroom settings, did not receive the additional music treatment. It is concluded that there was a
significant gain in the measured intelligence of the experimental group engaged in the music enrichment program and a
significant difference in favor of the experimental group in
the amount of change in intelligence. Both groups made significant gains in basic knowledge, communication, and social
behavior; however, there was no significant difference between
the 2 groups in the amount of mean change in these areas.

CHAPTER V:
EMOTIONAL DISTURBANCES

219. Ando, H., & Yoshimura, I. "Comprehension Skill Levels
      and Prevalence of Maladaptive Behaviors in Autistic
      and Mentally Retarded Children." *Child Psychiatry &*
      Human Development, 1979, 9, 131-136.

      Compared the verbal comprehension skills of 2 groups of
6- to 14-year-old children--47 autistic Ss and 128 nonorganic
MR Ss. Teacher judgments were used as measures of comprehension
skills and maladaptive behaviors. The following maladaptive
behaviors were assessed: self injury, attack against others,
destruction of property, hyperactivity, withdrawal, lack of
eye-to-eye gaze, stereotyped behavior, tantrums, and fear.
Comparisons were made between the Ss with maladaptive behavior
and those with it in each of the 2 diagnostic groups--autistic
and MR. Results show that the MR with hyperactivity or withdrawal had lower comprehension skill levels than those without these behaviors.

220. Ando, H., & Yoshimura, I. "Speech Skill Levels and Prev-
      alence of Maladaptive Behaviors in Autistic and Mentally
      Retarded Children: A Statistical Study." *Child Psychiatry &*
      Human Development, 1979, 10, 85-90.

      Assessed 47 autistic and 128 MR children and adolescents
from a special school in terms of 9 maladaptive behaviors, such
as self-injury, attack on others, destruction of property, hyperactivity, withdrawal, lack of eye contact, stereotyped behavior,
tantrums, and fear, as well as speech skill levels. Found that
withdrawing MR children had lower speech skill levels than those
who did not withdraw, and that the autistic children with self-
injury had lower speech skill levels than those without self-
injury.

81

221.   Balthazar, E.E., & Stevens, H.A. *The Emotionally Dis-*
       turbed Mentally Retarded: A Historical and Contemporary
       Perspective. Englewood Cliffs, N.J.: Prentice-Hall, 1975.

       Discusses the relationship between emotional disturbance
and mental retardation, both from an historical as well as a
contemporary viewpoint. Also, provides correct information
on differential diagnosis and treatment, and furnishes a broad
interdisciplinary range for program development and evaluation
in this area.

222.   Berman, M.I. "Mental Retardation and Depression." *Mental*
       Retardation, 1967, 5(6), 19-21.

       Diagnosed depression in the majority of older MR persons
referred for misbehavior. Suggests a re-definition of depression in terms of a more behavioral description.

223.   Bialer, I. "Emotional Disturbance and Mental Retardation:
       Etiologic and Conceptual Relationships." In F.J. Menolasci
       ed. *Psychiatric approaches to mental retardation*, 68-90.
       New York: Basic Books, 1970.

       Discusses the relationships between emotional disturbance
and mental retardation in terms of etiologic and conceptual
terms, taking into consideration the A.A.M.D. classification
system and certain aspects of the Lewinian Field Theory.

224.   Boberg, E. "Stuttering in the Retarded: I. Review of
       Prevalence Literature." *Mental Retardation Bulletin*,
       1977, 5, 90-100.

       Reviews published research on prevalence of stuttering
in MR populations as compared to populations of normally intelligent persons. Large differences found among prevalence
figures may be due to misclassification of a speech disorder
suffered by the retarded. Resolution of the conflict should
be undertaken as a first step in designing programs.

225. Borys, S.V., & Spitz, H.H. "Reflection-Impulsivity in
      Retarded Adolescents and Nonretarded Children of Equal
      MA." *American Journal of Mental Deficiency*, 1978, 82,
      601-604.

      EMR adolescents and nonretarded children of equal MA
were given the preschool and elementary forms of the Matching
Familiar Figures Test to assess reflection-impulsivity. The
authors found that the EMR adolescents did not differ significantly in accuracy and had somewhat longer response latencies
than did the nonretarded children. In view of these results,
it is unlikely that impulsivity contributed to the previously
reported performance decrement displayed by retarded individuals
on problem-solving tasks.

226. Bryson, Y., Sakati, N., Nyhan, W.L., & Fish, C.H. "Self-
      Mutilative Behavior in the Cornelia de Lange Syndrome."
      American Journal of Mental Deficiency, 1971, 76, 319-324.

      Four patients were observed with the Cornelia de Lange
syndrome (Type II) in whom compulsive self-mutilation was a
major feature. Each patient had a stereotyped pattern of
abusive behavior in which there was repeated trauma to the
same area. A total of 6 such patients have now been studied.
Self-mutilation may represent a distinctive feature of this
disorder and suggests a relationship between organic disease
and the expression of human behavior.

227. Campbell, B., & Grieve, R. "Social and Attentional As-
      pects of Echolalia in Highly Echolatic Mentally Retarded
      Persons." *American Journal of Mental Deficiency*, 1978,
      82, 414-416.

      Echolalia was examined in a sample of highly echolalic
MR individuals, which consisted of 11 adults and a 9-year-old
child. All Ss had been diagnosed as low grade (IQ 30-44).
When presented with a standard set of questions, under conditions differing in appropriateness for exchange of discourse
(e.g., questions presented with examiner and patient face-to-
face vs. questions presented with the examiner's face averted
vs. questions addressed to another person sitting silently
beside the patient), Ss' frequency of echolalia varied. Besides showing considerable sensitivity to aspects of discourse
exchange, Ss exhibited some limited capacity for processing
linguistic information.

228. Chess, S. "Emotional Problems in Mentally Retarded Chil-
      dren." In F.J. Menolascino, ed. *Psychiatric approaches
      to mental retardation*, 55-67. New York: Basic Books, 1970.

MR children's vulnerability to environmental stresses
may lead to the development of emotional disturbances. Four
categories can be distinguished: (1) problems related to brain
damage; (2) reactive disorders; (3) neurotic behavior; and
(4) psychoses.

229. Chess, S., & Hassibi, M. "Behavior Deviations in Mentally
      Retarded Children." *Journal of the American Academy of
      Child Psychiatry*, 1970, 9, 282-297.

Described the different frequencies of behavior and speech
categories in noninstitutionalized MR children.

230. Chess, S., & Korn, S. "Temperament and Behavior Disorders
      in Mentally Retarded Children." *Archives of General
      Psychiatry*, 1970, 23, 122-130.

Indicates that temperament influences the retarded child's
adaptiveness and has important implications for management.
Middle-class children living at home were studied. Results
indicate that certain patterns of temperament appear to inten-
sify the stresses to which the retarded child is especially
subject. The risk for developing a disturbance is greatest
in children who show irregularity in biological functions,
withdrawal responses, nonadaptability, predominantly negative
mood, and high intensity. Positive parental management of
a MR child with several signs of vulnerability may help achieve
better adaptation. Conversely, children who appear least at-
risk may manifest behavior disorders partly as a result of
adverse patterns of care and other environemntal pressures.

231. Craft, M. "Mental Disorder in the Defective: A Psychiatric
      Survey Among In-Patients." *American Journal of Mental
      Deficiency*, 1959, 63, 829-834.

Reports that, depending upon criteria used to determine
mental disorders, from 7 to 33 percent of a sample of MR in-
patients showed personality disturbance.

232. Cutts, R.A. "Differentiation between Pseudo-Mental Defectives with Emotional Disorders and Mental Defectives
with Emotional Disturbance." *American Journal of Mental
Deficiency*, 1957, 61, 761-772.

Attempts to find criteria for differentiating the Pseudo-
mental defective with emotional problems from the true mental
defective with emotional problems. This differential diagnosis,
when made, is usually in retrospect after repeated examinations;
but to be able to make the differentiation on an original examination would be of benefit to all concerned.

233. Dewan, J.G. "Intelligence and Emotional Stability."
American Journal of Psychiatry, 1948, 104, 548-554.

The examination of over 30,000 men shows a larger incidence of emotional stability among the MR than in the nonretarded.

234. Duckett, J. "Adaptive and Maladaptive Behavior of *Idiot
Savants*." *American Journal of Mental Deficiency*, 1977,
82, 308-311.

A comparison was made of 25 institutionalized idiot
savants and a control group of institutionalized retarded
persons matched for age, sex, IQ, and length of institutionalization. As a group, idiot savants were found to be somewhat
more disturbed and disturbing than their peers, although they
did not show extreme emotional disturbance nor reflect a clear
behavioral profile.

235. Foale, M. "The Special Difficulties of the High Grade
Mental Defective Adolescent." *American Journal of Mental
Deficiency*, 1956, 60, 867-877.

The special problems of the high grade mental defective
adolescent are considered. The seriously maladjusted mental
defective adolescent is discussed as well as the problems of
the institutionalized mental defective adolescent.

236.   Frankel, F., & Simmons, J.Q. III. "Self-Injurious Behavior
        in Schizophrenic and Retarded Children." *American Journal
        of Mental Deficiency*, 1976, 80, 512-522.

        Self-injurious behavior is a problem with some children
who are primarily nonverbal and low-functioning. This behavior
has resulted in management difficulties far out of proportion
to its incidence. In the present paper, the authors have considered possible operant and respondent paradigms instrumental
in the acquisition and maintenance of several different topog-
raphies of self-injurious behavior. Support for these paradigms
was gathered from existing epidemiological literature dealing
with humans and primates and from the literature concerned with
treatment of self-injurious behavior. Immediate outcome and
results of subsequent follow-up were presented as a function
of type of intervention, the nature of positive reinforcement
utilized, and the topography of the self-injurious response
involved.

237.   Frodi, A.M. "Contribution of Infant Characteristics to
        Child Abuse." *American Journal of Mental Deficiency*,
        1981, 85, 341-349.

        This review suggested that atypical infants/children
(with mental, physical, or behavioral abnormalities) are
at risk for child abuse. An explanatory model of abuse was
outlined and several studies described whose findings provide
support for the model. Some infants or infant attributes
are especially likely to be perceived as aversive and as
such may serve as aggression-facilitating stimuli. Other
factors that contribute to the probability of abuse are dispositions of the parent, such as hyperreactivity to noxious
stimulation. Such dispositions may be constitutional or may
have developed during negative transactions with the child.
Characteristics of the child and of the caretaker as well as
their social ecology all affect the likelihood of abuse.

238.   Gardner, J.M., & Giampa, F.L. "Behavioral Competence
        and Social and Emotional Behavior in Mental Retardates."
        American Journal of Mental Deficiency, 1970, 75, 168-169.

        The relationship between intellectual level and social
and emotional behavior (SEB) was examined in an institutionalized mentally retarded population. Two subjects were randomly
selected from each of 3 groups: moderately, severely, and profoundly retarded. Two judges recorded the frequency of inappropriate SEBs (e.g., screaming, hitting) during a half-hour

recreation period. Eight 30-minute samples were obtained for
the 6 subjects. The 3 groups did not differ significantly in
inappropriate SEBs. The independence of SEB from intellectual
functioning points to the need for their conjoint measurement,
rather than relying on such uni-dimensional measures as the
IQ or SQ.

239.   Golden, G.S., & Greenhill, L. "Tourette Syndrome in
       Mentally Retarded Children." *Mental Retardation*, 1981,
       19, 17-19.

       Tourette Syndrome, a condition beginning in childhood,
is characterized by both chronic motor and vocal tics. Bizarre
stereotyped movements, compulsive behavior, and coprolalia are
often present. In this study, six mentally retarded individuals
originally manifesting these symptoms are first thought to have
manneristic behavior. Prompt response to treatment with halo-
peridol exposes their true nature as tics associated with Tourette
Syndrome.

240.   Greyson, G., & Akhtar, S. "Erotomanic Delusions in a
       Mentally Retarded Patient." *American Journal of Psychiatry*,
       1977, 134, 325-326.

       An erotomanic delusion repeatedly precipitated by threat-
ened object loss was reported in a 46-year-old male MR patient.
The content of his primary delusion, that a teenager he saw in
church wanted to marry him, is the definitive characteristic
of erotomania although certain features of the patient's de-
lusional system differed from the syndrome. Some of the dis-
crepancies between the patient's psychosis and pure erotomania
may reflect his severe MR and his primitive, concrete interpretations of the threatened object loss. The patient's comparatively
unsophisticated variation of erotomania may reflect his limited
repertoire of ego defenses and his inability to project his own
needs onto others as abstract emotions.

241.   Guarnaccia, V.J., & Weiss, R.L. "Factor Structure of
       Fears in the Mentally Retarded." *Journal of Clinical
       Psychology*, 1974, 30, 540-545.

       This study explored the factor structure of fears in MR
children and young adults. Parents' ratings on the 81-item
Louisville Fear Survey for Children (LFSC) were obtained from
a mailed survey for 102 Ss who ranged in age from 6 to 21 and

had a mean IQ of 43. Four relatively independent and psycho-
logically meaningful factors emerged: Separation, Natural
Events, Injury, and Animals.

242. Jenkins, R.L., & Stable, G. "Special Characteristics
      of Retarded Children Rated as Severely Hyperactive."
      Child Psychiatry & Human Development, 1971, 2(1), 26-
      31.

      Matched 94 pairs of retarded children for age and year
of examination. Hyperactivity was rated as no problem in 1
S in each pair and as a severe problem in the other S. Findings indicate a higher incidence of CNS damage and/or dysfunction in Ss who were hyperactive than in those who were
not. Of 6 cases of hemiplegia, all were in the hyperactive
group, as were 7 of 8 cases of diplegia. A larger proportion
of the hyperactives had a history of convulsive seizures,
and more had a residual speech defect.

243. Krishef, C.H., & DiNitto, D.M. "Alcohol Abuse among
      Mentally Retarded Individuals." *Mental Retardation*,
      1981, 19, 151-155.

      Alcohol abuse among MR persons is investigated. Responses
to a questionnaire completed by officials of a sample of
Association for Retarded Citizens and Alcohol Treatment Programs across the country reveal the majority of MR individuals
identified in the survey as alcohol abusers are males. Most
abusers are not married and living arrangements vary. Problems related to drinking are arrests and difficulties at work.
Treatment methods deemed especially appropriate for MR alcohol
abusers are identified.

244. Menolascino, F.J. "Emotional Disturbance and Mental
      Retardation." *American Journal of Mental Deficiency*,
      1965, 70, 248-256.

      In 616 children under eight years of age, who had been
studied intensively as possible MR individuals, a total of
191 (31 percent) were noted to display emotional problems
of such a nature and extent to warrant a formal AAMD and/or
APA diagnosis. These 191 children formed two distinct sub-
groups: (a) MR and emotionally disturbed (24.5 percent of
the total group), and (b) primary emotional disturbance without mental retardation (6.5 percent of the total group). Thus,

nearly, one of every three children who were evaluated displayed prominent psychiatric problems. The children with
primary emotional disturbances further underscore the need
for routinely assessing emotional parameters in any child
suspected to be MR.

245. Menolascino, F.J. "Emotional Disturbances in Mentally
     Retarded Children." *American Journal of Psychiatry*,
     1969, 126, 168-176.

     The experience of a multidisciplinary team with 256
emotionally disturbed MR children are discussed, and descriptive diagnostic findings for four frequently noted types
of emotional disturbances are presented, along with treat-
ment-management considerations.

246. Menolascino, F.J. "Primitive, Atypical and Abnormal-
     Psychotic Behavior in Institutionalized Mentally Re-
     tarded Children." *Journal of Autism and Childhood
     Schizophrenia*, 1972, 3, 49-64.

     Five case reports are presented to illustrate primitive,
atypical, and abnormal (or psychotic) behaviors, said to constitute the three most common types seen in institutionalized MR
children and adolescents. Behavioral manifestations and specific
approaches to management and treatment are related to the histories of 5 boys, ranging in age from 6 to 14 years and represent-
ing, respectively, primitive behavior amidst delayed development, atypical intrafamilial communication patterns, atypical
behavior response of the child from a closely knit family,
childhood psychosis, and the rumination syndrome.

247. Menolascino, F.J. "Symposium on the Treatment of Behavioural
     Problems: II. Three Frequent Types of Behavioural Disturb-
     ances in Institutionalized Retardates." *British Journal
     of Mental Subnormality*, 1972, 28, (Pt. 2), 71-80.

     Presents the types of abnormal behavior of some MR per-
sons.

248. Menolascino, F.J., & Eaton, L. "Psychosis of Childhood:
      A Five Year Follow-up Study of Experiences in a
      Mental Retardation Clinic." *American Journal of Mental
      Deficiency,* 1967, 72, 370-380.

      A brief review of the literature on follow-up studies
of psychoses of childhood is presented. A five-year follow-
up report is given on 29 of a previously reported series of
32 cases of childhood psychosis. Questions regarding present
diagnostic categories are raised from the implications of
this and other studies. The need for further evaluations of
long-term treatment in the psychoses of childhood, especially
in the field of mental retardation, is underscored.

249. Montague, J.C., Jr., & Cage, B.N. "Self-Concepts of
      Institutional and Non-Institutional Educable Mentally
      Retarded Children." *Perceptual and Motor Skills*, 1974,
      38, 977-978.

      Twenty public school special education and 20 institu-
tionalized EMR children were compared on an experimental I
Feel--Me Feel self-perception scale. No significant differences
in self-concept were found between the 2 groups or between sexes;
all children had generally good appreciation of self-concept.

250. Ohwaki, S. "Behavioral Characteristics of Habilitated
      Retarded Persons." *American Journal of Mental Deficiency*,
      1974, 79, 385-390.

      An assumption that habilitated retarded persons had
higher social competence than nonhabilitated persons was
investigated by comparing 65 discharged residents of Lynchburg
Training School and Hospital who had completed vocational
training with 60 residents matched in age and IQ. The results
obtained from the hospital revealed that the habilitated group
fought less but attempted to escape and cursed more than the
nonhabilitated group. Social history indicated the existence
of cultural-familial components in the majority of the habilitated group. Psychometric scores, the Emotional Index of the
Bender Gestalt test, and an analysis of the medical diagnosis
supported the above finding. Since interpersonal adjustment
was an important factor in successful habilitation, an increased emphasis on counseling in vocational-training programs was suggested.

251. Pelechano, V. "A Behavior Disturbance Scale (ETC-1)."
     Analysis y Modificacion de Conducta, 1975, 1, 19-32.

     Evaluated 200 MR (117 males, 83 females) using a 60-item
behavioral checklist, the Escala de Trastornos de Conducta
(ETC-1). A factor analysis (rotation varimax) revealed 3
factors: submission-agression, psychomotor ataxia, and neurotic
symptoms. A correlation coefficient analysis indicated that
submission-agression was highly related to psychomotor ataxia,
but had little relationship with neurotic symptoms, and that
ataxia was correlated to neurotic symptoms.

252. Pershad, D., Kaushal, P., & Verma, S.K. "Neuroticism
     Scores of Mothers of Mentally Retarded and of Neurotic
     Children." *Indian Journal of Mental Retardation*, 1973,
     6(1), 24-27.

     Administered a 38-item Hindi Health Questionnaire to the
mothers of 25 MR children and of 21 emotionally disturbed children attending a child guidance clinic. The mothers of mentally
retarded children were found to be more emotionally disturbed--
i.e., more neurotic--than the mothers of emotionally disturbed
children.

253. Phillips, I. "Psychopathology and Mental Retardation."
     American Journal of Psychiatry, 1967, 124, 29-35.

     A study of 227 MR children and their families revealed
that emotional maladjustment more often than not accompanies
retardation. The author points out, however, that disturbed
behavior in the retarded is not due primarily to limited
intellectual capacities but to delayed, disordered personality
functions and disturbed interpersonal relationships with meaningful people in the environment.

254. Phillips, I., & Williams, N. "Psychopathology and Mental
     Retardation: A Study of 100 Mentally Retarded Children:
     I. Psychopathology." *American Journal of Psychiatry*,
     1975, 132, 1265-1271.

     Studied 100 MR children referred to a psychiatric clinic
due to the severity of their retardation. Found that 38 of
these children were psychiatrically disturbed, 13 had no psychiatric disorder, and 49 showed symptoms of characterologic,
neurotic, behavioral, or situational disorders.

255. Pilkington, T.L. "Symposium on the Treatment of Behavioural
      Problems: I. Psychiatric Needs of the Subnormal." *British
      Journal of Mental Subnormality*, 1972, 28, (Pt. 2), 66-70.

      Found that a sizable minority of the mentally ill MR
population would benefit from psychiatric contact. Treatment
methods are considered.

256. Pollock, H.M. "Mental Disease among Mental Defectives."
      American Journal of Mental Deficiency, 1945, 49, 477-480.

      Statistics obtained from a New York state hospital reveal
that the rate of first admissions among mental defectives is
several times as high as among non-defectives. The author
concludes that in mental defectives we have a group of persons with special susceptibility to mental disease. Unfortunately, this fact has not been taken into consideration in our
general treatment of subnormal children.

257. Rago, W.V., Jr. "Eye Gaze and Dominance Hierarchy in
      Profoundly Mentally Retarded Males." *American Journal
      of Mental Deficiency*, 1977, 82, 145-148.

      Previous research on gaze aversion has suggested that
avoiders are communicating subordination in the hierarchy of
social interaction. A study on aggression in profoundly MR
persons provided the objective measure required to determine
the relationship between duration of eye gaze and ranked position in a social group's dominance hierarchy. Results indicated that submissive individuals maintained significantly
longer eye contact as contrasted with dominant individuals.
Implications of the findings were discussed.

258. Reid, A.H., & Naylor, G.J. "Short-Cycle Manic-Depressive
      Psychosis in Mental Defectives: A Clinical and Physio-
      logical Study." *Journal of Mental Deficiency Research*,
      1976, 20, 67-76.

      Described four cases of short-cycle manic-depressive
psychosis in MR patients. Found that behavioral fluctuations
are correlated with alterations in sleep pattern, pulse rate,
and temperature.

259. Reiss, S., Levitan, G.W., & McNally, R.J. "Emotionally Disturbed Mentally Retarded People; An Underserved Population." *American Psychologist*, 1982, 37, 361-367.

The need to increase the supply of psychotherapeutic services for the emotional problems of MR people, as well as those of people with IQs between 70 and 80, is discussed. Low intelligence may increase the risk of emotional disturbance because it creates special adjustment problems while limiting the individual's ability to solve these problems. Low intelligence may decrease the opportunity for adequate psychotherapeutic services because of administrative, conceptual, and attitudinal reasons.

260. Revill, M.G. "Symposium on the Treatment of Behavioural Problems: IV. Manic-Depressive Illness in Retarded Children." *British Journal of Mental Subnormality*, 1972, 28(Pt. 2), 89-93.

Presents literature on the incidence of manic-depressive illness in children and MR persons.

261. Russell, A.T., & Tanguay, P.E. "Mental Illness and Mental Retardation: Cause or Coincidence?" *American Journal of Mental Deficiency*, 1981, 85, 570-574.

A sample of 93 patients admitted to an in-patient psychiatric unit for emotionally disturbed, developmentally disabled adolescents was studied in an attempt to clarify the relationship between intellectual functioning and psychoses occurring in the developmental period. The severity and duration of the psychosis, the presence of hallucination, and the degree of isolation of the child from his or her environment appear to be important factors influencing the occurrence of decreased psychometric test scores in the individuals studied.

262. Shukla, T.R., & Kroche, V. "A Study of Adjustment Problems of Mentally Retarded Children." *Indian Journal of Mental Retardation*, 1974, 7(1), 4-13.

Residential, health, social, and emotional adjustment of MR was investigated in 50 MR and 50 normal children. Maladjustment scores of MR groups were higher in comparison to those of the normal group. This finding held true for the other areas of adjustment. Group differences were highly significant for all areas of adjustment.

263.   Stephens, E. "Defensive Reactions of Mentally Retarded
        Adults." *Social Casework*, 1953, 34, 119-124.

        Reports that many MR people reduce their anxiety through
the defense mechanism of denial.

264.   Sternlicht, M. "The Assessment of the Emotional Dimension
        of the Social Functioning of the Retarded." Paper pre-
        sented at the annual meeting of the American Association
        on Mental Deficiency, Vermont, October 1966.

        Describes the various approaches to the assessment of
emotional factors in the social functioning of the MR person.

265.   Sternlicht, M. "The Concept of Death in Preoperational
        Retarded Children." *Journal of Genetic Psychology*, 1980,
        137, 157-164.

        Fourteen preoperational retarded boys and girls, as classi
fied by the failure to pass three conversation tasks, were inter
viewed for their concepts of death. Each S was asked, What make
things die?, How can you make dead things come back to life?,
When will you die?, and What will happen then? It was found
that the preoperational retarded Ss did not have realistic concepts of when they will die, or of the permanence of death.
They did, however, have realistic notions of how things die.
It was also found that the types of replies made to these
questions were related to their cognitive level.

266.   Sternlicht, M., Pustel, G., & Deutsch, M.R. "Suicidal
        Tendencies among Institutionalized Retardates." *Journal
        of Mental Subnormality*, 1970, 16, 93-102.

        The records of a group of 45 male and female suicidal
retardates, drawn from the largest institutional cross-section
of retardates in the United States, were examined for a number
of variables grouped into three categories: (a) statistical
parameters of the suicide problem among retardates; (b) psychological correlates of suicidal behaviour in retardates; and
(c) personality dynamics of the suicidal retardates. The
study sets forth a host of parametric and behavioural data
on suicide among retardates, presents a detailed psychological
analysis of a prototypical case, and advances a theory of retardate suicide.

267. Szymanski, L.S., & Tanguay, P.E. eds. *Emotional Disorders of Mentally Retarded Persons: Assessment, Treatment and Consultation.* Baltimore: University Park Press, 1980.

Discusses the various emotional disorders in mental retardation, and their assessment and remediation. Contributed chapters, with an essentially psychiatric bias. Includes an excellent discussion on psycho-pharmacology and mental retardation.

268. TeBeest, D.L., & Dickie, J.R. "Responses to Frustration: Comparison of Institutionalized and Noninstitutionalized Retarded Adolescents and Nonretarded Children and Adolescents." *American Journal of Mental Deficiency,* 1976, 80, 407-413.

Thirty adolescents (10 institutionalized retarded, 10 noninstitutionalized retarded, 10 nonretarded CA-matched) and 10 children (nonretarded MA-matched) were individually given the Rosenzweig Picture-Frustration Study (Children's Form). Responses were scored for direction of blame and reaction type, yielding nine frustration response categories. Three of the nine response categories showed significant group relationships. Retardation, institutionalization, and CA were all found to have an effect on responding, although analysis of response profiles showed all groups to be very similar in response patterns.

269. Waltzer, B. "Comparison of Institutionalized Mongoloids, Public School Mongoloids and Public School Undifferentiated Moderate Retardates for Three Emotional Factors." Doctoral dissertation, Rutgers State University 1965, summarized in *Dissertation Abstracts International,* 1970, 31, 1091A. (University Microfilms No. 70-16,591).

Testing the personality stereotype of mongoloids, it was hypothesized that there would be no difference between mongoloids and undifferentiated moderate retardates on the personality factors of aggression, adjustment, and extraversion. The results of this study cast doubt on the held mongoloid stereotype that describes them as being well adjusted, extraverted, and low in aggressive behavior.

270.   Weaver, T.R. "The Incidence of Maladjustment among Mental
        Defectives in Military Environment." *American Journal of
        Mental Deficiency*, 1946, 51, 238-246.

        Of 8,000 mental defectives surveyed, over half of the
group adjusted successfully in the Army. Four factors aided
adjustment: (a) personal assets, (b) a military program of
proper classification and assignment, (c) a program of group
psychotherapy, (d) utilization of social agencies. Three
factors aggravated maladjustment: (a) lack of foundation on
which to build personality, (b) personality deviations deeply
ingrained in the personality structure, (c) poor leadership.

CHAPTER VI:
CRIMINAL AND DELINQUENT BEHAVIOR

271. Addad, M., & Benezech, M. "Mentally Handicapped--Defini-
      tion and Study of Their Relation with Delinquency." *Revue
      de Droit Penal et de Criminologie*, 1980, 60, 443-462.

      A review of the existing literature on the criminogenic
effects of mental retardation shows that a low IQ does not
correlate directly with antisocial and criminal behavior.
Crime statistics show that the percentage of MR individuals
is only slightly higher among criminals than among law-abiding
citizens. However, mental retardation is not the immutable
result of brain damage or organic anomalies (true retardation),
or of functional disorders (pseudo-retardation). Retardation
also causes a dysfunction of cognition, volition, communication,
and assimilation of experience data in its subjects. A correlation between mental retardation and psychosis cannot be
denied. Criminal behavior can result from a failure of the
MR to assimilate intuitive and experimental data using the
inductive methods of children under 7 years of age. Like
infants, they are totally self-centered and subjective, and
lack inhibition mechanisms. Easily suggestible, they can
commit crimes at the instigation of intelligent criminals.
The MR are more frequently born among the lower socioeconomic
strata, into families where alcoholism, venereal disease,
mental disorders, and deviant behavior patterns are prevalent.
The MR feel the same need for love, group acceptance, and
peer appreciation as normal individuals. Frustrated and rejected from their early childhood, the MR may be driven to
commit criminal acts if this behavior brings them the rewards
of acceptance in the deviant subculture of the socially handicapped.

272.   Akesson, H.O., Forssman, H., Wahlström, J., & Wallin, L.
        "Sex Chromosomes Aneuploidy among Men in Three Swedish
        Hospitals for the Mentally Retarded and Maladjusted."
        British Journal of Psychiatry, 1974, 125, 386-389.

        Performed chromosome determinations of 117 male patients
in 3 hospitals for the MR and maladjusted who had a body length
of 180 centimeters or more. The finding of 13 patients with
gonosomal aneuploidy was overrepresented when compared with
the general population, suggesting that both excess X-chromo-
somes and Y-chromosomes may produce a predisposition for
socially deviant behavior in maladjusted MR persons.

273.   Bakeman, C.V. "The Developmentally Disabled Offender
        and Community-Based Services in Illinois." *Offender
        Rehabilitation*, 1976, 1, 89-100.

        Reports on a part of a study of the needs and problems
of developmentally disabled offenders, focusing on community-
based services for MR, cerebral palsied, and epileptic persons,
indicating a need for specialized programs and staff training
for these groups, as well as specialized living arrangements
and other services.

274.   Baker, D., Telfer, M.A., Richardson, C.E., & Clark, G.R.
        "Chromosome Errors in Men with Antisocial Behavior: Com-
        parison of Selected Men with Klinefelter's Syndrome and
        XYY Chromosome Pattern." *Journal of the American Medical
        Association*, 1970, 214, 869-878.

        A total of 876 males in prisons and facilities for the
mentally ill and MR underwent cytogenetic screening. Of the
23 Ss identified with sex chromosome errors, 7 with 47,XYY
chromosome pattern and 8 with Klinefelter's syndrome were
compared. Both groups displayed tall stature and elongated
lower segments; the XYY males averaged 3 inches taller than
the Klinefelter males. In contrast to 47,XYY males, Klinefelter
males uniformly displayed atrophic testes and buccal smears
positive for sex chromatin. Facial acne, ulcerous varicosities
of the legs, and neurological disorders were inconsistent features of both groups. The Klinefelter males of this series
had a mean IQ of 80, whereas the 47,XYY males had a mean IQ
of 84. Both groups manifested a wide spectrum of criminal
offenses and psychopathology, including psychosis.

275. Beckmann, J., Dupont, A., Erling, I., Jacobsen, P., Mikkelsen, M., & Theilgaard, A. "Report of Sex Chromosome Abnormalities in Mentally Retarded Male Offenders Including a Psychological Study of Patients with XYY and XXYY Karyotypes." *Journal of Mental Deficiency Research*, 1974, 18, 331-353.

Conducted a cytogenetic investigation of 99 MR male offenders. Eight Ss with sex chromosome abnormalities were found. Of these, the karyotype was 47,XYY in 6 cases, 47,XXY in 1 case, and 48, XXYY in 1 case. Ss with sex chromosome abnormalities were examined critically and by means of psychological testing (the WAIS, 2 verbal and 1 nonverbal memory test, the Bender-Gestalt, the Draw-A-Person test, the Rorschach, and the TAT). Criminal records, time of onset of the 1st criminal act, IQ, and body height were compared with those of 91 offenders with normal sex chromosome patterns. Psychological testing indicated that Ss with sex chromosome abnormalities had a relatively high IQ (range 63-68) compared with the other retarded offenders. Results of various subtests revealed that the Organization factor was greater than the Verbal Comprehension and Attention factors. A very short attention span was found in all of the Ss with sex chromosome abnormalities. Personality tests indicated that such Ss were characterized by impulsivity, immaturity, the use of primitive and ineffective defense mechanisms, and a low threshold of frustration. The study also included the cytological examination of 30 retarded schoolboys who demonstrated aggressiveness and who had been involved in petty larceny. One S with the Karyotype 47,XXY was found.

276. Bhagat, M., & Fraser, W.I. "The Meaning of Concepts to the Retarded Offender." *American Journal of Mental Deficiency*, 1970, 75, 260-267.

The semantic differential was administered to 81 MR subjects and 40 young offenders of average intelligence. The retarded offenders' responses to concepts relevant to delinquency were similar to those of their intellectually average counterparts, but there were significant differences. There was no evidence that the therapeutic milieu had engendered objectivity about self or surroundings.

277. Biklen, D. "Myths, Mistreatment, and Pitfalls: Mental
      Retardation and Criminal Justice." *Mental Retardation*,
      1977, 15(4), 51-57.

      Examined 3 major aspects of mental retardation and crimi-
nal justice: myths frequently associated with the relationship
of mental retardation and criminality, mistreatment of the MR
offender in the criminal justice system, and the perils of
reform in the field of mental retardation and criminal justice.
It is suggested that while many of the age-old myths have been
discredited through careful research, some myths still survive
today. Further, it is suggested that the extent of mistreatment endured by mentally retarded offenders has been inade-
quately researched. The discussion of reform measures includes
a review of court cases involving the retarded offender, as
well as a critique of commonly recommended "special" measures
for retarded people in the criminal justice field.

278. Blackhurst, A.E. "Mental Retardation and Delinquency."
      Journal of Special Education, 1968, 2, 379-391.

      Reviews information on various aspects of mental retarda-
tion and delinquency. Some of the conclusions, generalizations,
and implications concerning the characteristics of the retarded
delinquents, etiology of criminality among the retarded, relationship between intelligence and criminality, types of
crimes committed by the retarded, legal considerations, facilities for incarceration and treatment, educational and treatment practices, and preventive measures are discussed.

279. Brown, B.S., & Courtless, T.F. "The Mentally Retarded
      in Penal and Correctional Institutions." *American Journal
      of Psychiatry*, 1968, 124, 1164-1170.

      Report on the results of a nationwide survey to determine
the extent of retardation in prison populations, the criminal
offenses committed by the retardates, and the problems encountered by the personnel dealing with the incarcerated retardate.

280. Browning, P.L., ed. *Rehabilitation and the Retarded
      Offender*. Springfield, Ill: Charles C. Thomas, 1976.

      Professionals from the fields of psychology, rehabilita-
tion, law, and the criminal justice system explored the com-
plexities associated with a population of persons who are
both mental retardates and public offenders. Three of the
major areas addressed are: (a) the identification and description of retarded offenders; (b) their constitutional
rights and litigation with respect to such rights; and (c)
the legal system and its problems and implications for this
group.

281. Carroll, C.F., & Reppucci, N.D. "Meanings that Profes-
      sionals Attach to Labels for Children." *Journal of
      Consulting and Clinical Psychology*, 1978, 46, 372-374.

      Sought to identify relative meanings among professionals
of 3 clinical labels for children--MR, emotionally disturbed,
and juvenile delinquent--as well as an average or unlabeled
choice. 40 regular classroom teachers of grades 6 to 9 and
32 mental health workers responded on 2 questionnaires designed to measure their reactions to these labels, with 9
questions concerned with expectations for the child's success in school and work, implications for treatment strategies, and motivation to work with the child. The labels
conveyed clearly different relative meanings, and the 2 professional groups differed in a consistent fashion.

282. Clark, G.R., Telfer, M.A., Baker, D., & Rosen, M. "Sex
      Chromosomes, Crime, and Psychosis." *American Journal of
      Psychiatry*, 1970, 126, 1659-1663.

      Tested the hypothesis on the relation of XYY chromosomes
in males and tendency toward violence. A comparative study
was conducted using men with XYY chromosomes and men with
the Klinefelter syndrome (XXY). Using males from hospitals
for the criminally insane and from institutions for defective
delinquents, mental patients and MR, a small group of XYY
males and those with Klinefelter's syndrome were analyzed
and compared. The average height of the XYY male is 76 inches,
and body configuration appears normal for the height. It is
concluded that there seems to be no link between the XYY males
and violent criminal behavior. There appears to be little
difference between the XYY male and the Klinefelter male. The
XYY male's antisocial nature and tendency to violent crime is

possibly attributable to his "fearsome height." Sex chromosome abnormality may influence psychosocial adjustment but
other factors also may do so; hence, psychopathology and criminal behavior is not an inevitable deviance.

283.   Forssman, H. "The Mental Implications of Sex Chromosome
       Aberrations." *British Journal of Psychiatry*, 1970, 117,
       353-363.

The Blake Marsh Lecture for 1970, delivered before the
Royal Medico-Psychological Association, summarized the evidence that abnormal sex chromosome complement contributes to
mental retardation, psychosis, epilepsy, and personality
deviations, including antisocial conduct. A reasonable hypothesis is that the behavior problems stem from minimum
brain damage. The recent and distinct evidence suggests that
countless other forms of minimum brain dysfunction exist, which
indicates that reasons other than environment should be considered in determining causes of criminal conduct.

284.   Fraser, W.I. "A Retrospective and Cross-Sectional In-
       vestigation of a Deviant Subcultural Group." *American
       Journal of Mental Deficiency*, 1970, 75, 298-303.

Five hundred thirteen behaviorally disturbed retarded
and borderline retarded males from a Scottish therapeutic
community were studied retrospectively and by cross-sectional
analysis 10 years after the community terminated. The patterns of prior crime appeared to be unaltered by the therapeutic environment, contrary to earlier claims. Subsequent
offenders were recognizable by conduct in the hospital but
not by historical antecedents, other than prior offenses.
There was a spectrum of behavioral symptomatology between
the recidivist and nonrecidivist. The retardate required a
stable adult figure after discharge with whom he could identify.

285.   Frohlich, R., & Altdorff, V. "On Escapes from Clinics
       from the Youth Neuropsychiatrical and Psychological
       Aspects." *Psychiatrie, Neurologie und Medizinische
       Psychologie*, 1971, 23, 293-303.

Presents a qualitative analysis of circumstances relating to 55 youths who escaped from psychiatric clinics.
The population was characterized by antisocial behavior at

home, in school, and at work. Mental retardation was prevalent
among those who escaped. Hospitalization of delinquents with
nondelinquents presents problems which must be anticipated by
hospital management.

286. Gibbons, F.X., Gibbons, B.N., & Kassin, S.M. "Reactions
      to the Criminal Behavior of Mentally Retarded and Non-
      retarded Offenders." *American Journal of Mental Defi-
      ciency*, 1981, 86, 235-242.

      College students' attitudes toward MR criminal offenders
and their estimates of the types of crimes most often committed
by retarded persons were assessed through a survey. Based on
survey results, an experiment was conducted in which students'
reactions to one of two different types of crimes committed
by either a retarded or nonretarded person were examined.
Results indicated that the retarded offender received a lighter
sentence regardless of the type of crime, apparently because
the students thought that he had been coerced into committing
the crime and also into confessing to it.

287. Grimes, A.M. "Characteristics of Mentally Retarded Ju-
      venile Offenders in Retardation and Correctional Facili-
      ties in Texas." Doctoral dissertation, Texas Tech. Univ-
      ersity, 1976, summarized in *Dissertations Abstracts In-
      ternational*, 1977, 38, 726A. (University Microfilms No.
      77-16,030).

      Attempted to identify characteristics of MR juvenile
offenders in retardation and correctional institutions. A
number of characteristics differentiate the subjects.

288. Guidry, L.L., McBride, W.A., & Waters, T.J. "WAIS Per-
      formance of Forensic versus Civilly Committed Mental
      Retardates." *Psychological Reports*, 1978, 43, 723-726.

      Compared the WAIS performance of 34 forensic and 22
civilly committed mental retardates (mean ages 29.9 vs. 28.1
years) hospitalized in the same psychiatric facility. Foren-
sic retardates, in contrast to their civilly committed counterparts, scored significantly higher on the Similarities subtest and showed a somewhat consistent higher performance from
other WAIS scores, suggesting a trend that might reflect
"street wisdom" or intellectual assets of "survival value."

289.   Hafner, H., & Boker, W. "Mentally Disordered Violent
       Offenders." *Social Psychiatry*, 1973, 8, 220-229.

       Found that crimes of violence committed by 533 mentally
ill and MR offenders were quantitatively proportional to the
number of crimes of violence committed by the total population.
In affective psychoses and mental retardation, the risk of
committing an act of violence, which had to be calculated on
the basis of inexact data, was about 6 in 100,000 and was
10% of that for schizophrenia (5 in 10,000). Factors which
did not depend on the disorder, especially family and personality factors, seemed to be relevant for the disposition to
criminality. The disorder itself had different consequences,
generally seeming to postpone the manifestation of the act
of violence and thus raising the average age of the mentally
ill offenders.

290.   Hunter, H. "Kleinfelter's Syndrome and Delinquency."
       British Journal of Criminology, 1968, 8, 203-207.

       Surveyed male patients in hospitals for the subnormal
and found 17 chromatin positive males. Compared with a large
control hospital group, the Klinefelter group was consider-
ably more aggressive. Their aggression was mainly directed
against property and in terms of sex offenses against children.

291.   Idelberger, C.T. "The Mentally Retarded Criminal Offender:
       Finding Some Solutions for a Lost Cause." *Offender Re-
       habilitation*, 1978, 3, 161-170.

       Definitions of deviance and the process of labeling
individuals as deviant reflect prevailing societal values,
goals, and beliefs. Both the MR and the criminal offender
are labeled as deviant, and the dual classification makes
up a group of individuals labeled as defective delinquents
or offenders. This group falls under the domains of both
the mental retardation systems and the criminal justice
system. It has been bypassed by rights litigation and rul-
ings involving both the mentally retarded individual and
the criminal offender; this oversight reflects system and
public response to the mentally retarded offender as a group.
Such responses have a systematic basis that can be dealt
with through system change.

292. Jackson, N. "Educable Mental Handicap and Delinquency."
      Educational Research, 1970, 12, 128-134.

        In a sample population of 232 mentally handicapped ex-
pupils drawn from special schools and classes in a Scottish
city and county, 29.8% of the boys and none of the girls had
delinquent records. There was a marginal though not significant tendency for the delinquent youths to be more intelligent
than the nondelinquent youths. A significant relationship
was found between delinquency and (a) an absence of physical
defect, (b) family neglect, (c) abnormal family structure,
and (d) occupational instability. Those youths committing their
first offense after leaving school were found to be significantly
more intelligent than those whose first offense was committed
while of school age. A relationship was found between postschool
first offense, occupational instability, and high measured
intelligence.

293. Keilitz, I., & Miller, S.L. "Handicapped Adolescents
      and Young Adults in the Justice System." *Exceptional
      Education Quarterly*, 1980, 1, 117-126.

        Examines the demographic characteristics of, and offenses
committed by, juvenile offenders, and their placement in residential homes, detention facilities, and training schools.
Research indicates that emotional disorders, learning disabilities, and retardation are more prevalent among juvenile
offenders than among the general population. Three ration-
ales for this disproportionate prevalence are given: (1)
school failure, which creates the chain-learning disability,
poor school performance, low social perception, and dropout
and delinquent behavior; (2) susceptibility, which states
that learning disabilities are directly related to maladaptive behavioral characteristics; and (3) differential treatment, based on the failings of the criminal justice system.
Four models, based on different responsible jurisdictions
and varying degrees of educational programming, are described.

294. Kiyonaga, K. "A Study of Delinquency of the Mentally
      Retarded: I. The Rate of Delinquents Among the Mentally
      Retarded." *Reports of the National Research Institute
      of Police Science*, Tokyo, 1972, 13(1), 10-17.

        Examined the police and school records of 342 male and
214 female 20-year-old MR who graduated from special classes
in public junior high schools in Tokyo. School data included
IQ level, family background, and educational achievement. The
rate of delinquency was 10.8% for males and 0.9% for females.
Breakdown by IQ level indicated that the rate of delinquency
among MR males tended to decrease as the degree of mental deficiency increased.

295. Kiyonaga, K. "A Study of Delinquency of the Mentally
      Retarded: II. Relationships between Family Background
      and Delinquency among the Mentally Retarded." *Reports
      of the National Research Institute of Police Science*,
      Tokyo, 1973, 14(1), 64-71.

      Compared delinquency rates among 278 boys (IQ of 70 and
below) and 174 borderline and normal boys (IQ of 71 and above).
Comparisons were made in terms of home stability, occupation
of householder, economic status of family, and educational
level of the parents. The general delinquency rate was lower
among the MR than among the borderline and normal Ss. For
both groups, delinquency was higher among Ss from blue-collar
families than among those from white-collar families.

296. Knaape, H.H., & Kurth, E. "Children and Juveniles as
      Pyromaniacs." *Psychiatrie, Neurologie und Medizinische
      Psychologie*, 169, 21, 463-471.

      Obtaining pleasure from fire is a normal phenomenon in
the development of children, especially boys. The hypothesis
of pyromania is rejected in the sample of children examined,
many of whom were MR. The children had imitated careless acts
of adults in using matches around incendiary materials. Instruction of both parents and children in fire prevention is
strongly indicated. Misdeeds must be viewed in relation to
the level of personality integration of the youthful offender.

297. Lewandowski, D.G., & Saccuzzo, D.P. "Possible Differentia
      WISC Patterns for Retarded Delinquents." *Psychological
      Reports*, 1975, 37, 887-894.

      Under controlled conditions, an attempt was made to
assess the generalizability of WAIS hypotheses for the nondefective adolescent sociopath to 80 retarded 13- to 16-year-
old offenders. Groups were separated according to race and
sex, while IQ, socioeconomic status, and geographic location
were controlled. The criteria for selection of Ss were incarceration in a state juvenile correctional facility and a
Full Scale WISC IQ below 70. Results suggest that many WAIS
signs applicable to nondefective IQ ranges probably are not
appropriate for WISC scores of these retarded delinquents.
Post hoc analysis, nevertheless, provided some potentially
useful WISC signs for combinations of race and sex of retarded
delinquents.

298. Lomastro, J.A. "The Retarded Offender: A New Perspective."
     Doctoral dissertation, Brandeis University, 1976, summar-
     ized in *Dissertation Abstracts International*, 1976, 37,
     3185A-3186A. (University Microfilms No. 76-25,055).

     Studied the social adjustment of adult MR parolees.

299. MacEachron, A.E. "Mentally Retarded Offenders: Prevalence
     and Characteristics." *American Journal of Mental Defi-
     ciency*, 1979, 84, 165-176.

     The range of prevalence rates for retarded offenders
     reported in the literature varies from 2.6 to 39.6 percent.
     This wide variability appears to be due to the use of dif-
     ferent population bases and to the way intelligence is meas-
     ured. When these issues were explored empirically, prevalence
     rates for retarded offenders in two northeastern states were
     found to be only slightly higher than the prevalence rate of
     mental retardation in the general population. A second issue
     in the literature is identification of the predictors of of-
     fenders' offense severity, sentence length, and past recidivism.
     Results of this study showed that social and legal variables
     are better predictors than is intelligence, although no pre-
     dictors were particularly strong.

300. Marsh, R.L., Friel, C.M., & Eissler, V. "The Adult MR
     in the Criminal Justice System." *Mental Retardation*,
     1975, 13(2), 21-25.

     Adult MR are increasingly being processed through the
     criminal justice system. The Anglo-American concept of mental
     incompetence provides little protection to insure the special
     handling and treatment a retarded person requires. The re-
     tarded person, because of the lack of mental competence in
     addition to the intricacies of the criminal justice system,
     is often incarcerated. This incarceration does little to
     improve the retarded person. Recommendations are made to
     improve the detection of MR persons and handle them in a
     manner more suitable to their special needs.

301. Menolascino, F.J. "The Mentally Retarded Offender."
      Mental Retardation, 1974, 12(1), 7-11.

      Since the time of H.H. Goddard's investigations in 1914,
over 450 separate studies on intellectual dimensions of the
retarded offender have been published. It seem probable that
no other single characteristic of the MR has been so thoroughly
studied. Yet these investigations have not provided conclusive
evidence that intelligence level plays a role in delinquent
and/or criminal behavior. An overview of past and current
approaches to the MR offender is presented. Description of
a system of services to meet these individuals' needs is also
included.

302. Milner, K.O. "Delinquent Types of Mentally Defective
      Persons." *Journal of Mental Science*, 1949, 95, 842-859.

      A review of the social history and data of male and
female violent MR. Considered sexual and aggressive characteristics both before and during imprisonment.

303. Psarska, A.D. "Some Aspects of Delinquency in the Mentall
      Retarded." *Psychiatria Polska*, 1972, 6, 151-157.

      Studies 50 mildly MR male adults charged with various
criminal offenses (e.g., arson, homicide, and sexual offenses)
who were under psychiatric observation. Personality characteristics common to all Ss were discussed (e.g., feelings of
inferiority and a related need to compensate). An inappropriat
environmental attitude was also found to be characteristic
of the Ss, and it is suggested that this factor intensified
their deviant tendencies.

304. Rockoff, E.S. "The Mentally Retarded Offender in Iowa
      Correctional Institutions." Doctoral dissertation,
      University of Iowa, 1973, summarized in *Dissertation
      Abstracts International*, 1973, 34, 3194A. (University
      Microfilms No. 73-30,979).

      Described the MR adult offenders in Iowa correctional
institutions in terms of intelligence, and educational and
rehabilitative programs.

305.   Sanders, R.W. "Juvenile Delinquency and the Mildly Re-
       tarded Adolescent." *Medical Insights*, 1974, 6(3), 28-32.

       Juvenile delinquency is discussed in terms of the mildly
MR adolescent; actual case examples are cited. Three types of
delinquent behavior are identified: (a) the group delinquent
reaction; (b) the runaway reaction; and (c) the unsocialized
aggressive reaction of adolescence. Suggestions are given
for treatment of the MR adolescent's delinquency. Prevention
is recommended as the best treatment.

306.   Santamour, M., & West, B. *The Mentally Retarded Offender
       and Corrections*. Washington, D.C.: U.S. Government Print-
       ing Office, 1977.

       Provides a profile and problems of the MR offender in
correctional institutions. Describes rehabilitation programs.

307.   Schaller, E. "Mental Retardation and Juvenile Delinquency."
       Heilpaedagogische Werkblaetter, 1968, 37(2), 71-80.

       Evaluation of files of MR and delinquent youth revealed
that retardation was not the main cause of their delinquency.
All Ss showed a cumulation of various criminogenic factors of
an endogenic and exogenic nature, and milieu damage caused by
parental difficulties. Most delinquents were exposed to detrimental developmental influences during early stages or most
of their lives.

308.   Schilit, J. "The Mentally Retarded Offender and Criminal
       Justice Personnel." *Exceptional Children*, 1979, 46(1),
       16-22.

       MR individuals have in the past, and will continue in
the future, to come into contact with the criminal justice
system. This study investigated the knowledge and awareness
of police officers, lawyers, and judges in the areas of mental
retardation and the mentally retarded offender. The results
indicate that confusion occurs at all levels, and the dis-
pensing of justice might not always be just or equitable.

309. Shapiro, A. "The Mentally Retarded Offender." In P. Mittle
      ed. *Research to practice in mental retardation*, vol. 1,
      415-418. Baltimore: University Park, 1977.

      Presents different groups of MR offenders and suggests
the etiological factors of each group.

310. Silber, D.E., & Courtless, T.F. "Measures of Fantasy
      Aggression among Mentally Retarded Offenders." *American
      Journal of Mental Deficiency*, 1968, 72, 918-923.

      Compared fantasy aggression (as manifested in TAT stories)
of MR and nonretarded offenders. It was predicted that the
offenders would manifest more fantasy aggression than the
nonretarded, and that serious offenders among the retarded
would manifest more aggressive motivation than nonserious offenders. Contrary to expectation, the serious offenders manifested the least fantasy aggression directed outward; there
were no differences in amount of total fantasy aggression when
the MR were compared to the nonretarded. It is suggested that
the MR person may not experience any more frustration-induced
aggression than the nonretarded, but may be deficient in controlling anger when it occurs.

311. Smith, P.M., & Barclay, A.G. "Q Analysis of the Holtzman
      Inkblot Technique." *Journal of Clinical Psychology*, 1975,
      31, 131-134.

      The Q analysis for refinement of the diagnostic effective-
ness of projective tests was used and the Holtzman Inkblot Technique was administered to 3 behaviorally distinct groups of Ss:
20 normal, 20 delinquent, and 20 retarded black male adolescents
who resided in socioeconomically depressed neighborhoods. Medi.
and quartile scores were obtained from 19 of the 22 Holtzman
variables, and 4 factors were derived from factor analysis.
Definable subfactors appeared within the delinquent and retarde
groups, but loadings for normal Ss were primarily on 1 factor.

312. Sternlicht, M., & Kasdan, M.B. "Criminal Behavior in the
      Mentally Retarded: A Psychoanalytic Interpretation."
      Transnational Mental Health Research Newsletter, 1976,
      18(1), 1; 3-4.

      Concluded that the intellectual level is not the primary
etiology of criminal behavior patterns among the retarded, but
rather the entire structure and personality development of each
retarded individual is involved in the decision to commit a cri-

313. Svendsen, B.B., & Werner, J. "Offenders within Ordinary
      Services for the Mentally Retarded in Denmark." In
      P. Mittler, ed. *Research to Practice in Mental Retarda-*
      tion, vol. 1. 419-424. Baltimore: University Park, 1977.

      Supports the Danish policy to transfer the MR offender
to the ordinary services for the MR persons.

314. Tong, J.E., & McKay, G.W. "A Statistical Follow-up of
      Mental Defectives of Dangerous or Violent Propensities."
      British Journal of Delinquency, 1959, 9, 276-284.

      Followed-up male mental defectives who had been dis-
charged from institutions, and found that serious relapses
were uncommon. Also found that fairly long periods of training were required for some individuals for successful socialization, and that the various behavior factors associated
with a positive or negative prognosis were similar to those
of offenders in general.

315. Tutt, N.S. "The Subnormal Offender." *British Journal of*
      Mental Subnormality, 1971, 17(32, Pt. 1), 42-47.

      Conducted a detailed analysis of 63 admissions to a
"psychopathic" unit over a 5-year period. Wide variations
in the type of patients admitted were noted, which made it
difficult to provide facilities for all patients. The difficulty was increased by the location of the unit in a subnormal hospital of 400 beds where workshop and social facilities were aimed at the majority of the hospital population.
The staffing of the unit also presented difficulties, since
the staff were nurses trained in nursing of the mentally subnormal. It is suggested that many of these difficulties could
be overcome by changes in staff training and attitudes, allowing greater participation by patients in a shared responsibility situation.

316. Weingold, J.T. "Towards a New Concept of the Delinquent
      Defective." *Mental Retardation*, 1966, 4(6), 36-38.

      A new concept of prevention must be adopted to effect
such changes in the value system of society so that it will
accept the MR and make a place for them in that society.

317. Wildman, B.G., & Kelly, J.A. "Group News Watching and Discussion to Increase Current Affairs of Awareness of Retarded Adolescents." *Child Behavior Therapy*, 1980, 2(1), 25-36.

   Assessed the news awareness of 8 predelinquent or delinquent MR Ss (CA 13 to 17 years, IQ 40 to 70) using daily verbal news quizzes. In multiple baseline fashion, group TV newswatching plus brief discussion was sequentially introduced with 4 Ss and a TV news exposure-only condition was used with 4 Ss. While passive TV newswatching alone resulted in little change in news awareness, contingent upon the introduction of TV newswatching plus brief discussion, all Ss showed substantial improvement in their current affairs awareness. On several probe days, news quiz performance of the MR Ss was compared to the performance of 10 nonretarded high school students who viewed the same network news program; retarded Ss who received the TV plus discussion intervention performed at levels comparable to their nonretarded agemates on these pro\` days.

318. Woodward, M. "The Role of Low Intelligence in Delinquency *British Journal of Delinquency*, 1955, 5, 281-303.

   After reviewing pertinent studies, concluded that low intelligence plays little or no part in delinquency.

319. Wright, W.E. "Personality Intelligence and Social and Academic Behavior in Institutionalized Delinquent Boys." Doctoral dissertation, George Peabody College for Teachers, 1974, summarized in *Dissertation Abstract International*, 1975, 35, 6171B. (University Microfilms No. 75-12,458).

   Investigated the relationship among personality, intelligence, and behavior variables in institutionalized delinquent boys. Results show that institutionalized retarded delinquent boys had a less positive personality pattern than the intellectually average institutionalized delinquent boys.

320.   Zeleny, L.D. "Feeble-mindedness and Criminal Conduct."
       American Journal of Sociology, 1933, 38, 564-576.

       Lack of agreement among investigators regarding the re-
lationship between feeble-mindedness and criminal conduct is
found to be due primarily to a variability in standards for
feeble-mindedness and in the estimates of the amount of feeble-
mindedness in the non-criminal population.   Prominent studies
in apparent disagreement are found to be corroboratory when
reinterpreted in terms of relatively constant standards.
Criminals are found to be decidedly inferior when compared
with the traditional standards of Terman, and slightly inferior when compared with the United States Draft Army.   The
United States Draft Army is shown to be the best available
standard for the non-criminal population.

321. Abelson, R.B., & Johnson, R.C. "Heterosexual and Aggres-
      sive Behaviors among Institutionalized Retardates."
      Mental Retardation, 1969, 7(5), 28-30.

      Compared institutionalized retarded individuals identi-
fied in a census as frequently being aggressive (N=236) or
as frequently engaging in heterosexual behavior (N=125). The
two groups show almost no overlap in individuals comprising
them, and they differ markedly on a number of other census
items. The heterosexual group appears to demonstrate superior
social competence in a variety of areas when compared with
the Ss of the aggressive group, and also appears more competent
than the census population at large.

322. Adams, G.L., Tallon, R.J., & Stangl, J.M. "Environmental
      Influences on Self-Stimulatory Behavior." *American
      Journal of Mental Deficiency*, 1980, 85, 171-175.

      Effects of passive environmental conditions (quiet, radio,
and television) and manipulable objects (no toys, toys, toys
plus staff interaction) on stereotypic behavior were evaluated.
Four institutionalized MR residents with high rates of stereotypic behavior were observed in a multipurpose room of their cottage. Results showed significant lower levels of stereotypic
behavior under the quiet and music conditions as compared to
the television condition. There was no difference between
the three manipulable-object conditions.

323. Bailey, K.G., Tipton, R.M., & Taylor, P.F. "The Threatening Stare: Differential Response Latencies in Mild and Profoundly Retarded Adults." *American Journal of Mental Deficiency*, 1977, 81, 599-602.

One hundred twenty institutionalized MR adults were studied for response to a threatening stare, using a 2 (mild MR, PMR) x 2 (stare, no stare) x 2 (close, far) analysis of variance design. It was anticipated that the threatening-stare conditions would produce smaller response latencies for avoidance and aggressive behavior than would the no-stare condition, and that the stare would have greater impact on PMR than on mildly MR Ss, especially in the close conditions. These expectations were supported by the response latency data that yielded a highly significant main effect for stare and significant stare x MR and stare x distance interactions. The threatening stare served to reduce response latencies across levels of MR and distance and had the strongest impact up close for both the PMR and the mildly MR Ss, with the former Ss apparently affected more than the latter Ss. Although it was unclear whether the study dealt with primarily learned or unlearned behavior, it could be reasonably concluded that the findings were at least consistent with the phylogenetic continuity hypothesis.

324. Balla, D.A. "Relationship of Institution Size to Quality of Care: A Review of the Literature." *American Journal of Mental Deficiency*, 1976, 81, 117-124.

The existing empirical literature on the relationship of institution size to quality of care was reviewed. Quality of care was discussed along four dimensions: (a) resident-care practice; (b) behavioral functioning; (c) discharge rates; and (d) extent of parental and community involvement. Care has been found to be generally more adequate in smaller institutions. However, considerable variation in quality of care has been reported among small community-based facilities. Little evidence was found that the behavioral functioning of residents is different in institutions of different sizes. There are essentially no data on discharge rates of institutions of different sizes. There is some evidence suggesting that parental and community involvement may be enhanced in community-based facilities.

325. Balla, D.A., Butterfield, E.C., & Zigler, E. "Effects of Institutionalization on Retarded Children: A Longitudinal Cross-Institutional Investigation." *American Journal of Mental Deficiency*, 1974, 78, 530-549.

From four institutions for retarded persons, 103 children were initially examined on measures of MA, IQ, responsiveness to social reinforcement, verbal dependency, wariness of adults, imitativeness, and behavior variability. Approximately 2.5 years later those children remaining in the institutions were retested. The results indicated that response to institutionalization is a complex function of preinstitutional life, experience, the environments of the particular institution being considered, and of the sex and the diagnosis of the subjects. The children became less verbally dependent, less imitative, and more variable in their behavior during the course of the study. While IQ level did not change, MA increased. Children who showed greater behavior variability and who had a home to which to return were discharged more frequently. Objective characteristics of the institutions such as size and cost were not found to be related to the behavior and/or development of the children.

326. Balthazar, E.E., & English, G.E. "A Factorial Study of Unstructured Ward Behaviors." *American Journal of Mental Deficiency*, 1969, 74, 353-360.

A factor analysis of coping behaviors in a residential population of 288 more severely MR individuals is reported on. Eighteen factors emerged from the study. Each factor represented a behavioral domain within which individual members of the population responded in a consistent manner. The factors were established from 71 subscale items which were furnished by one section of the Central Wisconsin Colony Scales of Adaptive Behavior. Separate tables delineating the intercorrelations of the subscale items and a listing of the factors are provided. The reliability and validity of current testing practices, as well as the scaling methods for measuring direct observations of unstructured ward behaviors, are discussed.

327.   Balthazar, E.E., & Phillips, J.L. "Social Adjustment
       in More Severely Retarded, Institutionalized Individuals:
       The Sum of Adjusted Behavior." *American Journal of Mental
       Deficiency*, 1976, 80, 454-459.

       A measure which is used to count kinds of social behavior
in more severely MR residents was described in this study.
The measure is an aggregate or sum, and it is referred to as
the Sum of Adjusted Behavior. In this study, the authors
determined measures of social adjustment which are useful
for obtaining population parameters. Data concerning the
relationships between the Sum of Adjusted Behavior and CA
to MA, age at time of institutionalization, gender, medical
diagnosis, medication, and social behavior were discussed.
The relationships between adjustment and adaptive behavior
were also defined on the basis of the findings.

328.   Baran, S.J. "TV and Social Learning in the Institution-
       alized MR." *Mental Retardation*, 1973, 11(3), 36-38.

       Discusses the significance of television as a social
learning mechanism. Reports findings that MR children are
very likely to learn social behavior experientially from
television viewing, as a consequence of their high dependency,
low self-esteem, and heightened susceptibility to social
reinforcement.

329.   Blatt, B., & Kaplan, F. *Christmas in Purgatory: A Photo-
       graphic Essay on Mental Retardation*. Syracuse, N.Y.:
       Human Policy Press, 1974.

       Heavily studded with photographs, this volume criticizes
five residential institutions for the mentally retarded, and
the concept of large institutions ("warehouses") in general.
Also offers a model of an adequate residential setting.

330.   Blatt, B., Ozolins, A., & McNally, J. *The Family Papers:
       A Return to Purgatory*. New York: Longman, 1979.

       This brief book, studded with photographs, is a major
critique and chronicle of America's retardation institutions,
and represents a clarion call for further, hastier efforts
at deinstitutionalization.

331. Braginsky, D.D., & Braginsky, B.M. *Hansels and Gretels: Studies of Children in Institutions for the Mentally Retarded.* New York: Holt, Rinehart, & Winston, 1971.

    Analyzed two large New England institutions for the MR, and discusses the residents' institutional behavior and adaptations, and concludes that most "retardates" do not belong in special institutions (training schools).

332. Brown, J.S., & Guard, K.A. "The Treatment Environment for Retarded Persons in Nursing Homes." *Mental Retardation,* 1979, 17, 77-82.

    Jackson's Characteristics of the Treatment Environment (CTE) was administered to 130 staff members of eight nursing homes in one country to assess the quality of care given retarded persons. Principal findings were: (a) all homes fell short of the levels of patient autonomy and activity predicted for a therapeutic community; (b) autonomy and activity were strongly correlated; and (c) autonomy and activity levels were greater in homes with larger proportions of supervisory staff.

333. Butterfield, E.C., & Zigler, E. "The Influence of Differing Institutional Social Climates on the Effectiveness of Social Reinforcement in the Mentally Retarded." *American Journal of Mental Deficiency,* 1965, 70, 48-56.

    Holds that differing social climates result in differing performance on a simple motivational task. Socially deprived children are motivated for social interaction and support.

334. Cleland, C.C., & Dingman, H.F. "Dimensions of Institutional Life: Social Organization, Possessions, Time and Space." In A.A. Baumeister & E. Butterfield, eds. *Residential Facilities for the Mentally Retarded,* 138-162. Chicago: Aldine, 1970.

    A thorough discussion of the social organization of institutions for the MR.

335.   Craighead, W.E., & Mercatoris, M. "Mentally Retarded
       Residents as Paraprofessionals: A Review." *American
       Journal of Mental Deficiency*, 1973, 78, 339-347.

     This review provided a critical summary of studies em-
ploying MR persons as paraprofessionals. Such paraprofessionals
have worked successfully in some settings; however, they have
functioned in rather limited roles, serving primarily as reinforcing agents for specific target behaviors in specific experimental settings or as behavioral observers. Outcomes of
broader field research were ambiguous. Advantages which accrue
to the retarded paraprofessionals were presented, and suggestions were made for future work in this area.

336.   Cullari, S., & Ferguson, D.G. "Individual Behavior
       Change: Problems with Programming in Institutions for
       Mentally Retarded Persons." *Mental Retardation*, 1981,
       19, 267-270.

     Behavioral programs used in institutions for MR persons
are often ineffective in producing long-term changes. These
programs, which for the most part are based on applied research, are often implemented by poorly trained direct-care
staff, concentrate on changing the individual rather than the
environment, and are based on simple reinforcement principles.
An examination of these problems and suggestions of possible
causes and means for developing solutions are offered.

337.   Dailey, W.F., Allen G.J., Chinsky, J.M., & Veit, S.W.
       "Attendant Behavior and Attitudes toward Institutional-
       ized Retarded Children." *American Journal of Mental
       Deficiency*, 1974, 78, 586-591.

     This study demonstrated that aides' perceptions of the
attractiveness, likability, and mental level of residents
were related to the affective tone, content, and frequency
of aide-resident interactions. Residents who were seen
favorably on these attitudinal dimensions tended to receive
more positive, more social, and more overall interactions
with aides, as measured by reliable behavioral observations
on the ward. Suggestions for research on contingency training and staff-patient ratios, as well as implications for in-
service programs, were discussed.

338. Dillon, W.T. "Studies of Rigidity in Institutionalized Mentally Retarded Children." Doctoral dissertation, Florida State University, 1970, summarized in *Dissertation Abstracts International*, 1971, 31, 4584A. University Microfilms No. 71-6995).

Reports a pilot and primary studies of rigidity in institutionalized MR children.

339. Eyman, R.K., & Borthwick, S.A. "Patterns of Care for Mentally Retarded Persons." *Mental Retardation*, 1980, 18, 63-66.

Compared the characteristics of 10,998 developmentally disabled individuals (IQs 1 to 40+) residing in various institutional and community settings in Arizona, Colorado, Nevada, and California. Information on adaptive and maladaptive behavior was extracted from the Adaptive Behavior Scales. Results indicate that the more severely mentally retarded persons, with their attendant handicaps and maladaptive behavior, are still likely to be found in an institutional setting.

340. Eyman, R.K., Capes, L., Moore, B.C., & Zachofsky, T. "Maladaptive Behavior of Institutionalized Retardates with Seizures." *American Journal of Mental Deficiency*, 1970, 74, 651-659.

Data from 3 hospitals for the MR were analyzed in an attempt to cast light on specific areas of maladaptation of retardates with seizures. The results showed that aggressive behavior or attacks on patients, hyperactivity, arm-hand problems, and speech problems were all important factors in distinguishing between retardates with and without seizures. Such evidence suggests a relatively greater amount of brain dysfunction in retardates with seizures.

341. Glenn, L.E., Nerbonne, G.P., & Tolhurst, G.C. "Environmental Noise in a Residential Institution for Mentally Retarded Persons." *American Journal of Mental Deficiency*, 1978, 82, 594-597.

The study was designed to survey the noise characteristics in residence halls housing young MR children and to test the effects of this noise on speech-discrimination performance of the residents. The noise survey indicated that the mean level of the noise was 75 dB SPL (with the level greater than 70 dB SPL during 71 percent of the sampling time). The spectrum was similar in configuration to the long-time speech spectrum. Selected residents were tested for speech discrimination in quiet and noise conditions. Mean scores on the Word Intelligibility by Perception Identification test were 73.9 percent correct in the quiet and 44 percent correct in the noise conditions. The authors concluded that the residents, who already had a primary language-learning handicap, were being subjected to a possible secondary impediment resulting from their living environment.

342.   Grant, G.W.B., & Moores, B. "Resident Characteristics and Staff Behavior in Two Hospitals for Mentally Retarded Adults." *American Journal of Mental Deficiency*, 1977, 82, 259-265.

Results of part of a study aimed at evaluating the implications of different nurse staffing levels were reported. Two samples of 30 patients were observed in the two hosptials, and measures were obtained of the proportion of time they were involved in adaptive and maladaptive activities, the frequency with which they interacted in particular ways with the nursing staff, and their Adaptive Behavior Scale scores. When these various measures were examined, the authors found that those patients who needed more attention received it but not necessarily of the appropriate type. While such results are understandable and even perhaps predictable, they do serve to reveal a situation deserving remedial attention. The authors suggested that one possible means of countering this tendency to ignore the less attractive patients is for the nursing staff to be assigned much smaller groups of patients than is customary.

343.   Heller, T. "Group Decision-making by Mentally Retarded Adults." *American Journal of Mental Deficiency*, 1978, 82, 480-486.

The effects of group discussion and decision-making on subsequent decisions of MR residents of group homes were studied. Meeting in groups of four, the subjects discussed and attempted to make group decisions on interview questions. Between the pretest and the posttest, there was a greater increase in the quality of answers to the experimental than to the control questions. Leadership status correlated with individual participation rates and intital task competence, but not with verbal intelligence.

344.   Hemming, H., Lavender, T., & Pill, R. "Quality of Life
       of Mentally Retarded Adults Transferred from Large
       Institutions to New Small Units." *American Journal
       of Mental Deficiency*, 1981, 86, 157-169.

       Quality of life of MR adults was assessed in large in-
stitutions and after transfer to new small units. Total adaptive behavior of transferred residents increased in the new
units, especially after 9 months after transfer. Total maladaptive behavior first increased and then decreased. Adaptive
behavior increased in both higher and lower ability residents.

345.   Hull, J.T., & Thompson, J.C. "Factors Contributing to
       Normalization in Residential Facilities for Mentally
       Retarded Persons." *Mental Retardation*, 1981, 19, 69-73.

       Much evidence suggests certain aspects of environmental
normalization are related to improved adaptive functioning
among disabled persons. Although the characteristics of
clients are important, the nature of the residence is even
more important.

346.   Kalson, L. "M*A*S*H: A Program of Social Interaction
       between Institutionalized Aged and Adult Mentally Re-
       tarded Persons." *Gerontologist*, 1976, 16, 340-348.

       Reports on efforts to restore a major social role to
institutionalized aged persons through a social interaction
and socialization program. Thirty-four female and 14 male
residents participated in this program and were assigned to
either a control or experimental group. Ss met (at the home
for the aged) with 12 MR adults for an average of 20 2-hour
sessions over a 3-month period. Analysis of interview data
showed some evidence of increased role satisfaction and more
positive attitudes toward MR persons in experimental Ss.

347.   Kaplan, S., & Torisky, D. "Retarded Youth in Community
       Service: Parklands Payback Pilot Project." *Journal of
       Clinical Child Psychology*, 1972, 1(3), 26-29.

       Describes a proposed project in which private capital
will be given the opportunity to develop resort facilities
in state parks in return for the use of such facilities as
training grounds for the MR. The training will be for service
occupations and in social and recreational aspects of their
lives.

348.   Kass, K.A. "Role-Taking Ability and Social Competence
       in EMR Adolescents." Doctoral dissertation, Yeshiva
       University, 1979, summarized in *Dissertation Abstracts
       International*, 1980, 40, 3950A. (University Microfilms
       No. 8001263).

       Examined the relationship between role-taking ability,
selected motivational variables, and social competence among
EMR adolescents. No support is found for the hypothesis that
role-taking measures and/or motivational measures are related
to teachers' judgments on students' social competency.

349.   King, R.D., Raynes, N.V., & Tizard, J. *Patterns of
       Residential Care: Sociological Studies in Institutions
       for Handicapped Children*. London: Routledge & Kegan
       Paul, 1971.

       With the aid of extensive fieldwork, this book examines
the way in which MR are dealt with in various institutional
settings. After surveying the need for residential services
for this population, a discussion on the care and upbringing
of retarded children and on the theory of residential organizations is offered.

350.   King, T., Soucar, E., & Isett, R. "An Attempt to Assess
       and Predict Adaptive Behavior of Institutionalized
       Mentally Retarded Clients." *American Journal of Mental
       Deficiency*, 1980, 84, 406-410.

       One hundred forty-two institutionalized retarded clients
were assessed on the Adaptive Behavior Scale (ABS) within 6
months of their admission to a short-term residential facility
and approximately 12 to 18 months later. While Ss were found
to progress significantly on 7 of the 10 domains of Part 1 of
the ABS, no significant gains were noted on Part 2.

351.   Klaber, M.M., Butterfield, E.C., & Gould, L.J. "Respon-
       siveness to Social Reinforcement among Institutionalized
       Retarded Children." *American Journal of Mental Deficiency*
       1969, 73, 890-895.

       Children from a more socially depriving institution
elected to stay longer with a socially reinforcing adult than
children who were in a less socially depriving institution.

352. Kurtz, R.A., & Wolfensberger, W. "Separation Experiences of Residents in an Institution for the Mentally Retarded: 1910-1959." *American Journal of Mental Deficiency*, 1969, 74, 389-396.

Separations over a 50-year period from a midwestern state institution for the MR were analyzed. Likelihood for live and sanctioned release into the community was highest for residents admitted in adolescence. Death, the most common type of separation, was most likely to occur during the first year of residence, and in the lowest and highest age groups. Of infants admitted below age 2, 14 percent died within 3 months, and 45 percent within 12 months. While the reporting and analysis of death data is a relatively neglected area in studies of institutional population movement, it could provide suggestions for institutional program needs.

353. Lawrence, W. "Relationship of Climatological and Behavioral Variables among Profoundly Retarded Males." *American Journal of Mental Deficiency*, 1977, 82, 54-57.

This investigation was designed to determine the degree of relationship among five climatological and five behavioral variables among institutionalized profoundly retarded males. Target behavior of 50 PMR males was correlated with changes in barometric pressure, indoor and outdoor temperature, and indoor and outdoor relative humidity. Significant correlations were obtained between changes in barometric pressure and changes in the on-dormitory ambient noise level. It was concluded that the data provided some degree of support for the biometeorological position, which purports a relationship between certain kinds of behavior and climatological changes.

354. Lewis, M.H., MacLean, W.E., Jr., Johnson, W.L., & Baumeister, A.A. "Ultradian Rhythms in Stereotyped and Self-Injurious Behavior." *American Journal of Mental Deficiency*, 1981, 85, 601-610.

Institutionalized profoundly MR persons who exhibited stereotyped motor movements, including self-injurious behavior, were observed continuously in their typical environments for periods of 8 to 14 hours on each of several days. In addition to targeting stereotyped responses, the authors collected data pertaining to activities, settings, other behavioral states, and social interactions. Spectral and cross-spectral analyses

were conducted on data from each daily session. Power spectra
indicated a marked ultradian or less than 24-hour rhythm for
each subject on each day. Spectral density estimates were
thought to reflect the influence of rhythmic changes in the
institutional environment and, to a lesser degree, the influence of an endogenous rest-activity rhythm.

355. MacAndrew, C., & Edgerton, R. "The Everyday Life of
      Institutionalized 'Idiots.'" In T.E. Jordan, ed. *Per-*
      spectives in Mental Retardation, 62-75. Carbondale:
      Southern Illinois University, 1966.

      Presents a detailed and vivid description of the life
of profoundly MR institutionalized adults.

356. McCormick, M., Balla, D., & Zigler, E.   "Resident-Care
      Practices in Institutions for Retarded Persons: A Cross-
      Institutional, Cross-Cultural Study." *American Journal*
      of Mental Deficiency, 1975, 80, 1-17.

      Described institution-oriented and resident-oriented
care practices for institutionalized persons in the United
States and in a Scandinavian country. In main, found that in
both countries living units for severely retarded persons
were characterized by institution-oriented care practices.

357. Meile, R.L., & Burk, H.W. "Group Relationships among
      Institutional Retardates." *American Journal of Mental*
      Deficiency, 1970, 75, 268-275,

      Eighty-five institutionalized MR, some of whom were
members of a peer group and some of whom were isolates, were
compared for adjustment to the institution and conformity to
institution rules. The peer group socialized and supported
its members and they were more likely to deviate from formal
rules than the isolates. Similarity to others in personal
and social characteristics facilitated membership in a peer
group.

358.   Meyer, R.J. "Attitudes of Parents of Institutionalized
       Mentally Retarded Individuals toward Deinstitutionaliza-
       tion." *American Journal of Mental Deficiency*, 1980, 85,
       184-187.

       Parents of institutionalized MR persons were surveyed
through a mailed questionnaire to determine the placement they
preferred for their retarded children. An overwhelming majority
chose the institution over the group home and supervised apartment. Reasons for their choice centered on the availability
of quality of supervision, care, and other resources. The
resident's age, functioning level, and rated behavior were
not related to placement preference.

359.   Mitchell, A.C., & Smeriglio, V. "Growth in Social Compe-
       tence in Institutionalized Mentally Retarded Children."
       American Journal of Mental Deficiency, 1970, 74, 666-673.

       Two groups of 25 moderately and severely retarded chil-
dren were evaluated for social-competence development during
their first years of institutionalization. Children receiving
the routine care characteristic of state institutions made
no progress in Vineland social age; consequently, they showed
a significant decline of 10 points in average social quotient
(SQ). Children receiving an additional high-saturation teaching program increased in social age and maintained their preadmission SQs. Both groups were significantly different from
normal children in the comparative rate of development in various areas of social competence. Results suggest that young
moderately and severely retarded children require formal teaching in addition to routine attendant care.

360.   Mitchell, L., Doctor, R.M., & Butler, D.C. "Attitudes
       of Caretakers toward the Sexual Behavior of Mentally
       Retarded Persons." *American Journal of Mental Deficiency*,
       1978, 83, 289-296.

       A multidimensional questionnaire was administered to
staff members at three residential facilities for retarded
persons to determine their attitudes toward the actual and
potential sexual behavior of retarded persons. The questionnaire covered the areas of masturbation and heterosexual and
homosexual behavior. Dimensions were scaled to reflect pro-
gressively more intimate behavior, so that acceptability of
each response along the dimensions could be assessed. A mean
of 31.2 percent of those questioned felt that no sexual behavior,

not even simple physical contact, was acceptable for retarded
persons. This indicates that sex-education programs for retarded persons may be met with resistance by a substantial percentage of staff. Among those staff members who found it acceptable for retarded people to engage in sexual behavior, peak
acceptability occurred for heterosexual behavior. Sexual behavior in public, especially public masturbation, was considered a significant problem.

361.   Mulhern, T.J. "Survey of Reported Sexual Behavior and
        Policies Characterizing Residential Facilities for
        Retarded Citizens." *American Journal of Mental Deficiency*,
        1975, 79, 670-673.

        The result of a survey directed to administrators of 82
residential facilities for MR citizens were presented and discussed. The survey concerned sexual behavior among residents
and professional attitudes toward these kinds of behavior.

362.   Nihira, K. "Dimensions of Adaptive Behavior in Institu-
        tionalized Mentally Retarded Children and Adults: Dev-
        elopmental Perspective." *American Journal of Mental
        Deficiency*, 1976, 81, 215-226.

        Factor analyses were performed utilizing the subscale
scores of the AAMD Adaptive Behavior Scale, Part One, for
3,354 institutionalized MR children and adults. Eight different age groups were studied to determine: (a) the underlying dimensions of adaptive behavior measured by the scale,
(b) similarity of factor structure across ages, (c) whether
there were developmental changes revealed by factor scores,
and (d) the extent to which the above findings would be related
to level of retardation. Three salient factorial dimensions--
Personal Self-Sufficiency, Community Self-Sufficiency, and
Personal-Social Responsibility--appeared across a wide span
of age ranges from childhood through senility. The implication
of these factors was discussed in terms of the critical period
of development, rate of growth, and maximum level of growth
of subjects grouped by level of retardation.

363. Nihira, K. "Factorial Dimensions of Adaptive Behavior in Adult Retardates." *American Journal of Mental Deficiency*, 1969, 73, 868–878.

This study attempts to explore the basic parameters of adaptive behavior and the primary dimensions along which retardates differ from one another in coping with their environment. Objective descriptions of the coping behavior of 919 adult institutionalized retardates were obtained by means of newly developed behavior rating scales. A factor analysis of 22 variables delineated two major dimensions, Personal Independence and Social Maladaptation.

364. Nihira, K. "Factorial Dimensions of Adaptive Behavior in Mentally Retarded Children and Adolescents." *American Journal of Mental Deficiency*, 1969, 74, 130–141.

Objective descriptions of adaptive behavior of 313 institutionalized MR children and adolescents were obtained through a newly developed behavior rating scale. Factor analyses of the scale delineated three major dimensions: Personal Independence, Social Maladaption, and Personal Maladaption. In four different age groups, the data show that the obtained factor structure is relatively stable across a wide span of age range, from preadolescence through adulthood. Implications of the results are discussed in terms of adaptive mechanisms commonly used by the MR in coping with their environments.

365. Pandey, C. "Popularity, Rebelliousness, and Happiness among Institutionalized Retarded Males." *American Journal of Mental Deficiency*, 1971, 76, 325–331.

Two wards of institutionalized MR males were studied to determine the relationship among popularity, rebelliousness, happiness, and restrictiveness of setting. Ward personnel rated the subject's personality characteristics. Each subject was asked to name his "friends" and "enemies." Popularity was found to be related to a number of characteristics including intelligence on both wards and to youthfulness on the older, more restrictive ward. Rejection was more complete on the closed ward. Cooperativeness was more influential there, and the rebel was actively rejected. All rebellion was related to unhappiness, aggressiveness, and unpopularity. Happiness was related to passivity, cooperativeness, popularity, and infrequent rejection.

366. Payne, J.E. "The Deinstitutional Backlash." *Mental Retardation*, 1976, 14(3), 43-45.

This study elicited attitudes of parents of persons in large institutions in order to explore this phenomenon and to understand it better. The parents were in favor of maintaining the institution and were skeptical of the advantages of small group homes.

367. Pratt, M.W., Bumstead, D.C., & Raynes, N.V. "Attendant Staff Speech to the Institutionalized Retarded: Language Use as a Measure of the Quality of Care." *Journal of Child Psychology & Psychiatry & Allied Disciplines*, 1976, 17, 133-143.

An observational measure of adult speech to children, developed by B. Tizard et al, was modified and applied to residences for retarded adults. The measure categorizes the major functions of staff talk to residents as "control" and "information." Results resemble the findings of Tizard et al., i.e., "informative" staff speech was more complex and its frequency was associated with resident language comprehension abilities. The speech measure was related to another index of the quality of care provided in such facilities. Ability of resident speech "targets" was also found to affect the frequency of informative remarks by staff.

368. Prior, M., Minnes, P., Coyne, T., Golding, B., Hendy, J., & McGillivary, J. "Verbal Interactions between Staff and Residents in an Institution for the Young Mentally Retarded." *Mental Retardation*, 1979, 17, 65-69.

Patterns of verbal interaction between staff and residents in a Training Center for young MR persons was examined in this study. Conversation type initiations from staff elicited more verbal responses from residents than other types of verbal stimuli. Structured situations provided more verbal interactions than unstructured situations. There was a high frequency of ignore-type responses to resident-initiated verbal interactions. It is suggested that some features of the environment could be developed to improve language competence in MR people.

369. Rago, W.V., Jr. "Identifying Profoundly Retarded Sub-
      types as a means of Institutional Grouping." *American
      Journal of Mental Deficiency*, 1977, 81, 470-473.

      Dominance hierarchies were determined in 2 groups of 25
institutionalized PMR Ss as a means of identifying dominant
and subordinate subtypes. Ranks in the dominance hierarchy
were established by observing the amount of physical and non-
physical aggression initiated, the number of times assaulted,
number of different individuals assaulted by the S, spatial
utilization, and the average of the ranks attributed to each
S by the dormitory staff. Territoriality and aggression,
when analyzed by means of the formulation of dominance hier-
archies, were significantly differentiated among group members. Results indicate that institutional groupings based
on dominant and subordinate subtypes may be efficacious in
increasing programming efficiency.

370. Rago, W.V., Jr. "Stability of Territorial and Aggressive
      Behavior in Profoundly Mentally Retarded Institutionalized
      Male Adults." *American Journal of Mental Deficiency*, 1978,
      82, 494-498.

      A follow-up study of a group of profoundly MR institution-
alized male adults showed that territorial and aggressive patterns noted 19 months previously were substantially unchanged.
Behavior patterns were recorded particularly in regard to those
who initiated interactions (whether participants were peers or
staff), and the location of interactions (with regard to territories established by the Ss). The residents quickly established territories, and as patients were switched to new groups
they would adapt to the social outlines already existing within
the group. Once territories were established, they remained
unchanged unless a member was removed from the group or the
environment was altered in some way (such as by the removal of
a chair from one territory to another). This stability in
territoriality also was reflected in the stability of the
social-dominance hierarchy.

371. Rago, W.V., Jr., Parker, R.M., & Cleland, C.C. "Effect
      of Increased Space on the Social Behavior of Institution-
      alized Profoundly Retarded Male Adults." *American Journal
      of Mental Deficiency*, 1978, 82, 554-558.

      The social behavior of a group of institutionalized pro-
foundly MR male adults was observed under conditions of increased space. The findings demonstrated that an increase in

space of 29 percent significantly reduced the frequency of
aggressive acts occurring within the group. Also observed
was the effect of increased space on the residents' mobility
and nonaggressive interactions. Results were discussed in
relation to the residents' need for space.

372.   Reuter, J., Archer, F.M., Dunn, V., & White, C. "Social
        Milieu of a Residential Treatment Center for Severely
        or Profoundly Handicapped Young Children." *American
        Journal of Mental Deficiency*, 1980, 84, 367-372.

        Thirty-nine severely or profoundly handicapped young
children who lived in a residential treatment center were
Ss in a modified time-sampled observation study of social
behavior, state, and physical context. The study was conducted for 3 successive years. Although system-level changes
in the ecology of the institution over the 3 years did not
appear to affect the social-interaction indices, the developmental ages of the Ss were positively related to social opportunities and social behavior.

373.   Saunders, E.J., "Staff Members' Attitudes toward the
        Sexual Behavior of Mentally Retarded Residents." *Ameri-
        can Journal of Mental Retardation*, 1979, 84, 206-208.

        Seventy-five staff members from four private residential
facilities for MR adults were surveyed to elicit their attitudes
toward the sexual behavior and sexual knowledge of residents
in their care. Facility policies and programs applicable to
residents' sexuality were also the subject of inquiry. Comparable attitudinal surveys and studies dealing with the sexuality of MR persons were reviewed in the context of the present
findings.

374.   Shearer, A. *Handicapped Children in Residential Care:
        A Study of Policy Failure*. London: Bedford Square Press,
        1980.

        Traces the deinstitutionalization movement in England, and
why it has not been especially successful. Also outlines several reforms that are necessary in the field.

375. Scheerenberger, R.C. "Public Residential Facilities:
      Status and Trends." *Mental Retardation*, 1981, 19, 59–60.

      Updated information on the current status and trends of
public residential facilities in the United States was gathered.
Primary areas of concern include basic demographic data, population movement, resident programs, and administration, including budgeting and staffing.

376. Scheerenberger, R.C. "Public Residential Services for
      the Mentally Retarded." In N.R. Ellis, ed. *International
      Review of Research in Mental Retardation*, Vol. 9, 187–
      208. New York: Academic Press, 1978.

      Discusses the consequences of deinstitutionalization and
institutional reform via an analysis of the current status of
public residential facilities for the MRs, in terms of basic
demographic data, population movement, resident programs,
parental participation, placement/post-placement procedures,
and administration, including budgeting and staffing.

377. Schroeder, S.R., & Barrera, F. "How Token Economy Earn-
      ings are Spent." *Mental Retardation*, 1976, 14(2), 20–24.

      The consumer behaviors of institutionalized MR clients
in a sheltered workshop token economy revealed that they purchased discriminatively, budgeted their income, and displayed
Engel curves.

378. Schwartz, B.J., & Allen, R.M. "Measuring Adaptive Be-
      havior: The Dynamics of a Longitudinal Approach."
      American Journal of Mental Deficiency, 1974, 79, 424–
      433.

      The Adaptive Behavior Checklist was administered annually
to the residents of the Miami (FL) Sunland Training Center for
4 consecutive years. As a means of assessing adaptive behavior,
this checklist was used to provide feedback as to the progress
made by the residents, thus monitoring the effectiveness of
the institution in achieving certain behavioral objectives.
Data from a longitudinal study are presented along with the
means by which the results were communicated to the staff.
Correlations of the checklist with standard IQ scores were
discussed, as was the effectiveness of a revision of the
Adaptive Behavior Checklist.

379.   Sternlicht, M. "Social Relationships and Institutional
       Adjustments of Mentally Retarded Individuals: Sentence
       Completion Responses." Paper presented at the annual
       meeting of the American Academy on Mental Retardation,
       New Orleans, May 1977.

       Institutionalized MR individuals display perhaps unwar-
ranted optimistic feelings about the future, identify very
strongly and positively with the child-caring staff, display
somewhat more aggressive responses, have a need to be regarded
in a positive light, and view adult friendships as significantly
more important than peer friendships. Since the all-pervading
influence of direct child care staff is highlighted, it would
appear that this staff may be more significant in developing
adequate self-concepts than professional and/or administrative
staff.

380.   Sternlicht, M., & Bialer, I. "Psychological Aspects of
       Institutionalization in Mental Retardation." In I. Bialer
       & M. Sternlicht, eds. *The Psychology of Mental Retarda-
       tion*, 602-644. New York: Psychological Dimensions, 1977.

       Focuses upon the phenomenological nature of the institu-
tional experience and its psychosocial effects on the residents.
Suggests that institutionalization is not necessarily detrimental to later social adjustment, and that institutionalization
does not put the former resident at any social or economic disadvantage.

381.   Sternlicht, M., Bialer, I., & Siegel, L. "Relationship
       of Locus of Control, Self-Concept, and Modes of Adjust-
       ment in Retarded Residents." Paper presented at the
       annual meeting of the American Association on Mental
       Deficiency, New Orleans, May 1977.

       Found no relationship between self-concept and locus of
control in MR adolescents and adults. Furthermore, a positive
relationship between level of adjustment and locus of control
was found for male adolescents, and an inverse relationship
between locus of control and length of institutionalization
was found in female adolescents.

382. Sternlicht, M., & Deutsch, M.R. "The Value of Temporary Institutionalization in Habilitating the Mentally Retarded." *Mental Retardation*, 1971, 9(3), 37-38.

Holds that temporary institutionalization of the MR person can have a salutary effect upon the residents, as it allows for the acquisition of coping skills necessary in community living.

383. Sternlicht, M., Schalock, R.L., & Harper, R. "The Viability of Group Living Homes: The Implications of Semi-institutional Living." Paper presented at the annual meeting of the American Association on Mental Deficiency, Miami Beach, June 1979.

This study contrasted New York and Mid-Nebraska hostel residents, with regard to the manner in which they spend their time while in these community-based residences. Ten typical activities were selected for study, and the results are presented, together with their implications, particularly in the programmatic sphere.

384. Sternlicht, M., & Siegel, L. "Institutional Residence and Intellectual Functioning." *Journal of Mental Deficiency Research*, 1968, 12(Pt. 2), 119-127.

Institutionalization would appear to have a significantly depressing effect upon the intellectual functioning of retarded children, but not of retarded adolescents and adults, at least as measured by intelligence tests. With nearly all age groups, however, there would appear to be no institutional depressing influences upon performance abilities and capabilities. Also, visual-motor coordination is relatively unaffected by institutionalization. However, before any definitive conclusions can be drawn concerning the effects of institutionalization among MR, a longer-range longitudinal study needs to be performed, which would evaluate the effects of institutionalization upon a group of retarded infants and children, over a span continuing through their adult years.

385. Talkington, L.W., & Hutton, W.O. "Hyperactive and Non-
     hyperactive Institutionalized Retarded Residents."
     American Journal of Mental Deficiency, 1973, 78, 47-50.

     Institutionalized retarded residents classified as hyper-
active were compared on 15 variables to a matched group classified as nonhyperactive (N=211). Patient characteristics were
also analyzed on a post hoc basis. Only 4 variables (Disrupts
Activities, Stereotyped Behavior, Removes/Tears Clothes, and
Receives Tranquilizers) significantly differentiated the two
groups. The post hoc analysis revealed that hyperactivity
occurred more frequently in males and as ability level decreased.

386. Throne, J.M. "Deinstitutionalization: Too Wide a Swath."
     Mental Retardation, 1979, 17, 171-175.

     Deinstitutionalization of MR persons is questioned on
conceptual, scientific, and moral grounds. The issue of the
optimal institution is discussed, particularly institution
size. The relevance of operant research and practice to the
management, administration, and organization of institutional
services for the retarded is described.

387. Tognoli, J., Hamad, C., & Carpenter, T. "Staff Attitudes
     toward Adult Male Residents' Behavior as a Function of
     Two Settings in an Institution for Mentally Retarded
     People." *Mental Retardation*, 1978, 16, 142-146.

     Behavioral tracking observations of adult male residents
in a school for the MR were made in an enriched and deprived
setting on the ward. Various groups of professional staff
related to the ward were then asked to rate the ward activities
of the residents as to their "goodness" and "activeness." The
two settings elicited widely different behaviors and these
behaviors were evaluated differentially by the various professional staff members. The importance of environmental
props and the role of institutional staff members are discussed.

388. Wagner, P., & Sternlicht, M. "Retarded Persons as 'Teach-
      ers': Retarded Adolescents Tutoring Retarded Children."
      American Journal of Mental Deficiency, 1975, 79, 674-
      679.

      Investigated the effect of training MR adolescents in a
residential school to act as tutors for younger retarded children who were deficient in dressing and eating skills. The
effect of a tutorial program on both the adolescents (tutors)
and the young children (trainees), in terms of acquisition
and retention of self-maintenance skills for the trainees and
social and personal adjustment for the tutors, was examined.
The overall success of the trainees supports the view that
retarded persons can successfully instruct other retarded
persons.

389. Warren, S.A., & Mondy, L.W. "To What Behaviors Do Attend-
      ing Adults Respond?" *American Journal of Mental Deficiency*,
      1971, 75, 449-455.

      Responses of 15 attending adults to more than 800 samples
of behavior of 49 ambulatory institutionalized young regarded
children were recorded. The attending adults usually failed
to respond at all to either appropriate or inappropriate child
behaviors. When responses were made to appropriate behaviors,
they were likely to be encouraging, and thus were probably reinforcing. Responses to inappropriate behaviors were discouraging about twice as often as encouraging, providing potential
positive reinforcement for unacceptable behaviors. For all
behaviors, adult behavior appeared to offer children infrequent,
variable ratio reinforcement schedules.

390. Watkins, K.E. "Opinions of Staff Members Regarding the
      Sexual Behavior of Clients." *Exchange*, 1974, 2(2), 26-29.

      Answers to a questionnaire distributed to staff members
of the Fairview State Hosptial to ascertain the general attitudes toward the sexual behavior of the MR clients are reviewed.
Half of the respondents felt that sexual behavior among clients
represented a significant problem in treatment and half found
it a minor problem. Respondents demonstrated an open minded
attitude toward the acceptance of sexual behavior among institutionalized MR adults, leaning toward permitting behavior in
private rather than in public. Respondents also indicated a
desire for a clear set of guidelines for the management of
sexual behavior and for an effective sex education program
for patients.

391. Weber, D.B., & Epstein, H.R. "Contrasting Adaptive
      Behavior Ratings of Male and Female Institutionalized
      Residents across Two Settings." *American Journal of
      Mental Deficiency*, 1980, 84, 397-400.

      Twenty-two adolescent MR male and 22 female residents
from a state institution were compared on Adaptive Behavior
Scale-Part 2 ratings across 2 settings (cottage and classroom).
A multivariate ANOVA did not reveal an overall interaction
of sex and setting nor an overall effect for sex differences.
Results did indicate a significant overall effect for setting.
Significant differences were found in the following domains:
Rebellious Behavior, Stereotyped Behavior and Odd Mannerisms,
Unacceptable Vocal Habits, Hyperactive Tendencies, and Psycho-
logical Tendencies. Higher scores (negative direction) were
found in the classroom setting.

392. Weinstock, A., & Wulkan, P., Colon, C.J., Coleman, J.,
      & Goncalves, S. "Stress Inoculation and Interinstitutional
      Transfer of Mentally Retarded Individuals." *American
      Journal of Mental Deficiency*, 1979, 83, 385-390.

      Forty-four MR individuals were studied to determine if
the relocation syndrome can be averted in interinstitutional
transfer. Twenty-two persons who were transferred on a voluntary basis to a small, new, highly staffed facility and
given individualized attention in preparation for the move
were compared to a group of nontransferred matched control
persons on the Progress Assessment Chart and the Maladaptive
section of the Adaptive Behavior Scale, which were administered
prior to transfer and 1, 2, and 4 weeks after. The transferred
group displayed no lowered functioning in adaptive behavior and
no increase in maladaptive behavior. No relocation syndrome
was evidenced, as prerelocation preparation appears to have
averted the deleterious effects of transfer.

393. Westphal, C.R. "Variables Affecting the Efficacy of a
      Token Economy." *Mental Retardation*, 1975, 13(6), 32-34.

      This longitudinal study investigated variables affecting
the efficacy of a token economy used with 16 institutionalized
MR boys exhibiting disruptive behaviors. Four independent
variables, staff/resident ratio, consisting of reinforcement,
immediacy of reinforcement, and location of tokens, were manipulated to determine their effect on the number of tokens earned
and spent, and on the frequency of disruptive behavior.

394. Wills, R.H. *The Institutionalized Severely Retarded: A Study of Activity and Interaction.* Springfield, Ill.: C.C. Thomas, 1973.

    This study attempted to provide a greater perspective in the understanding of severely mentally retarded persons, via a specific investigation of practically all of their behavior in order to identify the relative significance of each type of activity and interaction initiated.

395. Witt, S.J. "Increase in Adaptive Behavior Level after Residence in an Intermediate Care Facility for Mentally Retarded Persons." *Mental Retardation*, 1981, 19, 75-79.

    Residential facilities for MR persons should be designed to maximize the behavioral status and development of the residents. In the present investigation, residence for approximately ten months in an Intermediate Care Facility for the Mentally Retarded (ICF/MR) leads to a substantial increase in the adaptive behavior level of 95 severely and profoundly mentally retarded former residents of a large state institution. Certain advantages provided by ICF/MR residence that could have provided this increase are discussed, e.g., improved environmental conditions and training, as well as other variables, both specific and general.

396. Upshur, C.C. "An Evaluation of Home-based Respite Care." *Mental Retardation*, 1982, 20, 58-62.

    Findings of an evaluation of a pilot home-based respite care program designed to serve severely MR disabled persons are reported. Data are collected concerning 91 requests for respite care services spanning a six-month period using questionnaires administered to both providers and families. Disability ratings are assigned to clients to determine whether more severely disabled clients are served than in the past. Results indicate that significantly more multiply handicapped clients are served successfully. Recommendations are given concerning expansion of home-based respite care for all levels of client disability.

397.   Zaharia, E.S., & Baumeister, A.A. "Technician Turnover
       and Absenteeism in Public Residential Facilities."
       American Journal of Mental Deficiency, 1978, 82, 580-
       593.

       Residential institutions have historically had problems
attracting and retaining reliable unskilled personnel to fill
technician-level positions. Even though there is little em-
perical evidence to support a relationship between staff stability and resident habilitation, there assuredly are such
effects. A first step toward assessing these effects, and
toward controlling costly technician withdrawal behavior
(specifically, turnover and absenteeism), is the use of a
common set of measures. The precipitants of employee withdrawal may be categorized into three areas that are subject
to empirical investigation and intervention: extra-institutional
management, and factors surrounding the individual worker.
Predictive research, for selection purposes has not yielded
much information that would be of use to administrators.
Traditional and more recent explanations were reviewed, and
some directions suggested for further research.

398.   Zigler, E., & Balla, D.A. "Impact of Institutional Ex-
       perience on the Behavior and Development of Retarded
       Persons." *American Journal of Mental Deficiency*, 1977,
       82, 1-11.

       Describes the different factors that contribute to the
effects of institutional experience on retarded persons. Concludes that the effects of institutional experience require
the consideration of the characteristics of the MR person,
his preinstitutional life experience, the nature of the institution, and a range of criterion behavior on the part of
the resident.

399.   Zigler, E., Butterfield, E.C., & Capobianco, F., "Insti-
       tutionalization and the Effectiveness of Social Reinforce-
       ment: A Five- and Eight-Year Follow-up Study." *Develop-
       mental Psychology*, 1970, 3, 253-263.

       MR children who had been examined 2 years after institu-
tionalization on a task used to assess motivation for social
reinforcement were examined on this task 3 years later. This
study reports results obtained at the third and fourth examination periods, 7 and 10 years after institutionalization. Children from highly deprived preinstitutional backgrounds showed

a greater decrease in their motivation for social reinforcement than children from less deprived backgrounds, indicating
that the institutional experience was more socially depriving
for children from relatively good than from relatively poor
homes. IQ changes during institutionalization were also
found to be related to the degree of preinstitutional deprivation.

400. Zigler, E., & Williams, J. "Institutionalization and
      the Effectiveness of Social Reinforcement: A Three-
      Year Follow-up Study." *Journal of Abnormal and Social
      Psychology*, 1963, 66, 197-205.

      Forty-nine children who had been tested on a simple
2-part satiation game 3 years earlier were retested on the
same game. These familial retarded children were divided
into high and low preinstitutional social deprivation groups,
and 2 reinforcement conditions were used. On the original
testing a positive relationship was found between social
deprivation experienced and the effectiveness of social reinforcement, with no reinforcement effect being found. On re-
testing, reinforcement effects were found, but no preinstitutional deprivation effects. Children's performance shows a
greater enhancement in the effectiveness of the social reinforcement for the low rather than for the high socially deprived Ss.

401.   Abramowicz, H.K., & Richardson, S.A. "Epidemiology of
       Severe Mental Retardation in Children: Community Studies."
       American Journal of Mental Deficiency, 1975, 80, 18-39.

       Twenty-seven community studies of severe mental retarda-
tion (IQ below 50) were reviewed. The prevalence rate of this
condition was about 4 per 1000 in older children; the rate was
somewhat higher in males. About one-half of severely MR children had associated handicaps. The cause of most cases of
severe mental retardation in unknown, but Down's syndrome
accounted for one-sixth to one-third of cases and a small
percentage were due to other chromosomal abnormalities, metabo-
lic diseases, or infection.

402.   Appell, M.J., & Tisdall, W.J. "Factors Differentiating
       Institutionalized from Noninstitutionalized Referred
       Retardates." *American Journal of Mental Deficiency*, 1968,
       73, 424-432.

       Attempted to establish objective criteria which would
differentiate retardates admitted to a residential facility
from those who were returned to their communities. Objective
criteria in the form of a Priority Waiting List Questionnaire
were suggested which could be used as a screening device in
the evaluation of retardates referred for admission. Factors
such a Living Conditions and Community Problems and Pressures
appeared to be the most significant in differentiating those
who were admitted from those who were not.

403. Baker, B.L., Seltzer, G.B., & Seltzer, M.M. *As Close as
      Possible: Community Residences for Retarded Adults.*
      Boston: Little, Brown, 1977.

      Describes a number of community residential models for
the MR as an alternative to institutionalization.

404. Bartnik, E., & Winkler, R.C. "Discrepant Judgments of
      Community Adjustment of Mentally Retarded Adults: The
      Contribution of Personal Responsibility." *American
      Journal of Mental Deficiency,* 1981, 86, 260-266.

      Criteria used to determine community adjustment of MR
adults were rated for importance by two groups of their employers, two groups of service-agency staff members, and one
group of parents to determine whether normative criteria differed across the groups. In a second study, case descriptions,
varying on the adjustment criterion of personal responsibility,
were presented to an additional sample from the five groups.
Results of discriminant function analysis showed that parents
and service-agency staff members differed markedly on the importance given to personal responsibility. Employers stressed
work-related criteria more than did the other groups.

405. Berkson, G. "Social Ecology of Supervised Communal Facili-
      ties for Mentally Disabled Adults: V. Residence as a Pre-
      dictor of Social and Work Adjustment." *American Journal
      of Mental Deficiency,* 1981, 86, 39-42.

      Matched groups of mildly MR people who lived with their
families, independently, or in a sheltered-care home were compared with respect to various measures of work performance and
social behavior in sheltered workshops. Differences between
the groups were negligible. The results suggest that residenti
placement by itself does not strongly correlate with productivi
or sociability.

406. Birenbaum, A. "The Changing Lives of Mentally Retarded
      Adults." In M.J. Begab & S.A. Richardson, eds. *The Men-
      tally Retarded and Society: A Social Science Perspective.*
      Baltimore, Md.: University Park Press, 1975.

      Observation of, and open-ended interviews with, 51 patien
who voluntarily left 3 large isolated state schools for the MR
to live in a community residence indicated gains in social behavior and independent functioning. On the basis of the examin
tion, it is concluded that: (a) massive and rapid resettlement

is unwise; (b) social skills needed to live in various residential settings and the appropriateness of socially learned
competencies in state schools for community living must be
defined; and (c) a model of the network of services required
by state school patients that meets the needs of the MR while
avoiding the dangers of overprogramming should be developed.

407.   Birenbaum, A., & Re, M.A. "Resettling Mentally Retarded
       Adults in the Community--Almost 4 Years Later." *American
       Journal of Mental Deficiency*, 1979, 83, 323-329.

       MR adults resettled at a community residence in a large
city from three state schools were found after four years to
maintain steady involvement in sheltered workshops to have
some relations with peers (but more restricted in personal
decision-making at home), and to participate less in the community's leisure activities.

408.   Birenbaum, A., & Seiffer, S. *Resettling Retarded Adults
       in a Managed Community*. New York: Praeger, 1976.

       Reports on a community residence for retarded adults,
called Gatewood, to which 63 men and women from 3 large isolated state schools were transferred. The origins of Gatewood,
its social organization, the experiences and responses of the
residents, and their participation in the larger community
are described.

409.   Bjaanes, A.T., & Butler, E.W. "Environmental Variation
       in Community Care Facilities for Mentally Retarded
       Persons." *American Journal of Mental Deficiency*, 1974,
       78, 429-439.

       Components of the environment of community care facilities
for MR persons, specifically the behavioral component, were
systematically examined. Studies of the behavioral environment in two board and care facilities and two home care facilities were reported. Differences in behavior, time-use patterns,
and characteristics of behavior indicated that: (a) there were
substantial differences in the behavioral components of community care facilities; (b) the board and care facilities examined were closer to the objective of normalization than were
the home care facilities; (c) more behavior was independent in
board and care facilities than in home care facilities; (d) exposure to the community was an important factor in normalization;

(e) the development of independent functioning appeared to be
related to the geographic location of the facility and involvement of the caretakers in the ongoing stream of behavior;
and (f) specific types of community care facilities were
associated with different outcomes.

410.   Bruininks, R.H., Meyers, C.E., Sigford, B.B., & Lakin, K.(
       eds. *Deinstitutionalization and Community Adjustment
       of Mentally Retarded People*. Washington, D.C.: American
       Association on Mental Deficiency, 1981.

       This volume was designed to aid in the process of evalu-
ating the effectiveness of deinstitutionalization and community
services. Discusses programs for enhancing the opportunities
for successful transitions to community life, and problems
faced in maintaining the momentum of the deinstitutionalization
movement.

411.   Burish, T.G. "A Small Community Model for Developing
       Normalizing Alternatives to Institutionalization."
       Mental Retardation, 1979, 17, 90-92.

       Describes a community-based program which provides the
MR with living conditions that are similar to the norms and
patterns of the nearby communities.

412.   Cohen, H.J., Kligler, D., & Eisler, J.A., eds. *Urban
       Community Care for the Developmentally Disabled*.
       Springfield, Ill.: C.C. Thomas, 1980.

       This edited work largely describes the transition in
the care and habilitation of developmentally disabled persons
from larger institutions to smaller, local community settings.
Community residential alternatives are reviewed in depth, as
are community supportive services, including treatment interventions.

413.   Collins, M.J., & Rodman, D.H. "A Residential Program
       for the Developmentally Disabled." *Social Work*, 1974,
       19, 724-726.

       Describes a network of 5 community residences for the
developmentally disabled established by a state institution
in cooperation with nonprofit organizations. Advantages of
the public-private partnership are detailed.

414. Crawford, J.L., Aiello, J.R., & Thompson, D.E. "Deinstitu-
     tionalization and Community Placement: Clinical and
     Environmental Factors." *Mental Retardation*, 1979, 17,
     59-63.

     A review of the clinical and environmental variables
related to placement in the community indicated (a) the occurrence of maladaptive behavior in community settings were predictive of institutional re-admission; (b) demographic and
functional behavior characteristics were inconstantly related
to success in the community; (c) sociophysical environmental
characteristics of residential alternatives influence behavior
in the community; and (d) the concept of "successful placement"
needs to be more explicitly and consistently defined.

415. DeSilva, R.M., & Faflak, P. "From Institution to Com-
     munity--A New Process? *Mental Retardation*, 1976, 14(6),
     25-28.

     A survey was conducted of all residents placed in the
community from a large facility, with social work intervention
over a 14-year period. The results indicate that substantial
movement of residents from the facility to the community has
been taking place for many years prior to a community-placement
concept becoming popular.

416. Elliot, R., & MacKay, D.N. "Social Competence of Sub-
     normal and Normal Children Living under Different Types
     of Residential Care." *British Journal of Mental Sub-
     normality*, 1971, 17, 48-53.

     MR adolescents living under different types of hospital
care and in the community, and two groups of normal children
living in an orphanage and in their own homes were compared
to determine possible differences in social competence. The
mentally retarded persons living in the community had more
social skills and higher verbal abilities than those under
different types of residential care, and long-stay in-patients
were inferior to short-stay patients. There were no significant differences in the social efficiency of the two groups
of normal children.

417.   Eyman, R.K., Borthwick, S.A., & Miller, C. "Trends in
        Maladaptive Behavior of Mentally Retarded Persons Placed
        in Community and Institutional Settings." *American Journal
        of Mental Deficiency*, 1981, 85, 473-477.

        Results from 426 retarded Ss (average age-12 years) demon-
strate that no significant time trend was present for either the
institutional or community groups, regardless of Ss' age and
level of retardation. Placement, level of retardation, and
age, however, were related to overall prevalence of maladaptive
behavior.

418.   Eyman, R.K., Demaine, G.C., & Lei, T. "Relationship Be-
        tween Community Environments and Resident Changes in
        Adaptive Behavior: A Path Model." *American Journal of
        Mental Deficiency*, 1979, 83, 330-338.

        The relationship between environmental ratings of com-
munity homes using factor scores derived from Wolfensberger
and Glenn's Program Analysis of Service Systems (PASS) and
changes in adaptive behavior of residents living in those
facilities was investigated. A path analysis was used to
relate resident characteristics, e.g., age, IQ, and intital
score on adaptive behavior, with six PASS environmental ratings
and both of these sets of variables with average annual change
in adaptive behavior over a 3-year period. The results showed
that a number of PASS scores were significantly associated
with positive change in adaptive behavior for specified types
of residents. The most general finding was that older, less
retarded residents improved in all aspects of adaptive behavior
in conjunction with positive ratings on items dealing with
comfort and deployment of staff, access to the home, local
proximity of services, and blending with the neighborhood.

419.   Fanning, J.W. *A Common Sense Approach to Community Living
        Arrangements for the Mentally Retarded*. Springfield, Ill:
        C.C. Thomas, 1975.

        The information in this book emphasizes the dimensions
and components of community residential care for the retarded
which enhance the fulfillment of their social, physical, recreational, legal, sexual, and emotional needs. In addition, it
points out the importance of practical matters, such as selecting an appropriate neighborhood.

420. Fendell, N. "Dining Club for Senior Citizens and Retardates." *Rehabilitation Record*, 1970, 11(4), 26-27.

Discusses a model for the effective interaction of MR individuals and elderly persons.

421. Gallay, E., Freedman, R., Wyngaarden, M., & Kurtz, N. *Coming Back--The Community Experience of Deinstitutionalized Mentally Retarded People.* Cambridge: Abt Books, 1978.

Discusses the behavior and interactions of formerly institutionalized MR persons, and some of the difficulties experienced.

422. Gottlieb, J., & Corman, L. "Public Attitudes toward Mentally Retarded Children." *American Journal of Mental Deficiency*, 1975, 80, 72-80.

The recent trend toward integrating MR children in the community and public school warrants examination of public attitudes toward these children. Factor analysis of questionnaire responses of 430 adults revealed four factors underlying attitudes toward retarded children: positive stereotype, segregation in the community, segregation in the classroom, and perceived physical and intellectual handicap. Older respondents, parents of school-aged children, and people with no previous contact with a retarded person tended to favor segregation of retarded children in the community. Results of this study suggest that attitudes of these groups must be addressed if retarded persons are to be successfully integrated into society.

423. Gottlieb, J., & Siperstein, G.N. "Attitudes toward Mentally Retarded Persons: Effects of Attitude Referent Specificity." *American Journal of Mental Deficiency*, 1976, 80, 376-381.

The effects of the specificity of the attitude referent on female adults' expressed attitudes were studied. Specifically, attitudes toward a "mentally retarded person" referent were compared with attitudes toward mentally retarded referents who were described in terms of their severity of retardation and CA. Results indicated that expressed attitudes toward a nondescript MR person referent were generally intermediate in favorability between mildly and severely retarded person referents. The response format of the attitude questionnaire (e.g., Likert, forced-choice) was also found to affect attitude scores differentially as a function of the referent employed.

424. Heal, L.W., Sigelman, C.K., & Switzky, H.N. "Research
     on Community Residential Alternatives for the Mentally
     Retarded." In N.R. Ellis, ed. *International Review of
     Research in Mental Retardation*, vol. 9, 210-249. New
     York: Academic Press, 1978.

     Examines and interprets the history of the institutional-
ization movement, and then reviews and integrates the literature
dealing with the movement from large, segregated residential
facilities to more cost-efficient, community-based, culturally
normative alternatives. Also discusses the research relating
to the successful placement of MR persons in the community.

425. Heller, T., Berkson, G., & Romer, D. "Social Ecology of
     Supervised Communal Facilities for Mentally Disabled
     Adults: VI. Initial Social Adaptation." *American Journal
     of Mental Deficiency*, 1981, 86, 43-49.

     Investigated the social adaptation of MR adults intro-
duced to two new vocational rehabilitation settings. Client
behavior was observed for 8 weeks after placement in an evaluation center and for an additional 8 weeks in subsequent work-
ship settings. During the evaluation period, clients' sociability increased with time in the program. In the later workshop
placement, the social milieu rather than time in the program
influenced the degree of client sociability.

426. Holley, S. "A Social Skills Group with Mentally Retarded
     Subjects." *British Journal of Social and Clinical Psychol-
     ogy*, 1980, 19, 279-285.

     Suggests that improvement in basic interaction skills,
including nonverbal components, will improve communication
and increase the social effectiveness of the MR in the community outside the hospital. An attempt was made to improve
7 mentally retarded Ss' (CAs 28 to 66 years; IQs 38 to 70)
basic interaction skills by means of social skills training
group. There was significant improvement in target behaviors
after training, and some improvements was maintained at 8
weeks follow-up. The study suggests that such training groups
might effectively improve the communication skills of MR Ss.

427. Holmes, R.F. "Characteristics of Five Community Living
      Arrangements Serving Mentally Retarded Adults in South-
      western Urban Pennsylvania." *Mental Retardation*, 1979,
      17, 181-183.

      The purpose of this study is to describe the character-
istics of five community living arrangements serving MR adults
in southwestern urban Pennsylvania.

428. Hull, J.T., & Thompson, J.C. "Predicting Adaptive Function-
      ing of Mentally Retarded Persons in Community Settings."
      American Journal of Mental Deficiency, 1980, 85, 253-261.

      Examined the impact of individual, residential, and com-
munity variables on adaptive functioning of 369 18- to 73-year-
old retarded persons (median IQ-54) using multiple-regression
to analyze scores on the Adaptive Functioning Index. Individual
characteristics (especially IQ) accounted for 21 percent of
the variance, while environmental variables, primarily those
related to normalization, accounted for 35 percent. The data
suggest that environmental normalization may be an effective
technology for the promotion of independent functioning of
retarded people as well as an ideology.

429. Jones, K. *Opening the Door: A Study of New Policies for
      the Mentally Handicapped*. London: Routledge & Kegan Paul,
      1975.

      Deals with the normalization concept, and how it has
been carried out in England. Also, discusses difficulties
in the implementation of these normalization principles.

430. Justice, R.S., O'Connor, G., & Warren, N. "Problems
      Reported by Parents of Mentally Retarded Children--Who
      Helps?" *American Journal of Mental Deficiency*, 1971,
      75, 685-691.

      Parents of 171 community-labeled retardates with mean
IQs of 79 were interviewed regarding the problems they have
with their retarded child, and the resources--personal, private,
and public--used to help with these problems. Perceived availability and effectiveness of services were also investigated.
It was found that parents reported they did not receive assistance from public or private resources for most of their problems. Further, a large proportion of parents, especially

minority group parents, reported that they did not know of
additional services which might help with their problems, or
reported that no services were needed.

431.   Kastner, L.S., & Reppucci, N.D. "Assessing Community
       Attitudes toward Mentally Retarded Persons." *American
       Journal of Mental Deficiency*, 1979, 84, 137-144.

       Although many researchers have found evidence of dis-
crimination toward retarded individuals in employment, education, and housing, attitude-survey researchers generally report
acceptance of retarded people in the community. To examine
this discrepancy, the authors compared responses on a survey
concerning retarded people of a "threat" group, who lived
near a house for sale that was described as "having the necessary characteristics" for a potential group home, and a "non-
threat" control group. Analyses between and across groups
yielded differences that have implications for public education efforts and the validity of the survey method for research
on mental retardation.

432.   Katz, E. *The Retarded Adult in the Community*. Springfield,
       Ill.: C.C. Thomas, 1968.

       Discusses various aspects of the MR adult residing in the
community, including programmatic considerations.

433.   Kelly, N.K., & Menolascino, F.J. "Physicians' Awareness
       and Attitudes toward the Retarded." *Mental Retardation*,
       1975, 13(6), 10-13.

       Community-based services for retarded citizens are in-
creasing as alternatives to institutional care. For community
services to reach their potential they must be recognized
and utilized by all professional groups, including physicians.
This study demonstrated that a sample group was fairly unfamiliar
with the local services for the MR-in spite of the fact that
the area had gained national recognition for its programs.

434.   Kraus, J. "Supervised Living in the Community and Resi-
       dential and Employment Stability of Retarded Male Juve-
       niles." *American Journal of Mental Deficiency*, 1972, 77,
       283-290.

       The study was concerned with the relationship of super-
vision in the community and 11 background variables to social
adjustment of 74 MR male juvenile state wards. Using multiple
regression analysis, it was found that supervision in the community has a highly significant positive relationship to all
measures of adjustment except delinquency. Delinquency was
associated with higher IQ. There was also a trend for higher
IQ to be associated with residential stability and less frequent
absconding. The number of institutional changes experienced
by the retarded males prior to community placement was related
negatively to their residential stability and acceptability in
employment. Length of stay with foster families and age at
the time of placement in the community were related positively
to their being unsettled in employment; age was also related
negatively to the frequency of absconding. There was a positive relationship between the number of foster home changes
prior to community placement and unacceptability of the retarded
males in paid accommodation.

435.   Kriger, S.F. *Life Styles of Aging Retardates Living in
       Community Settings in Ohio*. Columbus, Ohio: Psychologica
       Metricka, 1975.

       Discusses the needs and life style of aged MR persons.

436.   Kugel, R.B., & Wolfensberger, W. *Changing Patterns in
       Residential Services for the Mentally Retarded*. Washington,
       D.C.: President's Committee on Mental Retardation, 1969.

       This work basically discusses the concepts of normaliza-
tion and deinstitutionalization, with recommendations for alternative (community) residential settings.

437.   Landesman-Dwyer, S. "Living in the Community." *American
       Journal of Mental Deficiency*, 1981, 86, 223-234.

       The movement to deinstitutionalize and normalize the
lives of MR individuals has led to significant changes in
where people live and how programs are administered. In
this literature review, findings about the relationship between "successful" programs and size, staff to resident ratio,

cost, client characteristics, program type, community support,
family involvement, and peer relationships were selectively
highlighted.

438.   Landesman-Dwyer, S., Berkson, G., & Romer, D. "Affiliation
       and Friendship of Mentally Retarded Residents in Group
       Homes." *American Journal of Mental Deficiency*, 1979, 83,
       571-580.

The social behavior of 20 percent of MR residents in 18
group homes was studied. Found that moderately to mildly retarded residents, unlike the severely retarded, engaged in
"social" behavior when in groups, and in "neutral" behavior
when alone.

439.   Landesman-Dwyer, S., Sackett, G.P., & Kleinman, J.S.
       "Relationship of Size to Resident and Staff Behavior
       in Small Community Residences." *American Journal of
       Mental Deficiency*, 1980, 85, 6-17.

The daily behavior of 240 MR adult residents and 75 staff
members were analyzed in relation to facility size and other
environmental variables. For the 20 group homes studied, staff
behavior was remarkably homogeneous and generally unrelated
to facility characteristics. In contrast, resident behavior
differed across group homes. In larger facilities, residents
engaged in more social behavior, particularly with peers, and
were more likely to have intense, reciprocal friendships than
were those in smaller facilities. Despite more enriched staff-
resident ratios in the smaller homes, amount of staff-resident
interaction was not related to size. Overall, other environmental variables (e.g., location and social grouping) were
more closely associated with observed behavior patterns than
was size.

440.   McCarver, R.B., & Craig, E.M. "Placement of the Retarded
       in the Community: Prognosis and Outcome." In N.R. Ellis,
       ed. *International Review of Research in Mental Retarda-
       tion*, vol. 7. 145-207. New York: Academic Press, 1974.

Discusses the different types of studies done over the
years concerning the postinstitutional placement of the MR,
and discusses some of the many methodological problems of
such studies, as well as critically reviewing the overall
results to date. Concludes that, with the present state of
knowledge, placement is typically on a trial and error basis
and evaluation is mainly subjective.

441. Nihira, L., & Nihira, K. "Jeopardy in Community Place-
      ment." *American Journal of Mental Deficiency*, 1975, 79,
      538-544.

      As part of a broader research effort, a survey of the
adaptive behavior of 424 community-placed retarded persons
was conducted through small-group, tape-recorded interviews
with their 109 caretakers. From 1252 incidents of problem
behavior cited, 203 were judged to contain jeopardy. Seventy-
seven percent of these incidents involved jeopardy to health
and/or safety, 4 percent to general welfare, and 18 percent
contained legal jeopardy. In 79 percent of incidents, the
client jeopardized himself, in 12 percent he jeopardized a
fellow client, and in 9 percent he jeopardized a member of
the community at large.

442. Nihira, L., & Nihira, K. "Normalized Behavior in Community
      Placement." *Mental Retardation*, 1975, 13(2), 9-13.

      A survey of the adaptive behavior of 426 community-placed
MR individuals was conducted through small-group, tape-recorded
interviews with their 109 caretakers. From 1344 incidents collected, 194 were of positive or normative behavior. Of these,
123 involved gains in acquired skills, and 71 involved gains
in approved interpersonal relations. The findings suggested
that the respondents were primarily concerned about their
residents being able to care for themselves, and that caretakers found satisfaction in small gains as well as major
gains in the normative behavior by their residents.

443. Novak, A.R., & Heal, L.W., eds. *Integration of Develop-
      mentally Disabled Individuals into the Community*.
      Baltimore: Paul H. Brookes, 1980.

      This book deals with deinstitutionalization and its
relationship to community services. Basically it is a review
of previously published research, drawing upon a fairly large
group of sources and containing an extensive list of references.

444. Parks, A.W. "A Model for Psychological Consultation to
      Community Residences--Pressures, Problems, and Program
      Types." *Mental Retardation*, 1978, 16, 149-152.

      This study indicates the types of problems encountered
by community residences (halfway-house) staff in the development and maintenance of community-based programs for persons

with developmental disabilities. A further delineation of
some of the areas of concern suggests that staff pressures
might be alleviated through staff-centered consultation provided by psychologists. It is suggested that consultation
focus on staff frustrations, residents' problems that attending staff must respond to, and community problems. Maintenance of staff and prevention of client "re-institutionaliza-
tion" are cited as projected outcomes through use of this
consultation model.

445.   Reagan, M.W., Murphy, R.J., Hill, Y.F., & Thomas, D.R.
       "Community Placement Stability of Behavior Problem
       Educable Mentally Retarded Students." *Mental Retardation*,
       1980, 18, 139-142.

Follow-up community placement data were collected for
186 behavior problem EMR students at 6, 12, and 18 months
after discharge. Placement stability and placement instability
were analyzed for natural home, foster home, and group home
placements. Greatest stability throughout the follow-up period
was observed for students initially placed in their natural
homes. Comparable data for foster home and group home placements indicated decreasing placement stability throughout this
period. This decline, however, was largely the result of increasing movement toward less restrictive settings.

446.   Reiter, S., & Levi, A.M. "Factors Affecting Social Inte-
       gration of Noninstitutionalized Mentally Retarded Adults."
       American Journal of Mental Deficiency, 1980, 85, 25-30.

Studied the social integration of moderately and mildly
MR young adults. It appears that retarded people who grow
up in the community need help in order to become socially
independent.

447.   Romer, D., & Berkson, G. "Social Ecology of Supervised
       Communal Facilities for Mentally Disabled Adults: IV.
       Characteristics of Social Behavior." *American Journal
       of Mental Deficiency,* 1981, 86, 28-38.

Analyzed behavior categories for observations of 304
mentally disabled adults in relation to settings (sheltered
workshops and residential facility), personal characteristics
(age, sex, IQ, diagnosis, and desire for affiliation), and
characteristics of partners. Both settings and personal

characteristics predicted individual behavior rates for the
10 most frequently observed behavior categories. As many as
14 dimensions were extracted from behavior observed in more
intense dyadic relationships; these dimensions were strongly
related to characteristics of the Ss in the relationships.
Although more intelligent Ss exhibited higher rates of verbal
behavior, they were not more verbal in their intense social
relationships. Furthermore, Ss at all levels of intelligence
were sensitive to the intellectual characteristics of their
partners. Results suggest that the social behavior of mentally
disabled people is complex and sensitive to the presence and
characteristics of others; peer-group composition seems to
be critical to social adaptation in communal settings for this
population.

448.   Roos, P., McCann, B., & Addison, M., eds. *Shaping the
       Future: Community-based Residential Services and Facili-
       ties for Mentally Retarded People.* Baltimore: University
       Park Press, 1980.

       This work presents a very detailed overview of the various
programmatic and legal issues surrounding community-based residential services, including the impact of the law on recent
trends in service delivery.

449.   Rosen, M., Kivitz, M.S., Clark, G.R., & Floor, L. "Pre-
       diction of Postinstitutional Adjustment of Mentally
       Retarded Adults." *American Journal of Mental Deficiency,*
       1970, 74, 726-734.

       Twenty-nine demographic, psychometric, and behavioral
rating variables were evaluated as predictors of 22 criteria
of adjustment for a group of MR persons discharged to independent community status. Tests of perceptual-motor abilities
and behavioral ratings of employment potential showed the
highest number of predictive relationships with criteria;
tests of verbal abilities and ratings of social adjustment
were poor predictors. The results suggested that accurate
decisions regarding selection for discharge may ultimately
be made from psychometric scores and assessment of work performance within the institution.

450. Salzberg, C.L., & Langford, C.A. "Community Integration
      of Mentally Retarded Adults through Leisure Activity."
      Mental Retardation, 1981, 19, 127-131.

      This report demonstrates that simply establishing small
residences within a neighborhood, as a consequence of deinstitutionalization, does not appear to be sufficient to desegregate
MR adults. However, what is helpful is the utilization of age-
appropriate, commercially available leisure pursuits.

451. Schalock, R.L., Harper, R.S., & Genung, T. "Community
      Integration of Mentally Retarded Adults: Community
      Placement and Program Success." *American Journal of
      Mental Deficiency*, 1981, 85, 478-488.

      Evaluated the extent of community and program success
of 67 female and 99 male MR clients (average age-34 years;
average IQ=48) placed into a community-based program. Twenty
predictor variables measuring institutional factors, client
characteristics, training variables, and community characteristics were related to community or program success. Successful
placement was associated with sensory-motor and work skills,
appropriate social-emotional behavior, gender, and family
acceptance of placement and involvement with the interdisciplinary team. Program success was associated with language and
psychomotor skills, education received prior to placement,
community and institution size, and family involvement. Six-
teen percent were reinstitutionalized into either the state
mental retardation facility or a mental health facility.

452. Segal, R. "Trends in Services for the Aged Mentally
      Retarded." *Mental Retardation*, 1977, 15(2), 25-27.

      The focus of program development for the MR during the
last 20 years has been in the area of children and young adults,
and relatively little attention has been paid to the problems
of the aging MR person. Health care services, social and
emotional support, housing programs, vocational services,
recreational activities, referral services, transportation,
financial assistance, protective services, and support for
families of the elderly MR are needed. Although some community programs for the elderly MR have been implemented,
program development has been hindered by lack of trained
professionals, lack of transportation, discriminatory zoning
practices, limited job opportunities, negative community
attitudes, lack of funding, lack of agency coordination,

lack of community awareness, and difficulty in locating the elderly MR. It is imperative that programs be implemented to meet pressing health, social, and economic needs that confront the aged MR person.

453. Seitz, S., & Geske, D. "Mothers' and Graduate Trainees' Judgments of Children: Some Effects of Labeling." *American Journal of Mental Deficiency*, 1976, 81, 362-370.

Graduate students in a clinical practicum in mental retardation and mothers randomly chosen from a university community were asked to rate retarded and nonretarded children on characteristics reflecting social competence and interpersonal attractiveness and also on a social distance scale. The children rated were viewed on videotape in free-play interactions with their mothers. Each retarded child was shown once as an unlabeled child and once as a child labeled retarded. Mothers rated the retarded children as different from the nonretarded children on six of nine measures, regardless of label. When the retarded children were labeled, they were rated by mothers as significantly higher on items related to attractiveness then when they were unlabeled. Graduate student trainees' ratings did not discriminate between retarded children as a function of labeling, with one exception: like mothers, trainees rated retarded children as more likeable when labeled. However, both observer groups placed retarded children, regardless of status, significantly farther from themselves on the social distance scale than they placed nonretarded children.

454. Seltzer, G.B. "Community Residential Adjustment: The Relationship among Environment, Performance, and Satisfaction." *American Journal of Mental Deficiency*, 1981, 85, 624-630.

One hundred fifty three persons released from a state school for MR persons were studied with regard to two outcome measures of community residential adjustment: (a) adaptive behavior, as measured by the percentage of mastered skills that a subject performed regularly and independently and (b) subjects' satisfaction with aspects of their residential environments. Five environmental dimensions of six residential program types were examined. A multiple regression analysis was performed to explain the relationship between the measures of adaptive behavior and individual and environmental characteristics.

455. Spinak, J. "Normalization and Recreation for the Dis-
      abled." *Journal of Leisurability*, 1975, 2(2), 31-35.

      Discusses the increasing use in management of the MR
of the principle of normalization, under which effort is
directed primarily toward integrating the handicapped into
normal community life. The importance of coordination among
agencies and organizations is stressed. With growing independence the need for special programs will diminish, but
will not disappear entirely.

456. Sternlicht, M. "Variables Affecting Foster Care Place-
      ment of Institutionalized Retarded Residents." *Mental
      Retardation*, 1978, 16, 25-28.

      The variables that influence the probability of success-
ful foster care placement for MR individuals discharged into
the community are investigated. Four sources of variables
are identified: the resident, the foster parents or caretakers, the community, and the institution. The variables
are discussed relative to the present literature in the field,
and to the results of the author's experience. In conclusion,
guidelines for successful foster care placement are presented.

457. Stevenson, G. "The Community Adjustment of Moderately
      Mentally Retarded Adults in Los Angeles." Doctoral
      dissertation, California School of Professional Psy-
      chology, Los Angeles, 1979, summarized in *Dissertation
      Abstracts International*, 1980, 40, 5024B-5025B. (Univ-
      ersity Microfilms No. 8003255).

      Found that community adjustment of moderately MR adults
in Los Angeles is not a homogeneous concept, but rather a
reflection of significantly different dimensions of community
adjustment.

458. Strain, P.S., & Carr, T.H. "The Observational Study of
      Social Reciprocity: Implications for the Mentally Re-
      tarded." *Mental Retardation*, 1975, 13(4), 18-19.

      Presents findings from a national survey of 611 community
residential facilities and placements for retarded persons.
Funding, age and sex distributions of residents, staff re-
cruitment and training, and services offered are presented.
Results suggest that the community residential facilities

movement, as an alternative to institutionalization, is gaining
momentum and that these facilities provide opportunities for
residents of varying ages and disability categories to participate in school, work, recreational, and other community activities. The need for cooperation between administrators, residents, and community citizens to establish more positive results
is emphasized.

459. Sutter, P., Mayeda, T., Yee, S., & Yanagi, G. "Community
     Placement Success Based on Client Behavior Preferences
     of Careproviders." *Mental Retardation*, 1981, 19, 117-120.

The extent to which careprovider preferences in client
characteristics are matched to the actual characteristics of
clients is examined. Unsuccessful careproviders and clients
are found to be significantly more mismatched than successful
careproviders and clients in the areas of client maladaptive
behaviors. A more precise matching of careprovider preferences
to client behaviors at the time of placement might be expected
to increase the probability of placement success.

460. Sutter, P., Mayeda, T., Call, T., Yanagi, G., & Yee, S.
     "Comparison of Successful and Unsuccessful Community-
     placed Mentally Retarded Persons." *American Journal of
     Mental Deficiency*, 1980, 85, 262-267.

Examined differences in the characteristics of 17 unsuccessful and 60 successful community-placed adult clients.
Discriminant function analysis of data from the Behavior
Development Survey identified a maladaptive behavior factor
and sex to be significant discriminators between the 2 groups.
Unsuccessful Ss manifested a significantly higher frequency
of every maladaptive behavior assessed by the maladaptive
variable. More males than females failed in community placement.

461. Thompson, R.L. "The Development of Cooperative Relation-
     ships: An Alternative to Mandated Equality." *Mental
     Retardation*, 1978, 16, 138-141.

Cooperative relationships could become a substitute for
paternalistic, authoritarian measures in the provision of
services to retarded people. A review of the literature about
community services to the adult, or near adult, MR shows no
empirical studies that tested the differences between the

attitudes and responses of MR individuals participating in
cooperative relationships and those involved in authoritarian
ones. More effort is needed to establish and evaluate programs
that stress cooperative relationships between clients and
teachers.

462.   Tizard, J., Sinclair, I., & Clarke, R.V.G., eds. *Varieties
        of Residential Experience*. London: Routledge & Kegan Paul,
        1975.

    The studies reported in this book address themselves to
the question of why institutions which serve apparently similar
functions differ so much. The problems are approached through
the use of comparative methods. These involve measurement of
different dimensions of institutional care (e.g., difference
in ideology and in staffing), and the analysis of interrelationships among specific functional features which characterize
particular institutions.

463.   Upshur, C.C. "An Evaluation of Home-based Respite Care."
        Mental Retardation, 1982, 20, 58-62.

    Findings of an evaluation of a pilot home-based respite
care program designed to serve severely MR and disabled persons
are reported. Data were collected concerning 91 requests for
respite care services spanning a six-month period using questionnaires administered to both providers and families. Disability
ratings are assigned to clients to determine whether more severely disabled clients are served than in the past. Results indicate that significantly more multiply handicapped clients are
served successfully. Recommendations are given concerning ex-
pansion of home-based respite care for all levels of client
disability.

464.   Willer, B., & Intagliata, J. "Social-Environmental Factors
        as Predictors of Adjustment of Deinstitutionalized Mentally
        Retarded Adults." *American Journal of Mental Deficiency*,
        1981, 86, 252-259.

    MR adults placed from five state institutions were studied
2 to 4 years after they were placed in either foster family care
or community residences. Factors of the social environment that
were most predictive of individual adjustment were determined.
Adjustment was defined as behavior in five areas of functioning: self-care, behavior control, community-living skills, use

of community resources, and social support. Multiple regression analysis revealed that social-environmental factors and
other characteristics of community settings played an important
role in individuals' adjustment. Important features of the
social environment were similar across both settings.

CHAPTER IX:
VOCATIONAL AND OCCUPATIONAL ADJUSTMENT

465. Adima, E.E. "A Study of On-the-Job Characteristics of
Mentally Retarded Employees Judged to be "Good" and
"Bad" by Their Immediate Supervisors." Doctoral dissertation, University of Pittsburgh, 1974, summarized
in *Dissertation Abstracts International*, 1975, 35,
7751A-7752A. (University Microfilms No. 73-13,173).

The study considered the description of MR employees'
characteristics by their immediate supervisors. MR employees
who are considered "bad" by their supervisors are rated as
less able to deal with verbal instructions, as failing to
request additional materials, as unable to specify what was
unclear, and unable to transfer skills. They are also said
to decrease their productivity when there are changes in
routine.

466. Alper, S., & Retish, P.M. "The Influence of Academic
Information on Teachers' Judgments of Vocational
Potential." *Exceptional Children*, 1978, 44, 537-538.

Investigated (a) the extent to which academic information influences teachers' judgments of the vocational potential of the retarded, and (b) the importance of level of job
difficulty, teacher attitude, and academic skills for job
success. Analyses of responses of 86 work-study teachers
to 3 self-administered questionnaires supported the thesis
that teachers may be influenced by academic information when
making vocational decisions about their students. Knowledge
of IQ and academic achievement may also cause teachers to
underestimate or overlook more relevant vocational skill information.

467.   Becker, R.L. "Job Training Placement for Retarded Youth:
       A Survey." *Mental Retardation*, 1976, 14(3), 7-11.

       A survey of the types of jobs to which 1,438 MR youth
were assigned for on-the-job training in a work-study program
in 1972-1974 showed assignments to 185 different jobs in
14 major industries and miscellaneous classification.

468.   Bellamy, T., & Sontag, E. "Use of Group Contingent Music
       to Increase Assembly Line Production Rates of Retarded
       Students in a Simulated Sheltered Workshop." *Journal
       of Music Therapy*, 1973, 10, 125-136.

       Evaluated the use of group contingencies in increasing
the assembly line production rates of retarded and disturbed
workers in 2 experiments. The effectiveness of group contingencies in changing concurrent behaviors of group members
and the value of conjugately programmed behavior consequence
on production were examined. Normal public school resources
were used, and results demonstrate that group contingent
music, presented both episodically and conjugately, provided
an effective means of accelerating the assembly line production rates of retarded students.

469.   Berkson, G., & Romer, D. "Social Ecology of Supervised
       Communal Facilities for Mentally Disabled Adults.
       I. Introduction." *American Journal of Mental Deficiency*,
       1980, 85, 219-228.

       In the first of a series of papers describing social
relationships among mentally disabled adults in 4 sheltered
workshops, procedures for observing and interviewing clients
and staff members are explained and data on reliability and
general levels of social behavior are reported. Reliability
of social behavior was significant across time and situations,
but social-choice estimates were not very consistent across
staff, clients, and observations.

470.   Bitter, J.A., & Bolanovich, D.J. "WARF: A Scale for
       Measuring Job-Readiness Behaviors." *American Journal
       of Mental Deficiency*, 1970, 74, 616-621.

       A rating scale (Work Adjustment Rating Form) to predict
job readiness of retardates is described relative to the criteria of (a) systematic observation, (b) relevance, (c) reliability of observations, and (d) identification of behavior

patterns. Results demonstrate that a simple scale can predict job adjustment and that it holds promise for identifying meaningful behavior patterns. Futher research with the scale is recommended.

471.   Bodenmiller, F.W., & Sanders, R.M. "Decreasing Non-Compliant Behavior in a Sheltered Workshop." *Vocational Evaluation & Work Adjustment Bulletin*, 1977, 10(2), 25-31.

Used one client, a 26-year-old retarded male janitor-trainee who had spent 12 years in schools for the blind but was living at home, in a treatment program designed to overcome delay and debate as features of noncompliance with directives. After supervision was transferred to a special education teacher, the data for Baselines 1 and 2, each of 5 days, were obtained. The treatment that followed was for 5 weeks and included feedback, instructions, and social reinforcement from the supervisor. Three-day follow-up sessions were held after 3 and 7 weeks. Marked improvement from Baseline 1 to 2, to treatment, and to follow-up in compliance was noted.

472.   Boyan, C. "A Flexible Approach to Career Development: Balancing Vocational Training and Training for Independent Living." *Education & Training of the Mentally Retarded*, 1978, 13, 209-213.

Argues that rehabilitative efforts for MR adults have stressed vocational training at the expense of independent living skills (ILS) and that this area should be of major concern to professionals working in the field. It is suggested that ILS be systematically taught, starting with elementary school, and that later programs be designed to supplement vocational training in a balanced approach to helping retarded persons achieve full independence.

473.   Brandwein, H. "Social Problem Solving and Vocational Rehabilitation." Doctoral dissertation, Yeshiva University, 1980, summarized in *Dissertation Abstracts International*, 1980, 41, 1529A. (University Microfilms No. 8021227).

Found that moderately and mildly retarded adults who successfully achieved sheltered-worker status performed better on a social problem-solving test--THINK--than the dropouts from the vocational training program.

474. Brickey, M., Browning, L., & Campbell, K. "Vocational
      Histories of Sheltered-Workshop Employees Placed in
      Projects with Industry and Competitive Jobs." *Mental
      Retardation*, 1982, 20, 52-57.

Job placement histories of 73 sheltered-workshop employees
placed in Projects With Industry (PWI) or competitive jobs in
calendar year 1978 are examined during a 30-month period. Of
the 27 people placed in PWI positions, 48% were subsequently
placed in competitive jobs. Of the 53 competitive placements
in 1978, 60% were competitively employed as of July 1, 1980.
Job variables such as structure appear to be more important
to job success than employee demographic variables such as
IQ.

475. Brolin, D. "Value of Rehabilitation Services and Cor-
      relates of Vocational Success with the Mentally Retarded."
      American Journal of Mental Deficiency, 1972, 76, 644-651.

Investigated the efficacy of rehabilitation services for
retarded persons and variables related to vocational success.
Data on 193 former out-patients of a diagnostic center were
obtained. The subjects, mostly noninstitutionalized, ranged
in CA from 18 to 54 years and in IQ from 40 to 89. Three
independent raters judged the adequacy of services for each
client after the evaluation and these ratings were compared
with actual outcome. The findings upheld the importance of
rehabilitation services for the MR, especially males. Client
outcome was found to be particularly related to the interaction of certain client, family, community, and agency variables.

476. Brown, R.I. "An Integrated Program for the Mentally
      Handicapped." In P. Mittler, ed. *Research to Practice
      in Mental Retardation*, vol. 2, 387-393. Baltimore:
      University Park, 1977.

Presents a program dealing with MR individuals which
demonstrates the principles of coordinated training and
research in vocational, social, and home-learning skills;
integration of assessment and training; determination of
program levels by baseline performance; and structuring of
program into variable training steps leading to group and
individual placement in vocational areas.

477. Cass, M. "The Effects of Music on Retarded Individuals in a Workshop Setting." *Research & the Retarded*, 1975, 2(1), 18-23.

   Assessed the effect of music on work production, off-task behavior, social interaction, self-injurious behavior, and yelling out of 39 retarded 26- to 46-year-olds engaged in training in a workshop setting. Four types of music were played throughout morning and afternoon work sessions. Findings show that music did not significantly affect the behaviors studied.

478. Cleland, C.C., & Swartz, J.D. "Work Deprivation as Motivation to Work." *American Journal of Mental Deficiency*, 1969, 73, 703-712.

   The meaning of work for institutionalized or noninstitutionalized borderline and mildly retarded has been assumed to parallel the meaning of work for normals. The general prediction that work deprivation for "patient workers" would serve as a strong motivator to work was upheld, and the meaning of work to retardates was clarified.

479. Cleland, C.C., Swartz, J.D., Drew, C.J., & Talkington, L.W. "Charge Attendant Attitudes toward Working Residents." *Mental Retardation*, 1972, 10(4), 31-35.

   Used a questionnaire to determine the attitudes of 46 attendants toward their 301 student helpers. The student helpers' attitudes toward the more severely handicapped that they cared for revealed their primary job-oriented concerns to be time of payments, messiness of the work, and desire to change jobs. The attendants viewed student helpers as less aware of the needs of the severely handicapped than attendants. Ninety per cent of the attendants indicated they would not use student helpers as baby-sitters. Other motivations are discussed in relation to the competition between attendants and student helpers.

480.   Close, D.W., Irvin, L.K., Prehm, H.J., & Taylor, V.E.
       "Systematic Correction Procedures in Vocational-Skill
       Training of Severely Retarded Individuals." *American
       Journal of Mental Deficiency*, 1978, 83, 270-275.

       Seventy severely retarded adults were taught a vocational
assembly-skill task involving a difficult visual-motor discrimination. Comparisons of relative effects on trials-to-criterion
were made among two types of verbal-correction procedures and
three types of systematic physical-correction procedures. Reliable differences in effects occurred only between the three
systematic physical-correction procedures, with repeated
practice the most effective, physical prompts next, and ges-
tures the least effective. The results were interpreted as
demonstrating the efficacy of trainer-related training procedures in relation to stimulus-related strategies, as well
as relative efficacy among trainer-related correction procedures.

481.   Cohen, M.E., & Close, D.W. "Retarded Adult's Discrete
       Work Performance in a Sheltered Workshop as a Function
       of Overall Productivity and Motivation." *American
       Journal of Mental Deficiency*, 1975, 79, 526-529.

       Production times of high and low retarded adults in a
sheltered workshop were analyzed in terms of actual time
working as opposed to actual time not working and under conditions of standard and high motivation. Under standard
conditions, low productivity was primarily the result of
more time spent not working. High motivation attenuated
this effect. The results were discussed in terms of cognitive vs. motivational interpretations of individual differences in work performance.

482.   Coleman, A.E., Ayoub, M.M., & Friedrich, D.W. "Assess-
       ment of the Physical Work Capacity of Institutionalized
       Mentally Retarded Males." *American Journal of Mental
       Deficiency*, 1976, 80, 629-635.

       Educable and trainable mentally retarded males were
examined for physical work capacity. Analysis of results
indicated that the physical work capacity of the test population was 20 to 30 percent below that cited in the literature for nonretarded subjects of similar age and sex. Evidence also suggested that developmental and maintenance programs of physical fitness were required in order for mentally
retarded persons to qualify for and maintain employment on
most of the manual occupational tasks cited.

483. Cunningham, T., & Presnall, D. "Relationship between
      Dimensions of Adaptive Behavior and Sheltered-Workshop
      Productivity." *American Journal of Mental Deficiency*,
      1978, 82, 386-393.

      Factor analyzed the 24 domains of the American Associa-
tion on Mental Deficiency Adaptive Behavior Scale using a
sample of 217 adult retarded workshop clients. Of the 7
dimensions found to describe adaptive behavior, Personal
Independence, Social Maladaptation, and Personal Maladaptation
accounted for the majority of variance in the vector matrix.
Scores on each of the 7 factors were obtained for all Ss and
used to predict productivity in a workshop setting. A stepwise regression analysis yielded a significant regression
effect in which the factors of Personal Independence and
Social Maladaptation accounted for 25% of the variance in
salary and had a multiple correlation coefficient of .50 with
the predicted variable. It is concluded that adaptive behavior is a multidimensional variable, significantly affecting productivity in sheltered-workshop settings.

484. DeMars, P.K, "Training Adult Retardates for Private
      Enterprise." *American Journal of Occupational Therapy*,
      1975, 29(1), 39-42.

      Presents a community-based program to place MR persons
into work positions in private business and industry.

485. Dial, J.G., & Swearingen, S. "The Prediction of Sheltered-
      Workshop Performance: Special Application of the McCarron-
      Dial Work Evaluation System." *Vocational Evaluation & Work
      Adjustment Bulletin*, 1976, 9(4), 24-33.

      Related the McCarron-Dial Work Evaluation System (MDWES)
to work productivity and to entry wages, in a study at the
Dallas Rehabilitation Institute, using 40 retardates aged
16 to 47 years with 1 to 6 months in the Institute's sheltered
workshop. The 5 MDWES components measured were (a) verbal-
cognitive ability, (b) visual skills, (c) motor skills, (d)
emotional adjustment, and (e) integration-coping. Performance
on a group of selected workshop activities was the measure
of productivity, and from it a measure of wages was derived.
Multiple correlations for the MDWES variables were .79 for
production, .75 for hourly rate of payment, and .79 for piecework payment. Piecework employment paid clients exactly twice
as much as employment at hourly wages as a result of double
output by piecework clients.

486. Domino, G., & McGarty, M. "Personal and Work Adjustment
      of Young Retarded Women." *American Journal of Mental
      Deficiency*, 1972, 77, 314-321.

      The relationship of personal and work adjustment was
investigated in a sample of 35 young adult MR women working
in a sheltered workshop. For each subject clinical ratings
of general adjustment, personality ratings on five Sonoma
Check List dimensions (personal adjustment, self-confidence,
need achievement, need affiliation, and need endurance), and
work adjustment ratings (as measured by the work Adjustment
Rating Form) were obtained. The results support the hypothesis
that personal adjustment is positively related to work adjustment.

487. Dunn, D.J., & Kruel, D. "Individual Observation Using
      a Normed Behavior Observation System." *Vocational Evalua-
      tion & Work Adjustment Bulletin*, 1976, 9(3), 14-20.

      Selected "best" and "worst" workshop clients from among
a group of 10-15 workers making toy Christmas trains, by
unanimous staff agreement. Both were middle-aged white males,
single, retarded, and socioculturally disadvantaged, with a
history of institutionalization and 1 year in the program.
For 3 days the behaviors of both Ss were categorized as on-
task or off-task by point sampling every 5 minutes. Behaviors
of both workers were analyzed and compared with shop norms.
The "best" worker exceeded the shop norms in on/off ratio
and on-task, but not in off-task, which did not differ significantly from shop norms. Standard score comparisons were
made in 9 rating categories. Three showed no significant
differences on- and off-task, looking around, and idle, but
the other 6 showed the worst worker to differ from the best
and from shop norms with more talking on- and off-task, poorer
attending, less time on-task, and more "other" behavior (walk-
ing around from person to person and interrupting the work
of others). This observation schedule was evaluated as effective, and the profile showed that the "best" worker was more
attending, stayed more on-task, talked less, and showed less
"other" disruptive behavior.

488. Edge, W.L. "Emotional Adjustment of Mentally Retarded
     Adults Placed in Competitive Community Employment."
     Doctoral dissertation, Texas Woman's University, 1976,
     summarized in *Dissertation Abstracts International*, 1977,
     37, 4278A. (University Microfilms No. 77-737).

     Evaluated the emotional adjustment on the employment
status of MR adults placed in competitive community employment.
Found that there is a greater proportion of emotionally adjusted
individuals in the successfully employed group than in the un-
successfully employed group.

489. Fiester, A.R., & Giambra, L.M. "Language Indices of
     Vocational Success in Mentally Retarded Adults."
     American Journal of Mental Deficiency, 1972, 77, 332-
     337.

     This study involved the comparison of "success" and
"failure" retarded adults in sheltered workshops, on a variety
of psycholinguistic diagnostic tests. Unlike previous studies,
success or failure was defined in terms of actual productivity
rates. Nine out of 21 text variables significantly differentiated the 2 groups; all in the direction of the Success Group
having a higher mean score than the Failure Group. In addition,
a multiple regression equation was generated from the 4 test
variables which significantly correlated with individual
productivity. The results clearly confirmed the importance
of language and communication skills in the vocational functioning of retarded adults.

490. Fleres, C.N. "An Experiment in the Pre-occupational
     Education of Mentally Retarded Students on the Junior
     High School Level." *Education and Training of the
     Mentally Retarded*, 1975, 10(1), 26-29.

     Conducted a program to provide realistic simulated
career exploration opportunities for MR adolescents. Students were paid "school dollars" to perform services as a
nurse's aide, printer's helper, gas station attendant, mani-
curist, and electronics assembly worker. Dollars earned,
according to their performance, were deposited in the students'
checking accounts to be used in purchasing items from the
class store, thereby introducing the concept of banking.
Eight of 10 students responding to an oral questionnaire
said they felt earning money had been worth the effort, regardless of their feelings about working at a particular job.

Nine said they were happy to have participated, and 6 said they thought they had found an occupation to pursue in the future. Oral testing indicated that all students learned the fundamental concept of banking.

491. Foss, G., & Peterson, S.L. "Social-Interpersonal Skills Relevant to Job Tenure for Mentally Retarded Adults." *Mental Retardation*, 1981, 19(3), 103-106.

Social-interpersonal behavior areas most relevant to job tenure for MR adults are identified. Respondents to a questionnaire designed to identify these behavior areas were 64 job-placement personnel in sheltered workshops in 11 western states. A high level of agreement among the respondents was noted. Three of the four areas identified as most relevant to job tenure were concerned directly with the supervisor-worker relationship.

492. Friedenberg, W.P., & Martin, A.S. "Prevocational Training of the Severely Retarded Using Task Analysis." *Mental Retardation*, 1977, 15(2), 16-20.

Task analysis procedures were applied in the training of 2 EMR adults in the prevocational areas of a sheltered workshop. Each student was trained on both a hand and machine procedure for stapling labels on plastic bags, a task which requires multiple multidimensional discrimination. Training was successfully completed for both students within a short period of time, but a high unacceptable rate in subsequent production suggests that tangible reinforcement may be necessary to maintain low error performance in an inherently nonreinforcing task. Although machine stapling required longer training times, this disadvantage was offset by subsequent greater production and fewer errors following training.

493. Galkowski, T. "Adaptation of the Mentally Handicapped to a Working Life." *Revue de Neuropsychiatrie Infantile dt d'Hygiene Mentale de l'Enfance*, 1974, 22(1-2), 121-131.

Studied the work productivity and social acceptance of retarded adults working in a protected workshop. Thirty men, aged 19 to 25 years, were asked to perform 3 simple manual tasks. Two instructors rated the number and quality of the completed tasks. The social popularity of Ss was assessed through interviews with Ss and their instructors. Results indicated a significant relationship between intelligence level and work productivity. Most Ss were neither accepted nor rejected by the group as a whole, and the percentage of Ss with high popularity was small. Instructors were only slightly successful in rating the social acceptability of Ss. It is suggested that protected workshops create an exceptional environment, and that this must be taken into account in studies of the working retarded.

494. Garner, R.E., Lacy, G.H., & Creasy, R.F. "Workshops: Why, What, Whether?" *Mental Retardation*, 1972, 10(3), 25-27.

Discusses the origins, development, and problem areas of workshops for the MR.

495. George, M.J., & Baumeister, A.A. "Employee Withdrawal and Job Satisfaction in Community Residential Facilities for Mentally Retarded Persons." *American Journal of Mental Deficiency*, 1981, 85, 639-647.

This study was conducted to provide information concerning employee stability in community residential facilities serving MR persons. Information was collected on turnover, length of service, absenteeism, job satisfaction, and increased overhead costs as a consequence of the turnover rate for 21 randomly selected small and large community residential facility organizations that operated a total of 47 living units in Tennessee. Subjects included all house managers (full-time and relief) and administrator/supervisors in the 21 organizations for fiscal year 1978-1979. The results revealed a significant problem of controllable turnover of direct-service employees. The major factors contributing to this problem appeared to be (a) a lack of effective methods to orient, integrate, and maintain new staff members, (b) low pay and wide variations for amount and kind of work to be accomplished, and (c) a lack of training and support systems to deal with behavior problems presented by some residents.

496.   Gola, T.J., Holmes, P.A., & Holmes, N.K. "Effectiveness
        of a Group Contingency Procedure for Increasing Pre-
        vocational Behavior of Profoundly Retarded Residents."
        Mental Retardation, 1982, 20, 26-29.

Four profoundly MR middle-aged female residents in a
state institution Behavior Problems Program were trained
through the use of an interdependent group oriented contingency procedure to sit and later to work on prevocational
task. The results indicate that the group contingency procedure is highly effective in increasing both sitting and
work behavior and in decreasing inappropriate behavior. It
is concluded that such a procedure has applications for mentally retarded residents in a wide variety of settings.

497.   Gold, M.W. "Factors Affecting Production by the Retarded:
        Base Rate." *Mental Retardation*, 1973, 11(6), 41-45.

Determined based production rates of 20 retarded Ss
working 1 hour per day for 10 days and 3 hours per day for
10 days. Ss assembled a 14-piece bicycle brake under conditions of no reinforcement. The relationship between acquisition rate (how quickly Ss learned the skill) and production
rate was not significant, nor was the relationship between
production rate and IQ. The mean error rate for both groups
was very low. Data suggest that the MR are capable of producing, qualitatively and quantitatively, at a level above
what is presently acknowledged, even without conventional
reinforcement systems.

498.   Gold, M.W. "Research on the Vocational Habilitation of
        the Retarded: The Present, the Future." In N.R. Ellis
        ed. *International Review of Research in Mental Retarda-
        tion*, vol. 6, 97-147. New York: Academic Press, 1973.

Describes the present status of research on the vocational habilitation of the MR, which exists within a context
where the population with whom it deals is preceived by almost
everyone as being far less capable than is really the case.
Also, proposes 13 different directions for future efforts.

499. Goldberg, J., Katz, S., & Yekutiel, E. "The Effects of
      Token Reinforcement on the Productivity of Moderately
      Retarded Clients in a Sheltered Workshop." *British
      Journal of Mental Subnormality*, 1973, 19, 80-84.

      Investigated use of token economy with 7 moderately to
mildly retarded Ss in a sheltered workshop. Baseline levels
of production and preferences for reinforcing items were
determined over a 28-day period. Tokens were awarded hourly
and exchanged daily at first, with increasing intervals during
the 21 experimental days. Productivity increased by 42%
during reinforcement and dropped to below-baseline levels
after termination of reinforcement. The interaction of the
token reinforcement with the reinforcing effect of E's presence
and interaction is stressed.

500. Goldgraber, J. "The Effect of Job Enlargement on Pro-
      ductivity of Retarded Sheltered-Workshop Employees."
      Doctoral dissertation, Indiana University, 1977, sum-
      marized in *Dissertation Abstracts International*, 1978,
      38, 5392A. (University Microfilms No. 7801017).

      Investigated whether complex work tasks are best per-
formed in sheltered workshops by individual retardates or
when divided between a series of workers and performed in
assembly line fashion. Few significant differences are found,
yet the study results favor assembly line production.

501. Goldstein, H. "Social and Occupational Adjustment." In
      H.A. Stevens & R. Heber, eds. *Mental Retardation: A
      Review of Research*, 214-258. Chicago: University of
      Chicago, 1964.

      Discusses comparative studies of the social adjustment
of MR adults and their normal peers, as well as studies of
the vocational status of retarded adults, and concludes that
more services are needed in these areas.

502. Gorelick, M.C. "Assessment of Vocational Realism of
      Educable Mentally Retarded Adolescents." *American Jour-
      nal of Mental Deficiency*, 1968, 73, 154-157.

      The level of Vocational Realism of high school EMRs
was assessed; the relationship between realism and post-
high-school Employment Success was studied. Phase I included

886 tenth to twelfth grade EMRs drawn from 39 high schools.
Subjects for the second phase were 149 EMRs who had been
interviewed in Phase I and subsequently either graduated
from or dropped out of school. The hypothesis that the
Realistic EMR would be more successful in post-high-school
employment than the Unrealistic or No Plan EMR was not confirmed. Significant correlates with the level of Vocational
Realism were found.

503.   Grant, G.W., Moores, B., & Whelan, E. "Assessing the
       Work Needs and Work Performance of Mentally Handi-
       capped Adults." *British Journal of Mental Subnormality*,
       1973, 19, 71-79.

       Compared instructors' predictions of success or failure
on 8 specific tasks with actual individual performances of
27 mentally handicapped adults. There were an average of 6
inaccurate predictions of failure on each task, and estimates
of the number of trials that would be required to reach a
criterion exceeded actual numbers of trials taken. These
trends were particularly pronounced for female Ss.

504.   Greenspan, S., & Shoultz, B. "Why Mentally Retarded
       Adults Lose Their Jobs: Social Competence as a Factor
       in Work Adjustment." *Applied Research in Mental Retarda-
       tion*, 1981, 2(1), 23-38.

       Determined the primary reason for the involuntary termina-
tion from competitive employment of 30 mildly and moderately
MR individuals based on interviews with former employers and
others. Three "social" reasons (deficits in temperment,
character, and social awareness) and 3 "nonsocial" reasons
(production inefficiency, health problems, and economic lay-
off) were used to code the data. Support was obtained for 2
hypotheses: (1) that social incompetence plays at least as
important a role in explaining competitive job failures of
MR workers as do nonsocial reasons; and (2) that interpersonally
inept behavior (low social awareness), rather than emotionally
disturbed or antisocial behavior, appears to be the most frequent factor operating for those MR workers who are terminated
because of social incompetence. Vocational rehabilitation
implications are discussed.

505. Griffin, J.C. "Systematic Manipulation of Social Density
     Parameters with High and Low Level Retardates in a Work
     Setting." Doctoral dissertation, Texas Tech. University,
     1979, summarized in *Dissertation Abstracts International*,
     1979, 40, 1400B. (University Microfilms No. not available).

     Investigated the effects of social density upon work
performance of male retardates. Results show that increasing
levels of social density increase, in general, work performance.

506. Guarnaccia, V.J. "Factor Structure and Correlates of
     Adaptive Behavior in Noninstitutionalized Retarded
     Adults." *American Journal of Mental Deficiency*, 1976,
     80, 543-547.

     Forty MR adults working at a vocational training center
were rated by their counselors on the 10 behavior domains of
the Adaptive Behavior Scale. A factor analysis yielded the
following factors: personal independence, personal responsibility, productivity, and social responsibility. A regression
analysis of the 4 factors on the variables of age, sex, verbal
IQ, performance IQ, and maternal trust showed that the predictors together accounted for 75% of the variance in Factor 1
and very little of the variance in the other factors.

507. Halpern, A.S. "General Unemployment and Vocational
     Opportunities for EMR Individuals." *American Journal
     of Mental Deficiency*, 1973, 78, 123-127.

     Data from two broadly based studies concerning vocational
adjustment of educable retarded persons were examined with
respect to the presumed inverse relationship between adverse
community economic conditions and employment opportunities
for retarded workers. The data suggested that retarded persons are not automatically the losers in time of economic
hardship.

508. Halpern, A.S., Raffeld, P., Irvin, L., & Link, R.
     "Measuring Social and Prevocational Awareness in Mildly
     Retarded Adolescents." *American Journal of Mental Defi-
     ciency*, 1975, 80, 81-89.

     The Social and Prevocational Information Battery con-
tains nine subtests measuring social and prevocational awareness. It was developed and normed on secondary EMR pupils in

Oregon. The battery is easy to administer, orally presented
to eliminate reading ability as a determinant of performance,
and relatively simple to score and interpret. Information
concerning the standard error of measurement and predictive
validity indicates that this battery may be used for pupil
screening, monitoring pupil progress, or for program evaluation.

509.   Hanson, D.L., & Stone, L.A. "Multidimensional Percep-
        tions Regarding Actual and Potential Job-Placement
        Success of Mentally Retarded Adults." *Perceptual and*
        Motor Skills, 1974, 38, 247-254.

        Cognitive criteria used by professional counselors in
evaluating job placement success for MRs were investigated
in 10 institutionalized male MRs being considered for placement and 15 male MRs who were considered successful on-job
placement. Similarity estimations were made for pairs of
stimulus persons, where zero indicated no similarity and 100
indicated identity. Analysis of judgments by multidimensional
evaluation structure analysis provided results which scaled
actual and potential job placements on a number of meaningful
dimensions and suggested a method to specify clinical staff
consensus objectively.

510.   Hollender, J.W. "Prediction of Work Adjustment for
        Adolescent Male Educable Retardates." *Journal of Coun-*
        seling Psychology, 1974, 21, 164-165.

        The predictability of the client's perception of a
positive relationship with his staff supervisor regarding
a favorable work adjustment rating in rehabilitation workshop was studied, using data gathered from 25 16-year-old
male EMRs from a low socioeconomic level and at a metropoli-
tan rehabilitation center. Both work adjustment and the
client-perceived relationship were evaluated at 2 points,
separated by a one-month interval. Work adjustment and the
client-perceived relationship were not related in this sample;
however, high work adjustment ratings at the time of the
first evaluation were predictive of staff-rated frequency of
positive verbal interactions at the time of the second evaluation. Additional findings of a relationship between social
self-esteem and work adjustment were as predicted. An 18-
month follow-up indicated that good work adjustment in the
workshop was predictive of successful placement in competitive
employment.

511. Hunt, J.G., & Zimmerman, J. "Stimulating Productivity
      in a Simulated Sheltered Workshop Setting." *American
      Journal of Mental Deficiency*, 1969, 74, 43-49.

      Productivity in "exit ward" patients, participating in
a simulated workshop setting, was examined as a function of
introducing a bonus pay procedure. Work units completed per
hour served as the dependent variable, and coupons redeemable
for canteen items served as reinforcers. The bonus procedure
(a) significantly increased group productivity above that
previously obtained under non-bonus conditions, and (b) differentially maintained productivity at values consistently
higher than those obtained during temporally adjacent non-
bonus periods. While these results could have been accounted
for exclusively on the basis of the bonus procedure, they
could also have been influenced by verbal instructions given
in conjunction with that procedure.

512. Husson, Ph., & Verdalle, M. "Professional Employment of
      the Mentally Retarded: Psychometric Study: Psychological
      Enquiry." *Bulletin de Psychologie*, 1972-1973, 26(1-4),
      150-240.

      Tested hypotheses of similarity and independence between
vocational and intelligence test results for retarded vs. normal
Ss using the WAIS and selected vocational batteries. Results
indicate that retarded Ss were significantly inferior on the
vocational battery. The structure of aptitudes was different
for normal and retarded Ss. For the less retarded, the serious-
ness of the deficit in vocational aptitude was related to the
nature of the aptitude. Male Ss in both groups were better than
female Ss on tests of precision, and inferior on tests of manual
dexterity. The independence between intelligence and vocational
aptitude was strongest when the level of intelligence was high.
Study 2 tested hypotheses about attitudes toward employment of
the retarded. Two hundred and eighty-three questionnaires were
analyzed by category of personnel: administrative production,
or personnel divisions. Results show that attitudes were not
influenced by age, sex, or professional involvement of the
individual; assessment of information was influenced only by
the latter quality.

513. Ionescu, S. "Factors Predictive of Vocational Adaptation
      in Retardates." *Revue Roumaine des Sciences Sociales:
      Serie de Psychologie*, 1972, 16(1), 53-60.

      Classified 70 working retardates according to level of
work adaptation. The strongest factors distinguishing the
well-adapted from the poorly adapted were the scores on a
practical examination at the end of training school and the
absence of additional psychological problems. Other predictive factors included scores on other training school examinations, stability of parental family structure, length of
apprenticeship, and age at job qualification.

514. Irvin, L.K., & Bellamy, G.T. "Manipulation of Stimulus
      Features in Vocational-Skill Training of Severely Re-
      tarded Individuals." *American Journal of Mental Defi-
      ciency*, 1977, 81, 486-491.

      Fifty-one severely retarded adults were taught a diffi-
cult visual discrimination in an assembly task by one of three
training techniques: (a) adding and reducing large cue differences on the relevant-shape dimension; (b) adding and fading
a redundant-color dimension; or (c) a combination of the two
techniques. The combined procedure was found to be most
effective, the color coding fading next, and the relevant-
dimension cue disparity method the least effective. Concluded
that differences may exist in the efficacy of various vocational-
skill training procedures involving manipulation of stimulus
features.

515. Kapil, S.K. "A Follow-up Study of Post-School Activity
      Status in Relation to Selected Characteristics of the
      Trainable Mentally Impaired Students of Oakland Training
      Institute, Michigan." Doctoral dissertation, Wayne State
      University, 1980, summarized in *Dissertation Abstracts
      International*, 1980, 41, 1534A. (University Microfilms
      No. 8022814).

      Found that employment is related positively to EMR's
performance in a special school program.

516.   Kaufman, H.I. "Diagnostic Indices of Employment with the
       Mentally Retarded." *American Journal of Mental Deficiency*,
       1970, 74, 777-779.

       Using the Wechsler Adult Intelligence Scale (WAIS) and
the Reading and Arithmetic sections of the Wide Range Achievement Test, this study attempted to identify those cognitive
factors that discriminated between MR individuals who were
empolyed and those who were not employed.   The WAIS Comprehension subtest discriminated significantly between employed
and unemployed MR persons.   The results of the study indicate
the need for didactic programming relative to counseling and
work adjustment undertakings with the MR.

517.   Levy, S.M. "The Measurement of Retarded and Normal Work-
       ers' Job Performance through the Use of Naturalistic
       Observation in Sheltered and Industrial Work Environ-
       ments." Doctoral dissertation, University of Illinois
       at Urbana-Champaign, 1978, summarized in *Dissertation
       Abstracts International*, 1978, 39, 2868A. (University
       Microfilms No. 7820993).

       This study found that 2 MR adult workers considered not
viable for competitive employment by the workshop staff became competent industrial workers after receiving training
on an industrial job site.

518.   Lucchelli, G.J. "A Study of Job Performance and Related
       Factors of the Mentally Retarded Student." Doctoral
       dissertation, North Texas State University, 1976, sum-
       marized in *Dissertation Abstracts International*, 1976,
       37, 2142A-2143A. (University Microfilms No. 76-23,765).

       Studied the relationship between a variety of variables
and job performance of MR persons who received vocational
training.   The only predictors of job performance are the
intelligence quotient and impulse control.

519.   Malgady, R.G., Barcher, P.R., Davis, J., & Towner, G.
       "Validity of the Vocational Adaptation Rating Scale:
       Prediction of Mentally Retarded Workers' Placement in
       Sheltered Workshops." *American Journal of Mental Defi-
       ciency*, 1980, 84, 633-640.

       The validity of the Vocational Adaptation Rating Scale
(VARS) for predicting placement of MR workers in sheltered-
workshop settings was investigated.   The VARS was administered

by workshop supervisors to noninstitutionalized adolescents
and adults, ranging from severely to mildly retarded. Frequency and severity of maladaptive behavior in six domains
predicted the concurrent placement of retarded workers in
workshops, and also their placement one year later. Results
indicated low to moderate significant partial correlations
with concurrent placement and one year follow-up placement
(controlling IQ, age, and sex). Multiple-correlation analyses
indicated that the VARS provided significant increments in
predictable variance in workshop placements (13.8 to 16.1
percent) relative to predictions based on IQ, age, and sex.
Results support the instrument's incremental validity as a
measure to maladaptive behavior in vocational settings.

520.   Malgady, R.G., Barcher, P.R., Towner, G., & Davis, J.
       "Language Factors in Vocational Evaluation of Mentally
       Retarded Workers." *American Journal of Mental Retarda-
       tion*, 1979, 83, 432-438.

Vocational teachers described maladaptive social behavior of retarded workers in vocational training classrooms
and sheltered workshops. A rating scale was developed from
28 items measuring unacceptable language behavior. Twenty-
seven teachers rated (a) 196 retarded workers with respect
to the frequency of maladaptive behavior, and (b) the 28
items with respect to the probability that a given behavior
would result in termination of employment. Patterns of
language behavior of retarded workers were factor analyzed,
yielding two primary dimensions: verbal manners and communication skills. Irritating verbal manners were rated as more
likely to result in termination of a worker than were poor
communication skills. Both factors correlated significantly
with the AAMD Adaptive Behavior Scale, and communication
skills correlated significantly with the San Francisco Vocational Compentency Scale. Results suggested the need to re-
mediate maladaptive verbal behavior in sheltered or educational
settings and to assign workers to jobs in accordance with
their communication skills.

521.   Margalit, M., & Schuchman, R. "Vocational Adjustment
       of EMR Youth in a Work-Study Program and a Work Program."
       American Journal of Mental Deficiency, 1978, 82, 604-
       607.

Adjustment measures for students who took part in two
work programs for EMR graduates of special schools were compared. Fifty students took part in a work program (direct

placement in the work) and 50 students in a work-study program. The students, their parents, and their employers were
interviewed regarding vocational satisfaction and adjustment.
The work-study program graduates were significantly more
stable, satisfied, and adjusted than were the work-program
graduates (p<.001), but their professional opportunities
(reflected by the number of different jobs held) were limited.

522. McKerracher, D.W., & Orritt, C.P. "Prediction of Voca-
      tional and Social Skills Acquisition in a Developmentally
      Handicapped Population: A Pilot Study." *American Journal
      of Mental Deficiency*, 1972, 76, 574-580.

Found that intelligence was unrelated to vocational
progress, to the duration of programs, and to sex and age of
75 developmentally handicapped trainees.

523. Moore, S.A. "Reward Value, Goal Setting, and Work Per-
      formance of Mentally Retarded Adults." Doctoral dis-
      sertation, Boston University School of Education, 1979,
      summarized in *Dissertation Abstracts International*, 1979,
      40, 2559A-2560A. (University Microfilms No. 7923889).

Studied the effects of goal setting and reward value on
the work performance of MR adults. Found that conditions of
high reward value increased the production rates of MR subjects.

524. Morris, J.L., Martin, A.S., & Nowak, M.B. "Job Enrich-
      ment and the Mentally Retarded Worker." *Mental Retarda-
      tion*, 1981, 19, 290-294.

The effect of job enrichment on the production rate of
14 MR workers is evaluated. Job enrichment leads to increases
in standard rates of production for high IQ subjects and lower
rates for low IQ subjects. The effects of job enrichment on
high IQ subjects is consistent with previous findings with
MR subjects; however, the effects on low IQ subjects are unexpected, in that they are contrary to the findings for high
IQ subjects and those from previous research.

525. Myers, D.W. "A Comparison of Mentally Retarded Employees
      and Nonretarded Employees in the Federal Services in
      the Atlanta Metropolitan Area." Doctoral dissertation,
      Georgia State University--School of Business Administra-
      tion, 1972, summarized in *Dissertation Abstracts Inter-
      national*, 1972, 33, 20A-21A. (University Microfilms No.
      72-20,798).

      This study compared the MR and nonretarded employees in
federal service. Differences between the groups were found
in supervisory evaluation, turnover, age, salary level, and
length of employment. It is concluded that the federal program to encourage employment of the MR has been successful.

526. Nickelsburg, R.T. "Time Sampling of Work Behavior to
      Mentally Retarded Trainees." *Mental Retardation*, 1973,
      11(6), 29-32.

      Used time sampling procedures to study the work behaviors
of 30 MR (16 to 45 years) trainees. Fifteen Ss were rated as
successful and 15 as unsuccessful by their supervisors. Results indicate that the successful and unsuccessful Ss could
be distinguished by several work behavior characteristics concerning the amount of time each trainee was actually involved
in (a) attending to assigned task, (b) habitual sitting, standing, talking, joking, playing with others, and laughing on the
job, and (c) being away from assigned job station.

527. Porter, M.E. "Effect of Vocational Instruction on Aca-
      demic Achievement." *Exceptional Children*, 1980, 46,
      463-464.

      A study of vocational instruction for 70 mentally handi-
capped junior high school students showed that (a) career
development models can foster academic growth, (b) Ss may have
had skills that were not developed because of lack of reinforcement, and (c) internalized motivation may be an important
factor for achievement gains. Development of external locus
of control is important to promote learning effectiveness.

528.   Rapp, R.E. "A Normalization Approach to the Vocational
       Training of Mentally Retarded Adults." Doctoral disser-
       tation, University of Arizona, 1979, summarized in
       Dissertation Abstracts International, 1979, 40, 1410A.
       (University Microfilms No. 7920596).

       Compared the effects of training in a community work-
station to the effects of training in a rehabilitation workshop given to MR adults. Found that training given to MR
adults in the community work-station produced greater gains
in the development of vocational competencies than training
in the rehabilitation workshop.

529.   Richardson, J.B. "A Survey of the Present Status of
       Vocational Training in State Institutions for the MR."
       Mental Retardation, 1975, 13(1), 16-19.

       Reports results of a survey made of 203 state-supported
institutions for the MR in the US; 135 applicable replies
indicated changes in vocational training. Results show the
number of residents trained in actual working areas of institutions has dropped by about 20% and now represents only 64%
of training, as opposed to 100% estimated in a 1957 survey.
While only 31% of workers received payment of any kind in 1957,
90% currently receive payment, and 69% receive money. Only
20% of those employed full time in actual work areas, however,
earn more than $10.00 per week. Results of queries into in-
stitutional workshops, areas for training, and length of working days are also reported, and findings are compared with the
1957 survey.

530.   Richardson, S.A. "Careers of Mentally Retarded Young
       Persons: Services, Jobs, and Interpersonal Relations."
       American Journal of Mental Deficiency, 1978, 82, 349-
       358.

       Life histories and follow-up data at age 22 were obtained
for a total city population of children classified as MR (index
cases). Histories were also obtained at age 22 from matched
comparisons who at no time had been classified as retarded.
Matching was on age, sex, and social background. Placement at
school-leaving age and major occupation at age 22 were reported
for the index population. Those 22-year-old index cases not
receiving mental retardation services and their matched comparisons were examined on objective and subjective measures of
the jobs they held and selected indicators of interpersonal
relationships.

531.   Richman, J.S. "Background Music for Repetitive Task
       Performance of Severely Retarded Individuals." *American
       Journal of Mental Deficiency*, 1976, 81, 251-255.

Environmental manipulation in the form of specific
tempo background music was used to assist in the habilitation
of severely retarded persons. Thirty institutionalized
retarded males were tested on a repetitive manual performance
task judged to be similar to the type of tasks found in
sheltered workshops. Each subject received each of the background treatments noncontingently: no music, slow tempo music,
regular tempo music, fast tempo music. The results indicated
that the regular tempo of background music facilitated the
greatest improvement in performance, suggesting that the
effect of music on performance is more complex than the issue
of contingent presentation.

532.   Rosen, M., Halenda, R., Nowakiwska, M., & Floor, L.
       "Employment Satisfaction of Previously Institutionalized
       Mentally Subnormal Workers." *Mental Retardation*, 1970,
       8(3), 35-40.

The Minnesota Scale of Employment Satisfaction was
administered to 43 previously institutionalized MR persons
currently living and working independently in the community,
and to an additional 49 subjects drawn from the same population. Employment satisfaction of retarded workers was not
significantly different from that reported for large groups
of nonretarded unskilled and blue-collar workers. In both
groups, greatest dissatisfaction came from receiving inadequate
compensation and with being relegated to lowered status
positions in the company.

533.   Rosenberg, J.J. "The Effects of a Summer Work-Training
       Program on the Self-Concept of Mentally Retarded Adol-
       escents." Doctoral dissertation, Temple University, 1973,
       summarized in *Dissertation Abstracts International*, 1974,
       34, 4935A. (University Microfilms No. 74-1837).

Concludes that work-training programs for the MR are
highly successful when compared to the more conventional
sheltered-workshop approach.

534. Rudrud, E., Ferrara, J., & Ziarnik, J. "Living Placement
      and Absenteeism in Community-based Training Programs."
      American Journal of Mental Deficiency, 1980, 84, 401-404.

      A survey of client absenteeism in community-based train-
ing facilities was conducted. Results indicated that clients
who resided with their natural parents were absent more frequently than were clients who resided in community living
facilities. Found that absenteeism was unrelated to level
of intellectual functioning or age. Female clients tend to
be absent more often than male clients; however, the duration
of the absences are shorter, resulting in no significant difference between sexes in total days absent.

535. Rusch, F.R. "Toward the Validation of Social/Vocational
      Survival Skills." *Mental Retardation*, 1979, 17, 143-145.

      As the emphasis upon developing vocational employment
training programs for more MR adults continues to grow, the
need to identify skills, separate from performing one's
specific job tasks, becomes crucial. It is suggested that
there are social/vocational behaviors that, when acquired,
may contribute to long-term maintenance of employment. Social/
vocational survival skills are discussed.

536. Rusch, F.R., & Menchetti, B.M. "Increasing Compliant
      Work Behaviors in a Nonsheltered Work Setting." *Mental
      Retardation*, 1981, 19, 107-111.

      The training of one competitively employed person to
comply with fellow workers in a nonsheltered work setting
was attempted. Results indicated that practice and warnings
were successful in increasing positive compliant responding.
Sending the person home once also resulted in generalized
compliance to a third, untreated group of fellow workers.

537. Rylant, B. "A Sheltered Workshop in Belgium." *Mental
      Retardation*, 1972, 10(6), 36-37.

      This paper presents the program of a specific workshop
which is concerned with the essential goal of the personality
development of the retarded worker, rather than with economic
goals.

190   *Vocational and Occupational Adjustments*

538. Sali, J., & Amir, M. "Personal Factors Influencing the
Retarded Person's Success at Work: A Report from Israel."
American Journal of Mental Deficiency, 1971, 76, 42-47.

Predictors of rehabilitative success of retarded persons were examined hierarchically. Using work success (performance, output, and complexity of job activity) as the
grouping criterion, data were obtained on specific abilities,
personality characteristics, physical defects, and outward
appearance. Performance and output variables tend to be
more influenced by personality characteristics than by IQ or
specific abilities. Among specific abilities, motor coordination was most related to work success. Among personality
characteristics, perserverance was most highly related to
work success. Personality characteristics related to good
social adjustment appeared to be those required for work
success.

539. Sarata, B.P.V. "Employee Satisfactions in Agencies
Serving Retarded Persons." *American Journal of Mental
Deficiency*, 1974, 79, 434-442.

The work satisfactions of individuals employed by three
agencies serving retarded persons were examined. The results
contradicted the view held by most administrators that the
individual's level of overall satisfaction is determined
principally by his attitudes concerning employment in the
field of mental retardation. Rather, the data suggest that
satisfaction with the specific agency is the chief determinant
of overall satisfaction. Extensive contact with clients and
the perceived lack of client progress were found to be important sources of staff dissatisfaction. Finally, client-
related dissatisfactions were often attributed to agency or
staff deficiencies. Implications for altering administrative
practices were discussed.

540. Schreiner, J. "Prediction of Retarded Adults' Work
Performance through Components of General Ability."
American Journal of Mental Deficiency, 1978, 83, 77-79.

Performed a factor analysis on a set of variables used
to predict work performance or industrial rate for 127 MR
adults. Results indicate that there is a general ability
factor that can be partitioned into 3 components: cognitive,
visual-motor, and work sample/sorting abilities. The latter
2 components were more closely related to industrial rate

than was the former. Variables included S characteristics, standardized tests, ratings, and work samples. As a group, the work samples were the best predictors of industrial rate; the S characteristics were the poorest.

541.   Schroeder, S.R., & Barrera, F.J. "Effects of Price Manipulations on Consumer Behavior in a Sheltered Workshop Token Economy." *American Journal of Mental Deficiency*, 1976, 81, 172-180.

The consumer behavior of institutionalized retarded clients in a sheltered-workshop token economy were evaluated by changing prices in the workshop store. In the first experiment, it was found that clients displayed elasticity of demand, in that raising the prices of frequently purchased goods reduced the frequency and amount spent on more expendable items. Results from the second experiment showed that this change in spending pattern was not due to the relative modal unit price of item classes. The regulation of demand for consumer goods is a potentially useful way to maintain economic balance and effectiveness of a token economy.

542.   Screven, C.G., & La Fond, R.J. "An Application of an Avoidance Procedure to a Sheltered Workshop." *Psychological Record*, 1973, 23, 13-16.

Developed a timer-control device which was used to administer an avoidance procedure to 5 mentally-handicapped adults in a sheltered workshop. Ss' production rates and day-to-day stability increased with the use of mildly aversive consequences for inappropriate behaviors. Results indicate that providing feedback upon completion of work units improves trainee performance and workshop behavior.

543.   Siegel, K.A. "Modification of Workshop Productivity with an Operant-Self-Instructional Training Package." Doctoral dissertation, Bowling Green State University, 1976, summarized in *Dissertation Abstracts International*, 1977, 37, 5845B-5846B. (University Microfilms No. 77-10,895).

An operant-self-instructional training package was used to increase the productivity--a relatively complex sorting task--of 3 MR sheltered workshop employees and 1 MR student. Results indicate that the operant-self-instruction training package may be effective in reducing errors and stabilizing performance on workshop tasks with MR employees.

544. Sink, J.M. & Culligan, T.M. "Behavioral Disorders as
      Vocational Disabilities." *Journal of Applied Rehabilita-
      tion Counseling*, 1975, 6, 154-158.

      Discusses the implications of the decision to consider
cases which had been treated as behavior disorders as mentally
ill, MR, or physically handicapped. The effects of this
decision will be services to fewer offenders, the increase
of time required for client evaluation, and consequently the
delay of services to the client.

545. Song, A.Y., & Song, R.H. "Prediction of Job Efficiency
      of Institutionalized Retardates in the Community."
      American Journal of Mental Deficiency, 1969, 73, 567-
      571.

      A pilot study was conducted to identify which of selected
variables best predicted job efficiency of retardates in community employment. A predictor group of 18 cognitive, work,
and personality and demographic factors for the criterion
was hypothesized. Intellectual and work habit variables were the
most important predictors of later efficiency in the community
job when their relations to other variables were taken into
account. Race, sex, and withdrawn and aggressive behavior as
observed at the institution added little to the improvement of
prediction.

546. Sternlicht, M., & Schaffer, S. "Employing Mentally Re-
      tarded Ex-residents in the Institution." *Hospital &
      Community Psychiatry*, 1973, 24, 698-699.

      Following their discharge, 17 MR ex-residents were em-
ployed by the institution. The paper discusses the selection
and training of the employees, analyzed their predischarge
case histories and job-performance ratings, and compares the
results with previous research findings. The authors also
consider the advantages of employment in the institution of
former residence.

547. Stodden, R.A., Ianacone, R.N., & Lazar, A.L. "Occupational
      Interests and Mentally Retarded People: Review and Rec-
      commendations." *Mental Retardation*, 1979, 17, 294-298.

      This article reviews several studies regarding the choice
of occupational interests for the MR adolescent. Several concerns about current evaluation practices are discussed. Rec-
commendations are offered for a client-centered developmental
model, making the evaluation of occupational interests a viable
part of the clients' career/vocational development process.

548. Talkington, L.W., & Overbeck, D.B. "Job Satisfaction
      and Performance with Retarded Females." *Mental Retarda-
      tion*, 1975, 13(3), 18-19.

      Describes a study with 2 groups of 45 MR females designed
to explore the relationship between expressed satisfaction or
dissatisfaction in work assignments and associated performance.
Finding consistent with similar studies of nonretarded persons
are reported: job satisfaction was highly related to their
attendance, dependability, and general efficiency.

549. Tizard, J. "The Effects of Different Types of Super-
      vision on the Behavior of Mental Defectives in a
      Sheltered Workshop." *American Journal of Mental Defi-
      ciency*, 1953, 58, 143-161.

      Work productivity and behavior of MR boys does not differ
when their supervision is either strict or friendly, in contrast to the boys' behavior under laissez-faire conditions.

550. Townsend, J.W., Prien, E.P., & Johnson, J.T., Jr. "The
      Use of the Position Analysis Questionnaire in Selecting
      Correlates of Job Performance among Mentally Retarded
      Workers." *Journal of Vocational Behavior*, 1974, 4, 181-
      192.

      Investigated the efficiency of various existing measures
for predicting job performance of 121 MR 17- to 56-year-old
workers in a sheltered workshop. Using the Position Analysis
Questionnaire, 22 production-related jobs and 1 nonproduction-
related job were analyzed. Two job attribute clusters were
obtained. Correlations between 19 predictor variables (e.g.,
scores on the Vineland Social Maturity Scale, Wide Range
Achievement Test, Stanford Achievement Test, age, and extent
of secondary disability) and 5 criterion variables (supervisor ratings of job performance) were calculated separately
for Ss performing preferred jobs in each attribute group.
Results indicate that, contrary to past research, existing
measures are predictive of performance on some, but not all,
jobs in a sheltered workshop.

551. Wacker, D.P., Carrol, J.L., & Moe, G.L. "Acquisition,
      Generalization, and Maintenance of an Assembly Task by
      Mentally Retarded Children." *American Journal of Mental
      Retardation*, 1980, 85, 286-290.

      Four trainable MR children were taught a three-piece
assembly task. They were taught to verbalize the steps in
the designated sequence before assembling the objects. Their
performance was recorded in both the training setting and in
the regular classroom. Each child rapidly acquired the target behavior in the treatment setting and was successful in
generalizing and maintaining the behavior in an extra-treatment
setting.

552. Walls, R.T., Sienicki, D.A., & Crist, K. "Operations
      Training in Vocational Skills." *American Journal of
      Mental Deficiency*, 1981, 85, 357-367.

      Whether operations training reduces time and errors in
the acquisition of specific vocational tasks was investigated.
An operation is a particular response class that occurs in the
presence of a consistent stimulus. Subjects were mentally
retarded vocational-rehabilitation clients in a sheltered
workshop. Each subject was trained in either mechanical
operations (ABC) or wood operations (DEF) and subsequently
trained in two tasks involving ABC and two tasks involving
DEF operations. Significant time and error savings occurred
in task training when subjects had previously been trained
on the generic operations involved in those tasks. Results suggest that component operations to facilitate lateral and verti-
cal transfer to a variety of more specific job skills should be
taught in vocational-training programs.

553. Walls, R.T., Tseng, M.S., & Zarin, H.N. "Time and Money
      for Vocational Rehabilitation of Clients with Mild,
      Moderate, and Severe Mental Retardation." *American
      Journal of Mental Deficiency*, 1976, 80, 595-601.

      Mildly, moderately, and severely MR vocational rehabili-
tation clients comprised a random national sample of 600 clients.
One-half of the sample had been closed (services completed)
"rehabilitated," and half had been closed "nonrehabilitated."
Variables selected for analyses were time in referral, training and rehabilitation processes, dollars in evaluation,
facilities, all services, and earnings. Rehabilitated clients
tended to require more time in referral, less money for extended

evaluation and rehabilitation facilities, and earned more per week than the nonretarded clients. Severely mentally retarded clients required more time in training and higher costs for extended evaluation, rehabilitation facilities, and all services than the moderately or mildly retarded groups. A consistent interaction across five variables indicated that the greatest amounts of service in time and money went to the non-rehabilitated severely retarded group.

554. Weinberg, S.L. "The Effects of Verbal and Graphic Information Feedback on the Productivity of Mentally Retarded Employees in a Community Sheltered Workshop." Doctoral dissertation, Purdue University, 1976, summarized in *Dissertation Abstracts International*, 1977, 37, 5047A. (University Microfilms No. 77-1794).

Found that providing a MR worker with verbal and graphic information feedback about levels of his output can significantly enhance productivity.

555. Wimmer, D. "An Investigation of the Cognitive Content of Career Education for the Mildly Mentally Retarded." *Education and Training of the Mentally Retarded*, 1979, 14(1), 42-49.

Five career education curriculums were examined to (a) determine the cognitive content implicit in career education and its appropriateness for the mildly mentally retarded, and (b) identify levels of achievement as measured by selected test items in the cognitive domain of career education. The performance status of the mildly mentally retarded was compared with that of a nonretarded group, and the 60-item Career Education Cognitive Skills Item Battery is described.

CHAPTER X:
LEISURE-TIME PURSUITS

556. Adkins, J., & Matson, J.L. "Teaching Institutionalized
     Mentally Retarded Adults Socially Appropriate Leisure
     Skills." *Mental Retardation*, 1980, 18, 249-252.

     Six severely and moderately retarded, chronically insti-
     tutionalized females were exposed to a number of experimental
     conditions aimed at teaching an active leisure skill. Specific
     instruction in the task was the only condition that increased
     constructive use of time during leisure periods. Training
     generalized to a number of related tasks and was maintained
     during a 6-week follow-up.

557. Amary, I.B. *Creative Recreation for the Mentally Re-
     tarded*. Springfield, Ill: Charles C. Thomas, 1975..

     Describes the preparation and implementation of games
     and activities designed to meet the needs of the MR in a resi-
     dential facility, school, home, or other environment.

558. Black, M., Freeman, B.J., & Montgomery, J. "Systematic
     Observation of Play Behavior in Autistic Children."
     Journal of Autism and Childhood Schizophrenia, 1975,
     5, 363-371.

     The effect of environment upon the play behavior of
     5 autistic children was systematically observed in a stark
     environment, a theraplay unit, a playroom, and an outside
     play deck. The interaction of the autistic children with
     peers and objects was rated and revealed that object play was
     often manipulative, repetitive, and negative. Autistic chil-
     dren frequently related to multiple objects rather than their
     peers. Environment had little or no effect on play behavior.

559. Brace, D.K. "Physical Education and Recreation for
      Mentally Retarded Pupils in Public Schools." *Research
      Quarterly*, 1968, 39, 779-782.

      A nationwide survey in 1966 resulting from 1,589 returned
questionnaires sent to 4,022 schools officials in public schools
having MR pupils revealed that the retarded received inadequate
instruction in physical education and recreation.

560. Calder, J.E. "Service Delivery Patterns of Activity
      Programs within Selected Institutions for the Mentally
      Retarded in the USA and UK." Doctoral dissertation,
      Pennsylvania State University, 1979, summarized in
      Dissertation Abstracts International, 1979, 40, 2264A.

      A wide range of professional groups in the USA and UK
are involved in activity programs for the MR people. The
fundamental nature of recreation is universally recognized
and distinguished from activity therapy.

561. Calder, J.E. "Show Me How to Play: Recreation for the
      Mentally Retarded." *Australian Journal of Mental Retarda-
      tion*, 1972, 2, 111-117.

      Discusses the scope of recreation programs and their
contributions to the education of the MR. Particular attention is given to the role of physical recreation. The retarded have to be taught how to use community recreation
activities, and recreational counselors would be of benefit.
Recreation activities are needed to continue many of the
skills taught in school. Problems associated with meeting
the recreation needs of the MR are discussed, along with
factors concerning the organization and administration necessary to establish suitable recreation opportunities.

562. Carlson, B.W., & Ginglend, D.R. *Recreation for Retarded
      Teenagers and Young Adults*. New York: Abington, 1968.

      Presents general discussion on the utilization of recrea-
tion for the MR, with specific examples.

563. Compton, D.M. "The Untapped Reservoir of Human Energy." *Journal of Leisurability*, 1975, 2(3), 20-28.

     Describes the many ways in which failure to utilize the human resources of special populations (e.g., the poor, the aged, the retarded, and the handicapped) constitutes wastage of a valuable energy reservoir. Five steps that could be taken by park, recreational, and leisure agencies to tap this reservoir are outlined.

564. Corcoran, E.L., & French, R.W. "Leisure Activity for the Retarded Adult in the Community." *Mental Retardation*, 1977, 15(2), 21-23.

     Advocates planning and community action to provide retarded adults with opportunities to make use of local recreation and leisure time facilities. Proposes continuing education for the adult retarded.

565. Haun, P. "Recreation in Institutions for the Retarded." *Mental Retardation*, 1967, 5(6), 25-28.

     Holds that the same recreational or educational activity can be used for MRs in institutions.

566. Herr, D.E. "Institutionalized Adolescents' Perceptions of a Summer Camp Program." *Adolescence*, 1977, 12, 421-431.

     Fifty-one of 80 institutionalized adolescents responded to open-ended questionnaires in a 1-month summer camp. Ss' diagnostic classifications ranged from mental retardation and brain damage to schizophrenia and adjustment problems. Results suggest that Ss perceived camp as an excellent experience, from which they learned much.

567. Katz, S., & Yekutiel, E. "Leisure Time Problems of Mentally Retarded Graduates of Training Programs." *Mental Retardation*, 1974, 12(3), 54-57.

     Interviews with parents of graduates of sheltered programs in Israel disclosed parental concerns about the lack of suitable companions for the MR, and their isolation from society.

568.   Knapczyk, D.R., & Yoppi, J.O. "Development of Cooperative
       and Competitive Play Responses in Developmentally Dis-
       abled Children." *American Journal of Mental Deficiency*,
       1975, 80, 245-255.

       A behavior management procedure for training cooperative
and competitive social play was investigated. Subjects were
5 EMR children whose behavior and communication were deficient.
Using a token-praise-feedback procedure, increases in cooperative play as well as small increases in competitive behavior
was observed. Reinstating the token-feedback procedure after
reversal resulted in high levels of competitive play with no
change in cooperative play.

569.   Lebrun, S., & Hutchinson, P. "Human Sexuality: Expanding
       Self-Awareness in a Leisure Setting." *Journal of Leisura-
       bility*, 1977, 4(2), 6-8.

       Describes the operation and goals of Camp Kohai, a pro-
gram for children, adolescents, and adults who are MRs or have
learning disabilities or emotional and behavioral problems.
The program integrates learning and living with a program of
sex education which includes teaching self-awareness, concern
for others, and basic sensitivity.

570.   Li, A.K.F. "Play and the Mentally Retarded Child."
       Mental Retardation, 1981, 19, 121-126.

       A description of some of the play characteristics of MR
children and arguments for the importance of play for these
children is presented. The meager literature on play with
this group indicates the need for further research. Procedure
for the therapeutic use of play with MR children that have
emotional or behavior problems is suggested.

571.   Luckey, R.E., & Shapiro, I.G. "Recreation: An Essential
       Aspect of Habilitative Programming." *Mental Retardation*,
       1974, 12(5), 33-35.

       Discusses the importance of recreation to the total
system of habilitative services for MR persons, considering
the past and current trends. The parent-volunteer movement
and recent developments suggest that full normalizing potential
of recreational programming may be achieved in the future.

572. Matthews, P.R. "Recreational Patterns of the Mentally
      Retarded." Doctoral dissertation, Pennsylvania State
      University, 1976, summarized in *Dissertation Abstracts
      International*, 1977, 37, 7077A. (University Microfilms
      No. 77-9707).

      Found that the recreational activity patterns of lower
socioeconomic status MR elementary-age children are similar
to that of nonretarded lower and middle socioeconomic status
children.

573. Peters, E.N., Pumphrey, M.W., & Flax, N. "Comparison
      of Retarded and Nonretarded Children on the Dimensions
      of Behavior in Recreation Groups." *American Journal
      of Mental Deficiency*, 1974, 79, 87-94.

      Seventy EMR children were placed in adult-led recreation
groups of nonretarded children at a community center over a
4-year period to investigate the extent to which EMR children
can participate in such groups. The two dimensions usually
found in studies of child behavior were found in this setting
to be descriptive of the behavior of both the EMR and the nonretarded children. The EMR children scored lower on the dimension of Interest-Participation vs. Apathy-Withdrawal than
did the nonretarded children, but with some overlap of the
distributions.

574. Reiter, S., & Levi, A.M. "Leisure Activities of Mentally
      Retarded Adults." *American Journal of Mental Deficiency*,
      1981, 86, 201-203.

      Interviews were conducted with 44 moderately and mildly
retarded adults about their leisure activities. Comparisons
were made between these adults and nonretarded adults from
the general population who were matched for age and amount
of schooling completed. Results showed that the retarded
adults went out in the evenings and engaged in social visit-
ing significantly less frequently than did the general population. The two groups did not differ significantly with
regard to participation in a variety of daytime activities,
such as sports and excursions, or in a variety of home activities.

575. Roeher, A., Flynn, R., Hartnell, F., & Harshman, F.
      "Assessing the National Recreation Study." *Journal of*
      Leisurability, 1974, 1(14), 34-41.

      Critiques a report entitled Recreation Services for the
Handicapped by P. Witt by presenting the viewpoint of the
Canadian National Institute on Mental Retardation (NIMR).
It is stated that the report describes past and present problem and failures without analyzing them or providing proposals
for the future. Deficiencies in research methodology and a lack
of philosophical commitment are cited. The NIMR stresses the
normalization approach in treating the retarded, an approach not
stressed in the Witt report. The NIMR also concludes that the
Witt report's suggestion of voluntary coordination of services i
unrealistic, and that there should be more emphasis on citizen's
roles in planning services for the retarded.

576. Rosen, H.S. "Promoting Recreation Skills in Severely
      Retarded Children." *Revista Mexicana de Analisis de la*
      Conducta, 1976, 2(1), 85-99.

      Four studies using behavior modification procedures
were carried out in a summer camp attended by 5- to 15-year-
old mentally and physically retarded children. Ss ranged
from single Ss to entire classrooms, and camp personnel
served as experimenters. Results of the 4 studies show the
following: (a) day camps can be significant teaching settings
for young handicapped children; (b) children's participation
in healthy, physical activities can be increased by employing
behavior modification procedures; (c) indigenous camp personnel with proper training and supervision can carry out
behavior modification techniques without disrupting the normal
camp routine, and as a result have more time to supervise
children's activities; (d) behavior modification practices,
executed by existing personnel, can be carried out at a small
monetary cost.

577. Ross, D.M., Ross, S.A., & Kuchenbecker, S.L. "Rhythm
      Training for Educable Mentally Retarded Children."
      Mental Retardation, 1973, 11(6), 20-23.

      Intentional training and modeling techniques used in
teaching rhythm skills showed post-text improvement over a
group trained using traditional music techniques.

578.   Ryave, A.L. "Aspects of Storytelling among a Group of
       'Mentally Retarded.'" Doctoral dissertation, University
       of California, Los Angeles, 1973, summarized in *Disser-
       tation Abstracts International*, 1973, 34, 875A. (Univ-
       ersity Microfilms No. 73-18649).

       Describes and characterizes some aspects and mechanics
of storytelling among the MR. Provides a partial typology
of different types of series of stories based on the kind of
relationship between the stories in a series attended to,
and produced by, the retarded.

579.   Schilit, J. "Attitudes of Coaches and Educable Mental
       Retardates toward the Retardates' Participation in
       Interscholastic Athletic Competition." Doctoral disser-
       tation, Ohio State University, 1970, summarized in
       Dissertation Abstracts International, 1970, 31, 1652A.
       (University Microfilms No. 70-19357).

       Investigated the attitudes of coaches and EMR high
school students concerning the participation of the latter
on varsity and junior varsity interscholastic athletic teams.
It was found that the EMR were interested in participating
in athletics and that, in general, the coaches were positively
inclined toward permitting the EMR to participate in athletics.

580.   Sengstock, W.L., & Stein, J.V. "Recreation for the
       Mentally Retarded: A Summary of Major Activities."
       Exceptional Children, 1967, 33, 491-497.

       Discusses the platform, objectives, and activities of
various organizations in terms of their contributions to
recreation and physical education programs for the MR.

581.   Shisha, V.I. "Stimulating the Activity of Mentally
       Retarded Schoolchildren by Means of the Young Pioneer
       Club." *Defektologiya*, 1976, No. 2, 41-46.

       Young Pioneer clubs require and create suitable situa-
tions for certain desirable types of behavior, therefore
providing an opportunity to help retarded students to correct
or improve their behavior. A special summer camp was set up
for 17 5th-7th grade students, where getting together, conversation, distribution of assignments, and different practical
deeds took place. It was found that the Pioneer clubs can be
used very effectively to assist retarded children.

582.   Simpson, H.M., & Meaney, C. "Effects of Learning to
       Ski on the Self-Concept of Mentally Retarded Children."
       American Journal of Mental Deficiency, 1979, 84, 25-29.

       Changes in the self-concept of TMR children as a func-
tion of experience in a physical activity program were evaluated. The self-concept of a group of students was measured
before and after participation in a 5-week ski program. A
control group received similar pre- and post-measures of
self-concept but did not participate in the ski program. Significant changes in self-concept occurred among students in
the experimental, but not the control, group. Furthermore,
the magnitude of success in learning to ski was shown to be
positively and significantly correlated with magnitude of
change in self-concept.

583.   Sternlicht, M., & Hurwitz, A. *Games Children Play*. New
       York: Van Nostrand Reinhold, 1981.

       This is the first book of games designed specifically
to stimulate the psychological growth of developmentally disabled children. Discusses the psychological principles underlying play behavior, and traces the chronological stages of
play. Provides direct experience in the utilization of children's sensory facilities, memory, judgment, and creativity.

584.   Strain, P. "Increasing Social Play of Severely Retarded
       Preschoolers with Socio-dramatic Activities." *Mental
       Retardation*, 1975, 13(6), 7-9.

       Found that socio-dramatic activities increase severely
MR childrens' social play.

585.   Wehman, P. "Task Analysis in Recreation Programs for
       Mentally Retarded Persons." *Journal of Leisurability*,
       1978, 5(1), 13-20.

       Explores the use of task analysis, or breaking down of
individual behaviors, teaching them individually, and chain-
ing them together to produce the whole skill. Although task
analysis is highly accepted by educators, the difficulty is
to break down various behavioral objectives to determine when
the child achieves mastery in each step. Each step should
require increased precision, speed, or some other quantitative
improvement. The advantage of this system is that the child

is able to achieve mastery many times while learning, and therefore the rewards of mastery, both while accomplishing a realistic task and while working up to a higher level of goals.

586. Wehman, P.H. "A Leisure Time Activities Curriculum for the Developmentally Disabled." *Education & Training of the Mentally Retarded*, 1976, 11, 309-313.

Proposes a curriculum intended to provide retarded persons of all ages and functioning levels with a broad range of leisure time options, and to offer educators some sequence in which training may be given. The 5 tiers of play and leisure time activities included in this curriculum are (a) action on play materials, (b) passive leisure, (c) game activity, (d) hobby activity, and (e) active socialization. It is recommended that an effort be made to provide profoundly MR adults with play materials that are in line with their chronological age.

587. White, M.E. "Children's Games for the Adult Mentally Retarded." *Journal of Leisurability*, 1974, 1(2), 4-7.

Suggests that leisure programs for retarded adults are often overorganized, emphasizing childlike behaviors and activities. It is recommended that such programs encourage independence and teach normal adult social skills to retarded adults.

CHAPTER XI:
INDEPENDENT LIVING

588. Affleck, G.G. "Interpersonal Competencies of the Mentally
      Retarded." In P. Mittler, ed. *Research to Practice in
      Mental Retardation*, Vol. 2, 85-91. Baltimore: University
      Park, 1977.

     Discusses the importance of social-cognitive development
(particularly within a Piagetian model) for the achievement of
interpersonal competence among mildly and moderately MR individuals. Research data bearing on the association of social role-
taking ability with strategic interpersonal behavior also are
presented.

589. Altdorff, V. "A Method for the Psychometric Determination
      of Behavioral Properties for the Documentation of Case
      Files in Neuropsychiatry in Childhood and Adolescence."
      Psychiatrie Neurologie und Medizinische Psychologie,
      1973, 25(1), 27-37.

     Presents original questionnaires for measuring traits
of independence, industriousness, and social adaptation in
MR juveniles. Test-retest reliability is reportedly high.
Examples of the 3 questionnaires are presented.

590. Bass, M.S. "Marriage for the Mentally Deficient." *Mental
      Retardation*, 1964, 2, 198-202.

     This article discusses the possibility and advisability
of marriage for the MR, particularly in the light of increasing public acceptance of fertility control. Several scientific
investigations of sterilization are offered along with their
conclusions.

591.   Bauman, K.E., & Iwata, B.A. "Maintenance of Independent
       Housekeeping Skills Using Scheduling Plus Self-Recording
       Procedures." *Behavior Therapy*, 1977, 8, 554-560.

       Investigated the effects of 4 procedures on the mainten-
ance of meal preparation and housekeeping skills with 2 previously institutionalized 20-year-old males (an achondroplas-
tic dwarf and a mild retardate) in an independent living situation. Instructions, experimenter (E) scheduling plus self-
recording, partial self-scheduling plus self-recording, and
self-scheduling plus self-recording procedures were employed.
Results indicate that community living skills can be successfully managed in situations where strong external contingencies
are either difficult or undesirable to implement.

592.   Bell, N.J. "IQ as a Factor in Community Life Style of
       Previously Institutionalized Retardates." *Mental Retarda-
       tion*, 1976, 14(3), 29-33.

       Studied the community adjustment of previously institu-
tionalized MR persons. Found that IQ is positively related
to the subjects' employment and social relations.

593.   Brengelmann, J.C. "Psychological Problems in the Social
       Reintegration of Mental Retardates." *Analisis y Modifi-
       cacion de Conducta*, 1976, 2(2), 19-38.

       The problem of MR's reentry into the community as well
as predictive variables for a good prognosis for community
life were studied. Numerous measurement problems dealing
with the prediction of rehabilitation are presented.

594.   Brody, G.H., & Stoneman, Z. "Social Competencies in the
       Developmentally Disabled: Some Suggestions for Research
       and Training." *Mental Retardation*, 1977, 15(4), 41-43.

       A position for the development and instruction of social
competencies in developmentally disabled children is presented.
This conceptualization of social competencies is based upon
the beliefs that: (a) effective social functioning involves
a complex network of psychological processes, elucidated by
cognitive social learning theory; (b) social behaviors occur
within a context of frequently changing environmental settings;
and (c) effective social functioning requires social behavior
patterns to change qualitatively as the child matures.

595. Butler, E.W., Lei, T., & McAllister, R.J. "Childhood
      Impairments and Subsequent Social Adjustment." *American
      Journal of Mental Deficiency*, 1978, 83, 223-232.

      The relationship of a variety of childhood impairments
to subsequent social adjustment measures of occupations,
agency utilization, social participation, and arrest records
was examined. Generally, results indicated that impaired
persons adjust quite well in some respects but not so well in
others. There were differential social adjustments by type
of impairment and by age, sex, ethnicity, and socioeconomic
status. The data analysis suggests relationships between
impairment and social adjustment.

596. Crnic, K.A. & Pym, H.A. "Training Mentally Retarded
      Adults in Independent Living Skills." *Mental Retardation*,
      1979, 17, 13-16.

      Seventeen mildly retarded group-home residents were
trained in independent living skills and placed in independent living situations. Results showed that 14 residents
were able to move successfully to independence. Factors
found to be associated with successful independent living
included adequate psychological skills, behavioral living
skills, and accessibility of social support systems. Factors
associated with unsuccessful attempts involved anxiety-induced
behavioral regressions, the occurrence of overwhelmingly natural
consequences of behavior, and social isolation.

597. De la Cruz, F.F., & La Veck, G.D., eds. *Human Sexuality
      and the Mentally Retarded*. New York: Brunner/Mazel,
      1972.

      Presents a broad outline of the social and psychological
aspects of the sexual behavior of the MR.

598. Edgerton R.B., & Bercovici, S.M. "The Cloak of Compe-
      tence: Years Later." *American Journal of Mental Defi-
      ciency*, 1976, 80, 485-497.

      A sample of the persons in Edgerton's 1960-1961 study,
The Cloak of Competence, was revisited in 1972-1973. The
life circumstances of many of these persons had improved, but
predictions of the direction and nature of community adjustment in a number of cases proved to be inaccurate. The issue

of diversity in these cases and factors which make prediction
problematic, such as environmental variables (as opposed to
personal ones) and the effects of time on individual adaptation was discussed. Caution was suggested in looking at
short-term adaptation without considering these factors. The
importance of recognizing the individual's own definition of
success was also stressed.

599.   Fields, S. "Asylum on the Front Porch: II. Community
       Life for the Mentally Retarded." *Innovations*, 1974,
       1(4), 11-14.

       Maintains that many MR people, when provided with appro-
priate rehabilitative opportunities, can develop much more
self-reliance and independence than used to be thought possible.
One institution has found that by carefully selecting a neighbor
hood and by providing retarded residents with a job skill and
social education courses, many were able to make the transition to the community. In the past decade over 1,000 people
have been returned to community living by the programs reported.

600.   Floor, L., Baxter, D., Rosen, M., & Zisfein, L. "A
       Survey of Marriages among Previously Institutionalized
       Retardates." *Mental Retardation*, 1975, 13(2), 33-37.

       The ability of retardates to handle the responsibilities
of marriage and parenthood has been seriously questioned, but
few studies have explored the realities of this problem. This
report investigates the marital status of 80 previously institutionalized retardates, discusses possible effects of institutionalization, and suggests how rehabilitative programs can
improve the chances of future marital success.

601.   Floor, L., & Rosen, M. "Investigating the Phenomenon of
       Helplessness in Mentally Retarded Adults." *American
       Journal of Mental Deficiency*, 1975, 79, 565-572.

       Helplessness, or the inability to take effective action
in a problem situation, appears to involve both behavioral-
motivational and competence factors. As a personality characteristic, it may cause difficulties in community adjustment
for mentally retarded persons. Helplessness in a group of MR
adults was investigated through a set of behavioral and questionnaire measures specifically adapted for this population.
Similar measures were applied to a CA control group. Both

institutionalized and noninstitutionalized retarded subjects
exhibited significantly more signs of helplessness than did
the nonretarded control subjects. The results support the
hypothesis that helplessness is a meaningful personality
dimension among MR persons and can be objectively measured.

602.   Green, B.G., & Klein, N.K. "The Political Values of
       Mentally Retarded Citizens." *Mental Retardation*, 1980,
       18, 35-38.

       Findings indicate that MR adults are affected by the
process of political socialization much like their nonretarded
peers. Such data strongly support normalization, in that
shared political values are more likely to occur when MR
citizens interact with the larger society.

603.   Guarnaccia, V.J. "Factor Structure and Correlates of
       Adaptive Behavior in Noninstitutionalized Retarded
       Adults." *American Journal of Mental Deficiency*, 1976,
       80, 543-547.

       Forty MR adults working at a vocational training center
were rated by their counselors on the 10 behavior domains of
the Adaptive Behavior Scale. A factor analysis yielded the
following factors: (1) personal independence; (2) personal
responsibility; (3) productivity; and (4) social responsibiltiy.
A regression analysis of the four factors on the variables
of age, sex, verbal IQ, performance IQ and maternal trust
showed that the predictors together accounted for 75 percent
of the variance in Factor 1 and very little of the variance
in the other factors.

604.   Jones, L.A., & Moe, R. "College Education for Mentally
       Retarded Adults." *Mental Retardation*, 1980, 18, 59-62.

       Describes the attendance of college by MR adults.
Discusses financial assistance, curricular content, staffing
arrangements, and program components.

605. Kennedy, R.J.R. "The Social Adjustment of Morons in a
     Connecticut City: Summary and Conclusions." In T.E.
     Jordan, ed. *Perspectives in mental retardation*, 339-358.
     Carbondale: Southern Illinois University Press, 1966.

     Describes the adjustment of morons in five areas: namely,
family, marriage, employment, anti-social behavior, and social
participation.

606. McDevitt, S.C., Smith, P.M., Schmidt, D.W., & Rosen, M.
     "The Deinstitutionalized Citizen: Adjustment and
     Quality of Life." *Mental Retardation*, 1978, 16, 22-24.

     The adjustment of 18 people leaving a residential insti-
tution for MRs for independent status after completing rehabilitation programs was analyzed by means of personal interviews
conducted in the Ss' homes. The majority were of mild to
borderline intelligence. Most Ss were fully employed at
unskilled or semiskilled jobs. With the exception of the
few receiving welfare payments, Ss were middle-income working
class people with a median earned gross income of $6,670 an-
nually (1975). On the whole, Ss had limited knowledge of
their financial status and conducted few of their daily monetary transactions through a bank. As a group, they appeared
to be asocial rather than antisocial. Few participated in
community activities whereas they all spent many hours each
day watching favorite programs on their own television sets.
Ss generally had attained at least a minimal degree of adjustment in interpersonal relationships and had maintained at
least a minimal degree of independence. Almost all felt that
they would rather not be back at the institution.

607. Meyers, R. *Like Normal People*. New York: McGraw-Hill,
     1978.

     The story of a MR couple who marry, live in their own
apartment, and hold part-time jobs illustrates the changing
notions of human potential and various attempts to prevent
and overcome mental retardation.

608. Monson, L.B., Greenspan, S., & Simeonsson, R.J.
"Correlates of Social Competence in Retarded Children."
American Journal of Mental Deficiency, 1979, 83, 627-630.

The relationship of role-taking and referential-communication skills with social competence was assessed in 32 retarded children (mean IQ - 56.4; mean CA - 13 years, 7 months).
Significant associations were found between two types of teacher measures of children's social competence, between measures made by teachers and children themselves, and among scores of social competence and the skills of role-taking and referential communication. The findings suggest ways of assessing social adaptation more directly, which may be extended into specific interventions.

609. Osborne, A.G., Jr. "Voting Practices of the Mentally Retarded." *Mental Retardation*, 1975, 13(3), 15-17.

Many MR adults can vote in general elections competently if they are given the opportunity and some basic instruction in voting. This paper reviews the literature concerning the rights of the retarded to vote, the frequency in which the retarded actually vote, and the capabilities of the retarded to vote. The author concludes that with proper instruction our MR citizens are able to vote and that voting instructions should be made part to the curriculum for the retarded.

610. Reynolds, W.M. "Measurement of Personal Competence of Mentally Retarded Individuals." *American Journal of Mental Deficiency*, 1981, 85, 368-376.

The development and validation of the Personal Competency Scale, a 20-item rating instrument designed to assess competence of mentally retarded adults, was described. This broad bandwidth measure provides scores on three factorially derived domain scales. The three major dimensions of personal competence delineated were adaptive, cognitive, and affective competence. Correlations between the Personal Competency Scale and criterion variables, including IQ and Adaptive Behavior Scale scores, ranged from .61 to .75. Multiple regression and canonical correlations of .85 and .87, respectively, also strongly support the validity of this new measure.

611.   Saenger, G. *The Adjustment of Severely Retarded Adults in the Community.* Albany: New York State Interdepartmental Health Resources Board, 1957.

    This is the report of a study based upon interviews with the parents of over 500 severely MR adults, which was designed to obtain information concerning the adjustment of severely retarded adults residing in the community. Special attention was paid to the problems that the grown-up retarded person presented to his family and community.

612.   Schalock, R.L., & Harper, R.S. "Placement from Community-Based Mental Retardation Programs: How Well Do Clients Do?" *American Journal of Mental Deficiency*, 1978, 83, 240-247.

    MR clients (N = 131) placed during a 2-year period from either an independent living or competitive employment training program were evaluated as to placement success. Thirteen percent returned to the training program. Successful independent living placement was related to intelligence and demonstrated skills in symbolic operations, personal maintenance, clothing care and use, socially appropriate behavior, and functional academics. Successful employment was related to sensory motor, visual-auditory processing, language, and symbolic-operations skills. Major reasons for returning from a job to the competitive employment training program included inappropriate behavior or need for more training; returning from community living placement was related to money management, apartment cleanliness, social behavior, and meal preparation.

613.   Schalock, R.L., Harper, R.S., & Carver, G. "Independent Living Placement: Five Years Later." *American Journal of Mental Deficiency*, 1981, 86, 170-177.

    The placement success and quality of life of 69 MR persons placed into independent housing 5 years previously was evaluated. Eighty percent were still in their original independent housing placement. On the basis of multiple regression analysis, the most significant predictor variables were the behavioral skill areas of personal maintenance, communication, community integration, clothing care and use, and food preparation. Unsuccessful placements were related to bizarre behavior, nutritional problems, and inadequate home maintenance. Quality of life variables analyzed included

employment, finances, community utilization, leisure-time
usage, and friendship patterns. Analysis of the quality
of life variables presented a mixed picture—part of the
data reflected low income and possible loneliness; on the
other hand, community utilization occurred frequently and
involved normal activities. In light of the results, an
extended assistance-training model was presented.

614. Seltzer, M.M. "Retarded Adults as Workers: The Develop-
     ment of Competence." Doctoral dissertation, Brandeis
     University, 1978, summarized in *Dissertation Abstracts
     International*, 1978, 39, 3149A-3150A. (University Micro-
     films No. 7821715).

Investigated the success of retarded adults in their
adjustment to the role of worker. Found that the vocational
adjustment of retarded adults is complex, influenced by both
individual characteristics and environmental conditions.
Training programs, support services, and specific placement
policies for retarded adults are recommended.

615. Sitkei, E.G. "After Group Home Living—What Alternatives?
     Results of a Two Year Mobility Followup Study." *Mental
     Retardation*, 1980, 18, 9-13.

With the emphasis on placing more MR persons in community
residences rather than on institutionalizing, there is a need
to monitor the exodus from these homes and to determine what
alternatives are available to those who leave. The present
investigation has attempted to provide some answers from the
results of a nationwide sample of group homes. Personal interviews with operators provided information on the facility
and clients. One year and then two years later, the operators
were contacted again by mail to determine the status of residents at that time. The combined data of the two-year follow-
up became the basis for the reported information in this article.

616. Skaarbrevik, K.J. "A Follow-up Study of Educable Mentally
     Retarded in Norway." *American Journal of Mental Deficiency*,
     1971, 75, 560-565.

Information concerning the present status of 174 EMR
individuals, who had been discharged from vocational training
school for educable retardates in 1959 and 1960, was obtained
in 1967. Data with regard to economy, occupation, social life,

criminality, and official support were collected from several
official agencies. The information obtained indicated that
approximately 1/2 of the research population were self-support-
ing with a fairly good standard of living, and that only about
1/4 needed continuous official support. While most of the male
subjects were employed in industry or construction, a substantial number of the females were housewives. The relationship
between some personal variables and adjustment to society was
analyzed. This analysis emphasized the importance of other
handicaps as an important factor, in addition to low intellectual abilities.

617.   Stacy, D., Doleys, D.M., & Malcolm, R. "Effects of
       Social-Skills Training in a Community-based Program."
       American Journal of Mental Deficiency, 1979, 84, 152-
       158.

The effects of social-skills training upon the behavior
of 8 previously institutionalized MR adults, residing in
community group homes were evaluated. In comparison to a
control group, the subjects who received training showed substantial changes in the desirable direction for each behavior.
Generalization to unfamiliar situations was also noted. The
problems in placing retarded clients in the community without
social-skills training and the potential disadvantages of
inadequate training were discussed.

619.   Williams, R.D., & Ewing, S. "Consumer Roulette: The
       Shopping Patterns of Mentally Retarded Persons." *Mental
       Retardation*, 1981, 19, 145-149.

An attempt is made to develop information regarding the
commercial-product-purchasing behavior of mildly MR individuals.
To determine this, 11 participants are included in a mock shop-
ping exercise. The results indicate several serious deficiencies
in the purchasing strategies of the participants.

619.   Wilson, W. "Social Psychology and Mental Retardation."
       In N.R. Ellis, ed. *International Review of Research in
       Mental Retardation*, vol. 4, 229-262. New York: Academic
       Press, 1970.

Discusses mental retardation as a social problem, and
then discusses the MR individual in his social environment,
focusing upon his social success, his vocational success,
his self-concept, his image in the eyes of the layman, and
his relations to his family.

AUTHOR INDEX

Abelson, R.B., 321
Ables, B.S., 33
Abramowicz, H.K., 401
Adams, G.L., 322
Adams, M., 1
Addad, M., 271
Addison, M., 448
Addison, S., 93
Adima, E.E., 465
Adkins, J., 556
Affleck, G., 43
Affleck, G.G., 588
Aiello, J.R., 414
Akesson, H.O., 272
Akhtar, S., 240
Alcorn, D.A., 44
Alisch, C.J., 160
Allen, D., 43
Allen, G.J., 337
Allen, R.M., 378
Aloia, G.F., 131, 148, 149, 150
Aloia, S.D., 150
Alper, S., 466
Altdorff, V., 285, 589
Amary, I.B., 557
Amir, M., 538
Anderson, J., 29
Anderson, V.H., 138
Ando, H., 2, 3, 219, 220
Appell, M.J., 402
Archer, F.M., 372
Arndt, S., 20
Atkinson, A.C., 106, 107
Attwell, A.A., 79
Austin, G.J., 202
Ayers, D., 180

Ayoub, M.M, 482
Bacher, J.H., 151
Bailey, K.G., 323
Bak, J.J., 210
Bakeman, C.V., 273
Baker, B.L., 403
Baker, D., 274, 282
Baker, H.R., 25
Balla, D., 356
Balla, D.A., 324,325,398
Ballard, M., 152
Balthazar, E.E., 221, 326, 327
Baran, S.J., 328
Barcher, P.R., 519, 520
Barclay, A., 4
Barclay, A.G., 311
Barrera, G.J., 377, 541
Barsch, R.H., 45
Bartak, L., 5
Bartnik, E., 404
Bass, M.S., 6, 590
Bauman, K.E., 591
Baumeister, A.A., 397, 495
Baxter, D., 600
Beaver, R.J., 149
Becker, R.L., 467
Beckmann, J., 275
Bedrosian, J.L., 111
Begab, M.J., 63, 406
Bell, N.J., 592
Bellamy, G.T., 514
Bellamy, T., 468
Bender, L., 7
Benezech, M., 271
Bercovici, S.M., 598
Berger, M., 46
Berger, M.I., 47